PLANNING YOUR CHILD'S EDUCATION

Books by Charles H. Doebler
Planning Your Child's Education
Who Gets Into College and Why

Planning Your Child's EDUCATION

BY
Charles H. Doebler

Prentice-Hall, Inc., Englewood Cliffs, N. J.

Planning Your Child's Education by Charles H. Doebler
Copyright © 1971 by Charles H. Doebler
All rights reserved. No part of this book may be
reproduced in any form or by any means, except for
the inclusion of brief quotations in a review, without
permission in writing from the publisher.
ISBN 0-13-679779-2
Library of Congress Catalog Card Number: 75-148672
Printed in the United States of America T
Prentice-Hall International, Inc., London
Prentice-Hall of Australia, Pty. Ltd., Sydney
Prentice-Hall of Canada, Ltd., Toronto
Prentice-Hall of India Private Ltd., New Delhi
Prentice-Hall of Japan, Inc., Tokyo

To Eric, Chris, and Chad
As one cared for the others,
this book became possible

Acknowledgments

Any book like this must be the result of countless discussions, phone calls, interviews, and casual conversations with equally countless numbers of people. I am grateful to all of them for their questions and comments, which have been invaluable to me in forming the judgments I wrote about.

There have been a number of friends who have been especially helpful in specific areas, and I would like to thank them particularly: Dr. Eric Denhoff, for orienting me sensibly about the problems of child development, minimal brain damage, and its effect on educational progress; Dr. Roswell Johnson, who, as head of the health services of Brown University and as trusted confidant of many students, has a wealth of information on current undergraduate foibles; Mr. Evan West, Headmaster of the Providence Country Day School, who read and commented on the material covering the high school period; Dr. Gabriel Najera, who cheerfully allowed me to bounce my ideas on student behavior against his expertise as a psychiatrist.

To a number of others as well I owe a debt of gratitude: Mrs. Robert Woodcock, my typist; Mrs. Michael Carley, a skillful editor of mangled sentences; Don Michellinie, Fred David, Tom Collins, and Dave Desmarais, students who read the typescript and made comments, mostly helpful.

Finally, thanks to my wife, who didn't get in on this dedication, but produced the children who did.

Providence,
Rhode Island

Contents

Foreword

THIS IS NOT A BOOK ABOUT preparing for college, about the mysteries of college entrance, or about what your children are expected to do when they get there. Ideally, this book hopes to explain what goes on during the entire educational process your children (and even you) are likely to go through from start to finish, and how parents might make better plans with this information at hand. At the same time, one of the prime purposes I had in mind was to dispel some of the gratuitous mystery which has come to surround education and which seems (often with reason) to be designed to keep parents from knowing too much about what is going on.

For most families with children, educational planning is a major priority; the prospect of college looms over all other considerations in terms of its importance for the child's future livelihood and prestige. Future generations of families may be more concerned about the shape that graduate education will take, but for the moment college is still the major goal.

Like so many other goals which are universally desired, a college education has come to be thought of as an end in itself, rather than as another form of preparation and the last formal step for most people in a program which must be self-education thereafter. A college education is not a compartmented experience which is completed when the last degree is won, but an experience which is endless, and should be endlessly satisfying.

To many parents and students today this view of education has lost its meaning. College has become a necessity rather than a privilege, and a magic talisman to the right kind of life rather than an educational experience. Regardless of what a student may learn in college, by virtue of the degree conferred, his college education has the magic which can make ambitions become real, which can catapult Cinderella into the country club set or keep the children of college graduates safely in the middle class.

As a result, parents start the college race long before their children can understand what they are doing. Mothers worry over the effect of poor reading scores in the third grade, or whether the choice between Spanish and Latin in the eighth grade will be a deciding factor in getting into the Right College.

Considering the length of time which is devoted to this long-range goal and how important it is to parents, it is not surprising that their offspring have rebelled against the pressures, the length of time which it takes to get the proper credentials (and the length of time which accordingly they are kept in a state of dependence), and the implicit transposition of goals from education to union card.

While parents are concerned about the prestige of having children in college, and about the prestige of the college itself (although prestige alumni whose children were unable to make alma mater announce loudly how little it matters to them), their children have heard so much about education all their lives that they probably expect more than can ever be delivered.

With the frightening clarity of the young, they see and are disappointed by the faults which are apparent to them, but which are less clear to their elders, whose view nas been obfuscated by the "mystery" of education. The parents still believe in the system because they do not really understand it—either what goes on in the schools and colleges, or why their students often react in inexplicable and unsettling ways to the process.

This book is therefore designed to perform two functions: To help parents plan for the expected and the unexpected in the education of their children from the grades on up; to help parents understand some of the reasons behind the educational machinery and how these philosophies are likely to affect their children.

This book is not a technical document on how to raise your children to be superb students or to do well on the College Board tests. Nor does it tell you how to avoid the disappointments and frustrations that are likely to come up for you and your children, although it may explain some of them to you.

On the other hand, this book is not an attempt to summarize educational philosophy. This task remains for parents and children themselves to work out, since there is little likelihood of producing a successful student unless both parent and child have an understanding of what they are doing.

Instead, this book is designed to be a handbook, a useful tool which can provide parents with information based on considerable experience gained from working with both parents and children. I hope it will be helpful.

I

The Purposes of Education

NO PROCESS IN THIS COUN-
try is undergone so universally with so little understanding
as education. No one doubts the need for education; laws
have been passed making it mandatory until the age of
sixteen. Further, the outward signs of education are every-
where: authentic illiteracy is a rarity, the Book-of-the-
Month-Club is a corporation whose stock sells on the New
York Stock Exchange (and pays dividends), and college
enrollments have never been higher.

For many people education is an article of faith, too
important to do without and too complicated to understand.
Accepting the necessity for submitting their children to the
process, they send their children off to schools run by
specialized experts who bully the parents with their expertise and threaten them with dire results if they interfere in
the process.

In this respect, education and religion begin to look
strikingly alike. Both have practitioners who are initiated
into special mysteries, who alone are able to provide the

special result; and any lay person who violates the sacred canons runs the risk of excommunication.

An interesting case in point was the great reading debate of the late 1950s, when the lay public rose up, challenged, and essentially defeated the professionals, but in doing so generated all the heat, rancor, and irrationality that usually attend a religious or political discussion.

Although the general public can get excited about individual methods or situations in education, the process itself, and especially the philosophy behind it, remain a total mystery. Even though there has been a considerable surge of interest in the business of education by lay participants, it is still probably safe to say that although the mechanics of education are understood, the reasons behind the mechanics are very dimly understood, if at all.

To verify this statement, ask any student involved in education who is old enough to understand what is going on, "What is education?" The result is likely to be a backing and filling, a grasping at half-formed and unconnected ideas that could not be charitably termed a philosophy by any stretch of the imagination. What is more, the parents of current students are probably no better able to put into words what they feel the educational system should do.

There is no need to feel inadequate if this is the case, since experts with differing points of view have filled libraries with their theories of what constitutes a true education. As is the case with nearly all branches of learning that depend on thought and cannot be incontrovertibly proved by hard fact and research, different philosophies of education rise and fall, coming into popularity or disrepute as their promulgators do the same.

A striking example of this ability of vogues in educational method to take over the educational process was prevalent in the 1930s when the progressive schools were in full flower. As a somewhat perverted outgrowth of John

Dewey's teachings, progressive education not only let children learn by doing, but in some schools invited them to vote on those subjects which held the greatest interest for them. The results were quite often bizarre when this was carried to an extreme. A friend of mine who had been given the benefit of a progressive education in a private day school in New York City has yet to learn to write cursively, since this was never a subject approved by student vote. Even more remarkable and crippling is his inability to look up telephone numbers or words in a dictionary (he is a terrible speller) because, as he tells it, the alphabet came up for study regularly, but the majority of the class voted it down.

(A variation of this point of view, with a strong antagonism to memorizing as part of the learning process, is now current. I was discussing this concept with an undergraduate who said: "There is no need for any kind of memorization; understanding is the most important part of learning." I pressed the point, but he could not think of any use for rote learning of any sort—until I asked him how he expected to look up phone numbers. He saw the point, but it very nearly came to him as a new idea.)

Some definitions of education are sufficiently loose to include almost any philosophy or method, but they are really so loose that they can be bent in whatever direction is needed at the time. Such a point of view is the one that says education should enable a man to cope with his environment. In the present day, this means he must be able to communicate, to read, write, and speak intelligibly. He should have a smattering of background information which gives him a base for moving in his world in a knowledgeable way. For example, when he steps off a curb to cross a street, he should look first over his left shoulder, then over his right, to see if it is safe to cross. If he does not make this simple concession to his environment, he may get killed. Accordingly, one of the things mothers tell their children early is "Don't forget to look both ways before crossing the street." However, it is coping with the particular environment of this country which makes it necessary to look over the left shoulder first.

As the environment changes, so will a man's responses to it. Therefore, he must be trained to receive new information on a continuing basis and to adjust his actions or his attitudes accordingly. Again, on the simplest level, this means that our man, who has learned to look over his left shoulder first before crossing a street in the United States, had better look over his right shoulder first when crossing a street in London, and his response to this new situation had better be prompt.

Considering the amount of new information with which anyone today is flooded, some method of control has to be exercised to sort it out. The ability to store information easily, to record *in toto* any event that takes place, has guaranteed that records of recent history will be available for future generations. However, the sheer weight of the material threatens to swamp the purposes for which it was established. In a curious reversal of situations, historians of the future will have too much information, and the problem of sorting out the relevant from the irrelevant may become an overwhelming job.

Clearly, one of the most important jobs of education in enabling a man to cope with his environment is to make it possible for him to sort out what he has to know and to discard what he need not master. The classic story in this area is that of Conan Doyle's legendary Sherlock Holmes, who startled his friend and companion Dr. Watson by admitting that he did not know that the earth revolved around the sun:

> Now that I know it I shall do my best to forget it. . . . You see, I consider a man's brain originally is like a little empty attic, and you have to stock it with such furniture as you choose. A fool takes in all the lumber of

every sort that he comes across, so that the knowledge which might be useful to him gets crowded out, or at best is jumbled up with a lot of other things, so that he has a difficulty laying his hands upon it. . . . It is of the highest importance, therefore, not to have useless facts elbowing out the useful ones.

Although the concept of not overburdening one's mind with facts that are unrelated to everyday use is a sound one, the process of selection and comparison is not one which can be taught quickly or easily. First, it requires a high initial level of information, since it is necessary to make comparisons with existing information in order to decide whether the new is important or not. Long before a student is able to make judgments of this sort, he must have acquired a considerable store of background information to use as a guide. And yet, before he can go on to the next step that will enable him to make his way in a complex world, the student must learn to decide what is important.

This next step is to coordinate the material he has gathered on one area or one problem in order to come up with a conclusion, a recommendation, an opinion, or a decision.

A simple example of this process can be seen every day as a pedestrian starts to cross a street, sees a car coming, makes a judgment as to whether he can cross the street before the car will be on him, and, having made rapid calculations on the speed of the car, the width of the street, and his own pedestrian speed, decides he can cross the street safely. Since a number of pedestrians are injured each year, it is clear that not everyone is able to make perfect judgments on even so simple a situation. However, the rudiments of all decision-making are bound up in this fairly simple example, except that the results of deciding to cross the street are not mired by any intellectual or moral issues involving rightness or wrongness. And there is one further and probably more important difference: After crossing the street, although the action required a fairly complicated set of evaluations and decisions, there was no need to inform the world afterward of what was decided.

In most decision-making, such communication of the results of the decision-making process is of genuine concern. Whether the decision by a foreman to dig a foundation trench at a certain place must be relayed to the laborer who will dig it, or a tax lawyer has finally come up with a complicated but legal solution to his client's financial problems, the resulting decision is not a personal one—that is, one which the maker keeps to himself. Rather, it must be passed on to others, and if the decision-making process is to be at all useful, it is necessary that it be conveyed with unmistakable clarity to the person who wants the information.

Thus the question of communication becomes established not just in the inward direction toward the individual—as in the cases of street signs or directions on how to open boxes or how to get from Plum Beach to Pine Street—but also in an outward direction, too, as it becomes necessary to tell others what you think, what to do, or what conclusions you have reached. This is a circular process, because it is impossible to take in enough information to be able to make judgments unless the inward communications are well developed.

Conversely, there is usually little point in making a decision of some complexity unless the outward communications system itself is capable of handling such complexity. Complexity does not necessarily mean big words or obscure words or difficulty of comprehension. In fact, the more sophisticated the mind, the more it is willing to deal with complicated subjects in a simple way. It might well be considered a form of intellectual insecurity to try to impress the listener with your knowledge by describing a conclusion or a decision in terms which are deliberately difficult to understand. A college dean of my acquaintance could not resist making metaphysical discourses to the students of his college in the most ponderously abstruse language. I once asked an undergraduate who had just heard one of these effusions what he thought of them. "Gratuitously obfuscatory," said the student, in a neat parody of the dean's style, which proves that college students are usually as bright as the people who teach them.

If, in order to cope with his environment, one must gather information (reading), make judgments on the worth of the information gathered (comparison), put together the important or connected facts to produce a decision or conclusion (synthesis), and, finally, announce the result to whomever is interested (communication), then how is this complicated process taught? Further, although this pattern of reading, comparison, synthesis, and communication was most notably described by Cardinal Newman as the proper basis for a liberal education, is it proper as a prototype for all education, or should there be a difference between the education of those who are able to enjoy the luxury of education which is not absolutely designed to enable them to make their living directly from what they have learned, and the education of those for whom economic uncertainty makes a practical education necessary. The struggle between the practical and the nonpractical aspects of instruction is only one of many that have made the field of education a bloody battleground for many years.

In actuality, this difference of opinion appears to be the difference between theory and practice, between those who see education as an ideal and those who are concerned with it for the economic survival of their children. But this is not entirely true, for many institutions in this country whose curricula are not directly responsive to the parents of the enrolled students still feel strongly that education must have a direct and tangible result, and that the most sensible aim of education is the preparation of the recipient to perform some useful task that will enable him to earn a living.

Although it is certainly an oversimplification, it is safe to say that the practical orientation of American education is a direct result of the spirit of free enterprise: You go to school to learn how to make a living.

It is perhaps again a perversion of the theories of John Dewey, the great American prophet of education, to say that much of the vocational flavor of higher education in this country stems from his general concept that a student learns by doing, and that he should be doing things which are concrete and understandable in terms of the end product. To this end, Dewey promulgated the idea of problem-solving as the best motivational device in learning, at whatever level. That is, if a student wants to learn how to repair a car, build a house, or cook a meal, there are certain background skills and pieces of information which must be acquired before this can be accomplished. With the specific goal as a carrot before him, the student then learns all the things he must in order to achieve his end, whether it be electricity or physics to repair the car or the ability to read so that a recipe can be followed.

Methods based on problem-solving are not practical for teaching on a mass basis, even though problem-solving is indeed a powerful motivation for learning. Chief among the drawbacks of problem-solving methods is the fact that as each student goes his separate way in the business of solving his own particular problem, there is little opportunity for the teacher to transmit a body of knowledge in an orderly fashion. While it is true that this knowledge will be useful later to the problem-solvers, if there is no apparent immediate use for it, there is none of the motivation present which makes problem-solving such an attractive learning inducement.

Nevertheless, it is not surprising that courses studied in school and in college, based on Dewey's ideas as adapted to more general use by the concept of making what needs to be learned as readily practical and hence palatable as possible, are often measured by the yardstick of their usefulness, not in abstract, but in specific terms.

One of the clearest and earliest victims of practicality was the study of Latin. Latin is a dead language: no extant society speaks it, the Roman Catholic Church has recently abandoned it for its services, and even Harvard College now prints its diplomas in English, although not without a considerable protest from the traditionalists. As a dead language it has no place in a curriculum increasingly crowded with necessary subjects, and many critics helped to remove it.

Its apologists, on the other hand, spoke of Latin as a kind of mental barbell—it was splendid exercise and training for the mind. The practicalists retorted that studies of the carryover effects from learning Latin indicated there was no evidence that the study of Latin made a mind stronger or better able to cope with new information than did the study of anything else considered more practical.

The curious result is that, despite these apparently sensible attacks on it, Latin continues to survive, and even to flourish to an extent, perhaps because it is deeply satisfying to study its literature, its structure, and its influence on other languages. There is an even better and more practical contemporary reason. Since English grammar is almost universally the most poorly taught subject of the entire curriculum, the study of Latin does give some training to its students in the structure and grammar of the English language. As for the purely practical results, it is my observation after reading admission folders for many years that it is possible to tell from the results of the College Board Achievement examination in English Composition whether a student has studied Latin or not; if the score is higher than the verbal aptitude score, the chances are the student studied Latin.

Practicality and relevance should go hand in hand; that is, the importance of any one subject for the student's future has to be assessed by the student. The concept of relevance has been nearly beaten to death in recent years by those who cannot project the usefulness of many standard disciplines in the liberal arts curriculum. To such people a subject which cannot be clearly seen as subsequently useful either in making a living or in solving the problems of the world must be irrelevant.

An ambitious undergraduate recently presented his problem to me. He was getting Ds in his major, economics, and was worried about the effect this would have on his admission to a graduate school of business. It was difficult, if not impossible, to explain to him that to study economics on the undergraduate level and then follow with a graduate study of business might be achieving practicality at a cost of sterile narrowness, and that even business schools themselves recommend broad undergraduate study before going to business schools.

The limitations of the problem-solving approach to education lie in its assumption that if the subject has no immediate usefulness in the eye of the student, then it is not relevant to his future. If this is so, how is it possible to teach students the basic skills of gathering information, making judgments on it, putting the judgments into some workable pattern, and then telling someone else about them? Further, is such a pattern of education as valid for a limited intellect as it is for a good one? If not, where is the dividing line, and how sharply should it be observed? These are only a few of the most pressing dilemmas that education must solve in one way or another. Pedagogy has already offered varied solutions and has been offering them for centuries. But the questions have particular force now because of the vast increase in the population that will undertake education, not only at the secondary level but also beyond it, and because of the need for an educated citizenry that can understand some of the problems of government and make sensible decisions at the polls.

Finally, probably the least understood of all the problems which face education are those of aesthetics and leisure which do not seem, at first glance, to be practical concerns at all. As our country grows more crowded, there is a genuine need to have the mass of people understand that natural beauty must be preserved and that man-made objects should conform to some broad general concept of planning and taste; otherwise we will perish of ugliness in a jungle of used car lots and Humburger Heaven drive-ins. In this general category of aesthetics and leisure also goes concern about pollution of air and water, and the pressing problem of waste and waste removal. Parenthetically, anyone who has seen the streets of Copenhagen and those of New York might well ask how the Danes have inculcated in their citizens a sense of neatness, and whether this can be accomplished anywhere else in the world.

Less understandable, because it would seem to be on the surface a pleasurable dilemma, is the lurking threat of leisure. Automation and a high level of productivity are concentrating the working day, and soon the working week, into smaller and smaller pieces. For at least one union, the twenty-five hour work week is already at hand. A recent suggestion by a distinguished economist, to institute a three-day work week of ten-hour shifts each in order to keep machinery working steadily for six days a week, seems to be unappealing except for the three-day week.

Cursory studies of "liberated" employees who have shorter work weeks both in this country and abroad indicate that, for the most part, workers in this position will take second jobs if they are available. A minority report says that in one union the response to the shorter work week was idle husbands at home, drinking beer and watching television—no great crime except to their resentful wives who were still spending "overtime" hours running the house.

No amount of concern or study about the possible corrosive effects of too much leisure is likely to make a dent in a union's demand for a shorter work week, but the pattern seems clear—that our education at present provides no resource or training for a totally new need, leisure, and that the need to consider this in planning education seems inescapable.

It is perhaps anomalous that the very class (a dangerous word to use in America, but sociologists can prove classes exist) most likely to be able to handle leisure on the basis of training and inclination is the least likely to have the problem. That is, the educated managerial class is more likely to find cerebral pursuits an agreeable way to spend time, but, being managers, its members are not likely to have an overabundance of leisure because of the natural tendency of paperwork to yield to Parkinson's Law.

Although educators apparently have not been concerned with these two problems of the future, it has been a fascinating topic for the Utopists who have dared to guess intelligently about the future. *1984* by George Orwell and *Brave New World* by Aldous Huxley are two such attempts and are either so perceptive or so overworked that they both have become schoolboy bibles—usually read as a pair during high school for book reports. This does not gainsay the fact that Huxley had a keen scientific mind and a remarkable imagination, and his solutions, although more palatable on the surface than dreary Orwellian defeatism, are quite as frightening. Huxley planned for leisure, and he planned for consumption. As a matter of fact, in his new world everything was planned, including a man's station in life, which he was conditioned to accept and even to enjoy. Working-class humans were taught to enjoy sports, to use consumer goods, to abhor beauty, and to obey. In order to make the system work, even the top level of intellect, the Alphas, were conditioned from birth, and none were permitted free thought. Such a controlled existence is repugnant to our way of living, but there is more than a germ of truthful realization in the world that Huxley set up.

A practical question arises and rearises for anyone trying to design a perfect system of education: Should education attempt to do the same thing for everyone, or are some students "more equal than others"? In teaching a student to cope with his environment, is it sensible to have the future mechanics learn how to become mechanics as the best way to cope with their environment, or are other things as important for their future roles as citizens? In the problem-solving school of education, the student will learn those things which he discovers he will need. Thus a mechanic will learn to read when he discovers this is the only way he can get the information out of a service manual. Presumably he will learn mathematics in presenting bills or figuring dimensions, horsepower, tire pressure, or whatever. But what about the abstracts that every citizen of a republic is called upon to assess—the way to vote, to assess the candidate at hand, to decide whether the arguments he presents are logical and intelligent or not? Who will teach him to read critically, so that he can decide whether or not the reports he is reading are slanted? If, up to this point, he has been chiefly concerned about repair manuals and has learned to read for that purpose, what possible training will he have had in abstract thinking?

I am not trying to suggest that very many students now have such a narrow education as this mythical mechanic, but, in the question of practical education for a practical end, the degree of specialization and the time it takes become critical questions—regardless of whether the student will eventually become a mechanic or a college professor of sociology. In this way, the professor can be as limited in his interests and his outlook as the mechanic, although his specialization should have come at such a later date that he is more broadly educated. Yet, because of his position as a teacher, he should embody such professional principles of education as receptivity to ideas that oppose his, and subsequent objective thinking.

The question naturally arises as to what extent an education can be broad if it is so abstract that it kills enthusiasm for learning? Further, if the ability to learn abstract concepts without being particularly concerned about the subsequent use of the knowledge gained is directly proportional to intelligence, who shall decide where to draw the line separating the necessary general education from the specifically practical that is needed to earn a living?

Actually, I am reasonably certain that a student who feels the need for a practical education is drawn in that direction not so much by the level of his intelligence as he is by his family's background and their attitudes toward education. The meaning of "liberal" in the phrase liberal arts is likely to be that the student in question comes from a comfortable background and that he, in fact, can enjoy the luxury of a nonpractical liberal arts education because he has been liberated from the economic pressures which are so often the matrix of the educational thinking of parents. Thus he is likely to have a liberal education followed by practical specialization in graduate school; the less affluent will insist on the practical vocational training earlier.

The differences in parental attitudes are so important in shaping children that it has been possible to determine what kind of background a child has encountered as early as six months of age. This should come as no surprise, because as parents move to the upper end of the social scale they realize the importance of education accordingly, and gear their lives to getting it for themselves and providing it for their children. The only surprise is that the results can be detected so early.

In the same way, the amount of money which a school system is willing to spend on each pupil is not in itself a guarantee of how good an education any child can get, but it probably is the best single indicator of the attitudes of parents and pupils about education, and high tuition expenses are symptomatic of a high valuation of education.

The importance of parents in determining attitudes raises several difficult problems in determining how education should operate on an ideal basis and how it has to operate in practice.

Ideally, each child should be trained to the top level of his ability in those areas where he is best suited. It is pointless, for example, to attempt to give a student of limited ability anything beyond the essentials of abstract education. If, in high school, he were taught (in addition to subject material, and by means of that instruction) the rudiments of "education"—that is, how to proceed independently to find out things he needs to know, to acquire the rudiments of aesthetics and the basis for logical thinking and communication—he could then be given whatever vocational training seemed appropriate, either in high school or at the junior college level.

On the other hand, a student of high capability should be given the maximum preparation for an extensive education, and should be allowed the maximum depth and lack of specialization until the graduate level, in order to give him the greatest amount of time to identify and develop his interests.

In both these extreme cases, we are considering ideals without the complications which inevitably arise in actual situations. These complications are two: (1) the difficulty of determining ability without a possibly serious degree of distortion; and (2) the distorting effect of parental attitudes on a child's education.

An example of the first complication is the case of a limited child born to college-educated parents, who will be treated as a college preparatory student in the face of any but the most obvious contrary evidence. An unwillingness to face the fact that a student is not college material is the trademark of too many parents, and school guidance offices can cite many cases where parental insistence has resulted in frustration, despair, and failure.

In a case of the second complication, a potentially bright student who is born into a family which does not have education as a primary goal and which is not interested in books, reading, ideas, and the wide variety of other attitudes which go with being highly educated, is not likely to be able to get from his family the kind of support and encouragement his long education needs. Even if this family is able to assume a considerable part of the expenses of education (not all well-educated people are rich, nor are all the educationally ignorant poor), they will be unwilling to make the financial sacrifices which are necessary and which the educated middle class has come to expect as one of the conditions of existence.

But an even more trying problem to schools and parents is the uncertain or varying validity of the intelligence tests, or whatever is used to determine ability. It is hardly a novelty to doubt the efficacy of standardized tests. Years before the problem became acute because of the need to identify students from impoverished backgrounds, Professor Banesh Hoffman of Queens College had published a number of diatribes against the College Board, the most ubiquitous of the standardized test makers for the college-bound group of students. Despite Professor Hoffman and a number of other complainants, the fact remains that there is little else that can be counted on, particularly in a public school situation where the tests are perforce administered on a mass basis.

Since Chapter VIII will deal with the pitfalls and advantages of testing, I do not wish to expand on this theme at the moment except as it bears on the problem of counseling

children at some point in their schooling about what kind
of program to take.

Performance alone cannot be the key. A dean of Case
Western Reserve University told me recently that one of
their worst counseling problems is the engineering student
who has worked at top efficiency throughout his high
school career, but who simply does not have the additional
margin of effort or ability needed in the greater competition
of college.

Test scores alone do not measure potential accurately or
consistently. Every counselor has a repertoire of anecdotes
about the students who had poor scores and who went on to
be successes in college.

In the face of conflicting information on test scores and
performance, and in the face of the fact that, while middle-
class parents are going to push their students, working-
class parents may very well not be sophisticated about the
possibilities of education available to their children, what
kind of policies can be set as to where general education
leaves off and specific education for vocational purposes
begins?

There is, fortunately or unfortunately, no absolute answer. While, on one hand, teachers deplore the pressures
that parents put on their children in driving them to
performance above what can be reasonably expected, on
the other hand, teachers and school systems are often
plagued by a system which has been set up to take care of
the majority. Sensitivity, flexibility, and individuality are
the keys to ideal counseling, and no small part of that
flexibility should be a teacher's recognition that a parent
can be right. The converse, of course, is true as well.

In subsequent chapters I will deal with some of the
questions raised here, such as the proper evaluation techniques for the identification of talent and what a parent can
expect from his children, some further thoughts on the
nearly unconsidered problems of leisure and aesthetics,

and, of course, some means for a parent to evaluate the current process ofeducation and what it is likely to accomplish for, or do to, his child.

As for the business of a liberal education and how to impart it convincingly, there is no question in my mind that, even at the primary level, this is superior training which can be of benefit to any citizen—the extent of his education in the liberal tradition depending on the extent of his abilities, with the more limited students receiving specific training early, and the more talented going furthest before specialization.

This kind of education is more involved with development of attitudes than with any specific hard and fast skills. It does require the development of skills of accuracy in reading and communicating; it does require skill in analysis and synthesis to do all the jobs the liberally educated man must be able to accomplish—to gather, judge, and communicate. But a sense of the importance of liberal education, an awareness that any idea or opinion is subject to review in the face of new or conflicting information are attitudes, and attitudes are considerably more difficult to promulgate than skills.

One of the reasons it is so difficult to develop an attitude of receptivity and open-mindedness in students is that teachers themselves too seldom demonstrate it in their own classrooms. It would be improper to lay the blame for teacher inflexibility on the colleges that train our primary and secondary school teachers. But wherever the blame rests, I have heard too often the complaint from students in freshman English courses that a grade on a composition often tallies with the extent to which the student's views are agreeable to the instructor. In general, this is a valid criticism of a great deal of teaching.

To develop a receptive and open-minded point of view requires a great deal of personal security, for if a student, at whatever level, presents an idea which has merit, and if, on being evaluated, it appears that the student's idea is better than the teacher's, the teacher then has been publicly exposed (or so he might feel) as less bright or less well informed than the student. Perhaps this is acceptable at the graduate student level, but it unquestionably becomes harder to take as the educational scale descends. At the primary level, where the most important attitudes about education are first instilled in the students, it is most important for the teacher to demonstrate receptivity to ideas. But this is precisely where such receptivity is least likely to be demonstrated, because most teachers do not have a sufficient sense of personal security to allow themselves to be given new ideas or to be corrected by a small child.

Part of the fervor of the reading debate centered around a similar kind of situation. The practice if not the philosophy of teachers at the lower grade level is that the teacher must be infallible; otherwise the students will be confused rather than instructed. But with parents teaching their children to read before they reached school, the result was confusion in teachers and students about how to go on from there.

It is certainly true that the learning processes which must be undertaken in the earliest primary grades are so complicated that there is need for a forceful presentation on the part of the teacher. However, the teacher should be more than a dispenser of unquestioned wisdom. Certainly there are opportunities even in the earliest grades to develop the equivalent of discussion groups which could weigh various aspects of any question under discussion, whether it be about the Indians being cheated out of their homeland (which actually came up in my wife's nursery school class recently), or about whether bunnies really lay Easter eggs.

The conscious development of an attitude of reason and receptivity early could and would carry over into more advanced grade levels, where teachers must be trained to expect, even to welcome, questions which might seem to threaten them. It is here, however, that human nature seems to stand in the way of achieving such a goal. And yet if the formal aspects of teacher training could underscore the importance of this sort of attitude, it could be accomplished. Now, when the educational establishment is in a state of siege over its methods, practices, and purposes, is an ideal time to consider a considerable overhaul in the methods and philosophies of training teachers.

Since parents are among the very last consulted about educational philosophies (except when they protrude themselves, as they did in the great reading debate of ten to twelve years ago), it is not likely that schools will take seriously any comments or feelings a parent may have about his child which are contrary to the classroom experience. Yet there are times when a parent is right and the school is wrong. What is more, because a *child* is the special unique property of one family, whereas a *student* is only one of many in a school, the parent can and will spend more time and money attempting to straighten out a child who is resisting education than the school ever can.

The fine line between intuitive understanding of a child's ability and willful self-deception about his lack of ability is hard to draw. In general, parents are completely justified in verifying their intuitions by going to special testing consultants, for example, who can administer highly individualized tests in a highly sophisticated and sensitive way. Assuming that the testing service is genuinely good and not given to sugar-coated hyperbole (and many are), the parents should be willing to abide by the judgments of the testing service.

In turn, schools should be willing to abide by the judgment of services which are legitimate even though outside the school system, and to make adjustments in curricula, sectioning, counseling, and the other machinery of the school in accordance with this new information. Receptivity to new ideas should include receptivity to new testing information on the child of a particularly fractious set of parents, as well as receptivity to what goes on in a classroom. Teachers trained to say "I don't know" at the proper time must be able to say this to parents as well.

This would be the ideal situation for both sides are operating with a maximum of rational broad-mindedness in the best interests of the student. Unfortunately, the battle lines have been drawn for too many years, and many teachers, who have come to see themselves as an embattled minority, feel put upon by parents. Again, the development of attitudes becomes important. The training of teachers should include instruction in the basic concepts of what the product of education is supposed to be. Most important, some philosophy of what education should do (as opposed to instructional theories) should be discussed in broad detail—with teachers, as part of their training; with parents, as part of a continuing indoctrination at the schools; and finally, with the students themselves, in accordance with their maturity and ability to understand why they are doing what they are doing.

If this nirvana of educational philosophy could be established, there is no question in my mind that we would have better schools, better teachers, and most important, a vastly better finished product.

II

Methods of Education

IN ONE WAY, THE FACT THAT almost all parents are remarkably ignorant about the processes of education during their children's time in school is a blessing. The intricacy of the process is so great, the chances for failure, bad instruction, and discouragement so frequent, that if these things were rationally considered by parents, they would be scared stiff. Having come through the mill themselves relatively unscathed, they now think of education as an ordinary, inescapable fact of life that is handled by experts who know what they are doing and from which their children will emerge as easily as they have.

Although Mother will certainly shed a few tears when Bobby goes off to his first school class, she is more concerned that her baby has grown up than she is worried about any difficulties Bobby may have as a student. Yet, in one way or another, Bobby's remaining education, and possibly the course of his future life, can be affected by his success or lack of it in those first school classes.

If he is successful from the first, if he gets good reports on his behavior, his neatness, his ability to color pictures, his ability to pay attention and follow directions, the chances are that he will continue to be a good student through school. Please note the phrase "good student" does not necessarily imply anything about the nature and extent of what the student learns. The good student is the one who does what he is told, is dutiful, attentive, nondisruptive, and, in the proper sense of the word, docile. That is, he is a highly teachable child, and will probably remain so. In the same way, girls in our society tend to be more docile than boys; inherently, they are more likely to be good students, even while young.

Perhaps this phrase should be "particularly while young," because it is especially in the pre-school differences between boys and girls that the classroom suitability of girls shows up. Boys try more dangerous games, are physically more aggressive, get "killed" more often as the result of play than girls. Girls, on the other hand, are more likely to be emulating domestic situations, playing house, dressing dolls, and skipping rope while boys are building forts and playing cowboys and Indians.

In fact, the natural disparity between boys and girls is so great that some generalizations can be made about sex and a child's response to the early years of school. In general, boys seem to have more difficulties and natural bars to learning than is true for girls. For that reason, barring unforeseen circumstances, a boy who has not demonstrated any learning or behavior problems at the beginning of his schooling is apparently free from many of the problems associated with his sex and is likely to be a good student throughout his early academic career—i.e., up to the seventh grade, a major point in the education process. A sensitive and perceptive teacher might be able to establish the existence of a child's difficulties (or lack of them) as early as the first grade; certainly by the completion of the third grade, there should be enough evidence to go on.

Conversely, girls are less likely to have educational problems. Therefore, if a girl does show behavior or learning problems early, she is likely to have scholastic difficulties which conceivably could dog her throughout her entire school career.

Like all generalizations, this one must necessarily be hedged with qualifications: the teachers must be observant and intuitive in their judgments; bad days or a bad period must not be judged as typical of the child's overall performance. For example, at this period a child's jealousy of a new baby in the house can touch off resentment and a bid for attention which often takes the form of classroom crankiness.

As simply as possible, the answer to the implied question of what determines the probabilities of success in early school lies in attitudes and maturity. Maturity is of great importance, especially neuro-motor maturation, by which I mean the normal development of such neuro-muscular coordination as is related to the whole intricate process of learning. Understandably, this includes the proper development of inner coordination from eye to brain and from ear to brain, but there is also considerably more requirement for muscular coordination and gross motor control than the uninitiated ever think is necessary when they consider sedentary occupations like reading and writing, that require very little obvious activity or movement.

Boys tend to mature later than girls. A study of school failures in the earliest grades, made in connection with a study of brain dysfunction, shows that the very young male has the highest predilection for learning failure. Like all studies, this one also is subject to exceptions. Some children mature faster than their age would indicate and become among the most successful learners, but in general it is fair to say that the younger the child enters school, the greater is the probability of his having trouble, and that this is more true of boys than of girls.

The arbitrary dates set by many school systems often trap parents into sending their children to schools before they are really ready. It is probably wise, therefore, for parents of a child who falls on the distinctly young end of the age group that enters kindergarten or first grade to try to find out how mature their child is in relation to others in his group. This is one of the excellent reasons for nursery school in that it places the child in a school-like social environment where his behavior in a group and his responses to a learning situation, no matter how rudimentary, can be observed. Although I think the educational lobbies of the various state legislatures have carried certification of teachers almost to the point of futility, it is certainly true that the recent push to have nursery school teachers meet certain standards of training is a good idea, if implemented correctly.

The good nursery school teacher, with or without the proper training credentials, is one who can intuitively feel out those children who are going to have learning difficulties in the increasingly organized schooling of kindergarten and the first grade. Sometimes the teacher's prognostications have a basis in observed fact; sometimes they reflect no more than a hunch about a student.

Parents are likely to be touchy about the ability of their little ones, and as a result many nursery school teachers are reluctant to speak up in more than very general terms about a child's progress. It is the parents' responsibility, therefore, particularly if their child is at the young end of the scale, to make pointed inquiries of the nursery school teachers about their evaluations of the child's probability of success. If there is any considerable doubt, it is then wise to consider postponement of what would normally be the next step, whether it be from nursery school to kindergarten, or from kindergarten to first grade. Consultation might include talking to counselors in the school system and to the child's pediatrician.

Just as maturity can make an important difference even at the lowest level of education, so too can the attitudes of the people who surround the student—fellow students, parents, older brothers and sisters, even new arrivals.

Parents are probably the first and strongest influence of all. In a home where education is clearly important, where parents read books and speak grammatical English, students will pick up these attitudes from their parents, which then may be reinforced by their fellow students. Children from backgrounds which have little understanding or experience with education are likely to be somewhat unresponsive to any school situation, even in nursery school. When placed with children who are "serious" about education, their attitudes should veer around to some kind of alignment with that of the group. The positive reinforcement of the home is a necessary beginning for scholastic success, just as the continuing reinforcement of fellow students is important. It is on the basis of the Coleman Report, showing that students took their educational cues from their peer groups, that the highly controversial concept of school busing took shape: The most efficacious motivators of students are other students (who in turn are started in this motivation by their parents and the home situation).

Older brothers and sisters can be helpful to the younger ones. By having explored the unknown territory first and, of course, by telling the younger ones about their adventures, they serve to dispel some of the fear of uncertainty. Moreover, the older children, who are apt to be intoxicated with their newfound knowledge, are anxious to pass it on, and there inevitably will be some amateur teaching.

If the older brothers and sisters are happy with school and if the relationship between the older and younger children is good, then the results will be good. "Sibling rivalry," a phrase dear to the heart of child psychologists, however, does raise its ugly head, and occasionally takes the form not of competition, but of retirement from competition. A child who has a number of highly successful older brothers and sisters and who feels that someone else is getting the lion's share of the family attention (the second child, the next to the last child) may decide to avoid odious comparisons with the rest of the children by retreating from competition entirely. In a classic case of this sort, the child will find some excuse for not drawing a picture when asked or, after drawing one, will destroy it before it can be shown, saying he did not like it. Once started, this kind of behavior is difficult to reverse, because it is apparent that one of the most powerful inducements to academic achievement is previous success in school. The child of average ability who retreats from learning because of the fear of competition is likely to be branded as a slow learner or a nonlearner by teachers, unless the school or the teacher is unusually sensitive to the varieties of negative learning situations. In this case, the help of a psychologist or child psychiatrist seems indicated, but the identification of the many other potential problems needs the attention of a fairly sophisticated team: pediatric neurologist, psychiatrist, clinical psychologist, educational specialist, speech and language specialist. Since it is unlikely that many school systems will be able to afford such an extensive array of diagnostic machinery, concerned parents in most school systems must rely on sensitive and intuitive teachers, and on their own instinctive feelings about their children.

Too many teachers have been worn down by parents who do not want to hear any comments which either are negative or merely seem negative to them. The parent who takes up the cudgels in his child's behalf is not likely to get anything from a teacher but platitudes. If a parent can persuade a teacher that he really wants to know about his child's experiences and attitudes in school, and will not take umbrage at anything a teacher says professionally, then it is possible to build a relationship which can be highly useful to all concerned—parent, teacher, and child. Unfortunately, too many parents have exhausted the teacher's willingness to believe parents' claims to open-mindedness, and it is not uncommon to find that any kind of parent-teacher exchange is discouraged.

On the other side of the coin, parents are completely at the mercy of the school system for the quality and the type of teacher their children will have in those first few important years when, very often, the academic die is cast.

For the young student who has all the right qualifications—appropriate maturity for his age, intelligence, concerned but not anxious parents, and emotional good health—the degree of competence and understanding of his first teachers is important, but not so vital as it can be for other students less fortunate than he; such a child is likely to survive the educational process hardily.

But other less fortunate students may have problems which are less obvious, even to eyes of teachers who have seen generations of students come and go. The victims of these problems may appear to be stupid, inattentive, resentful, or fractious when in reality they are suffering from hidden conditions which prevent them from being as good students as they otherwise might be. The net result is that they are likely to be failures in school at an early age. Failures by their own standards, that is, or simply not successes. There is a great deal of difference. To be a failure in school ultimately means not to move to the next higher grade, but the situation really does not have to reach that point in order to discourage a child; if he does not do as well as his parents expect him to or as well as others he considers equals, he may think himself a failure. At such a tender age, it is probably overstating the case to talk about success and failure, because the students themselves have not learned to think in such stark terms. It is perhaps more reasonable to say that the students who are successful find school highly enjoyable; those who are not successes dislike school, or parts of school, or find other school activities in which they can be more successful. It is scarcely remarkable to point out that success breeds satisfaction and the probability of continuing success. The lack of it in any area may eventually produce a total retirement from any kind of competition.

For example, a recent study of high school dropouts in Rhode Island showed, to the surprise of the man making the survey, that a dropout was not a person who, while still a student, had abandoned academic activities in favor of athletics or other extracurricular endeavors, but one who had been a complete nonparticipant. In other words, before finally dropping out of school, he had withdrawn from any kind of competition in school, presumably because none of them had given him satisfaction.

While some of the attitudes of very young students are certainly important, what produces them is more important. A lack of success can make a child less than enthusiastic about school, but a few successes can probably bring him quickly around again. However, what makes early success most necessary is the dependence of learning on what has gone before. That is, almost all the school experience depends on the ability to read, and any delay in reading efficiency slows up all the subsequent educational process. Thus, learning the process of reading is absolutely essential. Considering the complexity of translating sound to paper and then back to sound again, it is remarkable that the ability to read is common and that the literacy rate anywhere is as high as it is. It is not so remarkable that constant refinements and changes have been tried over the years to make learning to read easier.

It became quite clear that the results have not always been happy when the great reading war broke out in the

mid 1950s. Although this was certainly not the first time
methods for teaching reading had come under attack, it was
probably the first time they had been considered so enthusiastically by a wide public. To quote Jean Chall in her
book *Learning to Read: the Great Debate*:

> Such a period began in 1955 in the United States with the
> publication of Rudolph Flesch's *Why Johnny Can't Read*.
> This book took the nation by storm. It stayed on the
> best-seller lists for over thirty weeks and was serialized in
> countless newspapers. Although the general press reacted
> favorably to it, reviewers in educational periodicals al-
> most unanimously rejected it.

The battle was fought chiefly over the two major methods
of teaching reading—word recognition and phonics. The
word recognition method is based on the ability of a child
to recognize a group of letters as a group and to identify
them for what they are and what they mean. When he sees
"ball" printed, he does not break it down into components,
and, indeed, would not be able to. It becomes a complete
learned unit which in turn becomes a visual symbol for
ball. Once a basic vocabulary is built up by this method,
instruction is given in the values of the components that
make up each word so that a totally new word, one which
has not been repeated in a reading primer enough times to
produce recognition, can be identified.

There is much to be said about these two systems, both
for and against. Because word recognition is based on the
word seen as a whole, there is little spelling learned by
syllabification; the word (or word's spelling) all comes out
in one piece. This fact led Flesch to conclude that word
recognition techniques encouraged guessing on the part of
students, who would guess at an unfamiliar word if it were
sufficiently like a familiar one. If a child disgorges the
letters of a word in a slightly different order from the way
he digested them, the word will be spelled wrong, but the

child will be unlikely to be aware of it. Thus I have seen more students whose college applications tell me they have studied the "paino" than I care to remember. One can also recognize "schloarship" and "Darthmouth," words spelled the way their authors remember having seen them, as products of word recognition reading techniques. On the other hand, English spelling and English pronunciation are in notorious disagreement, so that the child who learns to spell words by the phonic method does not have all the advantages on his side. When I see an applicant who has participated in "atheletics" I know that he probably has learned by the phonic (or some related) method, because he is spelling it the way he pronounces it.

Curiously, the television generation has reinforced the original premise of the word recognition school of reading by proving to every parent that it is not necessary to know the alphabet in order to read. Any preschool child who watches television is likely to astonish his parents at a tender age by caroling out "Coca-Cola" or "Esso" when he is driven past the appropriate sign. This is reading, and it is word recognition. However, it is word recognition in a very special form; "Coca-Cola" printed on a piece of paper in other than the characteristic script will not be recognized. It is the entire design of the words that is identified.

Learning words this way is not unlike learning Chinese ideographs; there are thousands to be learned and recognized. However, since Western civilization has invented and modified a code by which speech can be translated to paper, it seems much simpler to learn the code. Probably one of the reasons that the word recognition school grew up and flourished so enthusiastically is that the code in English is so enormously complicated. Consonants like g can have a number of different values (George, grocery, having, garage) and vowels like o can move all over the place (to, look, over, off, come), to say nothing of the diphthongs, some of which are separated by an intervening consonant (*can* becomes *cane* because of the mysterious activity of an added *e*). Small wonder that foreign visitors are baffled by English, and the wonder might well be that so many of our children learn to read at all.

Phonics, the method of teaching reading by teaching the child the phonetic values of the alphabet and then teaching him to put the pieces together into a pattern which conveys the sound and the meaning on the paper was the original method of teaching reading. This usually involved a great deal of rote drill in memorizing sound patterns, but the more relaxed view of teaching that began in the 1920s and '30s was against the drudgery and unimaginativeness of rote learning. For whatever reasons, the phonetic system was out and the word recognition method became the accepted method in reading until recently when the pendulum began to swing the other way.

It should not be inferred that there were only two methods ever advanced for learning to read. Reading methods and studies of the results are among educators' favorite forms of research. Methods have run the gamut from the entirely predictable, which produces reading books suitable for satire ("See Jim. See Jim go. Go, Jim, go."), to a remarkable self-teaching method which involves an electric typewriter which calls out the name of the letter struck. In this way, and through the means of letters or numbers projected on a screen, to be reproduced by the child on his typewriter, the child can be taught to read at a remarkably early age—sometimes as early as two years. The author of this unique method, which has generated a good deal of publicity, is Omar K. Moore, who feels he has developed a reading program in which the interest and problem-solving ability of the child himself determines the effectiveness of the result. Since his method is unique, and involves a great deal of special and complicated equipment and a high degree of individual attention, its use has been chiefly experimental to this point.

Other methods of reading have centered around texts printed in key colors to denote special words and sounds, have combined phonics and word recognition in varying degrees, and have concentrated on the material covered in the readers as a prime source of reform. For example, Dan and Nan, two favorite central characters in a reading series, were clearly white, middle-class, and suburban. All fine for the white, middle-class, suburban reader, but what about a youthful reader who was not in any of these categories?

The new reading primers identify with the city dwellers, and the pictures are street scenes. Hydrants have replaced trees, and the participants are multi-colored, as opposed to a previously all white cast in a suburban setting. This is a sensible reform which has little to do with method but a great deal to do with possible motivation, and it has been widely adopted with apparently good results.

What about the different methods? Now that the debate seems temporarily settled in favor of the phonic method once more, and now that scientific studies have been mobilized to prove the efficacy of differing methods, what is the conclusion? Any examination of studies on reading quickly tells us that the experts are reluctant to agree, even when they are presented with the same studies and are asked to draw conclusions. It is dangerous, therefore, to say that any study or set of studies *proves* anything in the field of reading. However, there are some conclusions made about the teaching and learning of reading which seem safe to accept. They are that:

> 1. Knowing the letters of the alphabet and the sounds they stand for, before learning to read, can help a child greatly in the process of learning to read;
>
> 2. In the first three grades, knowledge of the letters and sounds of the alphabet seems to have a greater influence than intelligence on reading ability;
>
> 3. Beyond the third grade level, knowledge of phon-

ics and the general level of reading seem to go hand in hand: a student whose knowledge of phonics is low tends to read at a lower level.

On the other hand, not all students whose knowledge of phonics is good are necessarily good readers. And as a student progresses through school, the correlation between intelligence and reading ability increases steadily.

Again, although the evidence of studies is apparently open to differing interpretations, a greater number of reading problems and spelling problems seems to develop for students taught by the word recognition method than for those taught by a phonic method. But, although the current evidence seems to support the phonic method solidly (the whole history of reading is punctuated with scientific studies which can turn over previously made scientific studies), there is still the mystery of why some students cannot learn to read. Their difficulty seems to bear no relation to any particular teaching method. Usually if these problems are caught in time, they can be conquered by patience, by careful individual attention, and by an elastic shifting of methods which sometimes goes directly against what is considered the "best" method at the moment. In other words, anything that might work is used because it is so vitally important that a child learn to read. The tragic aspect of the dyslectic child is that his inabilities may not be related to intelligence at all, but his reading disability nevertheless may stamp him as "slow" or possibly "ineducable." Often the only people who still believe in the child are his parents, and in many cases they are right to do so.

Before considering the possibilities that may keep a child from being as good a student as his ability warrants, consider for a moment the incredibly complicated code which man has devised for communicating and what is needed to decode this elaborate system.

In order to decode his system, the student must know the

language—which he does. By the time a child has reached the age of four, generally the lower limit for the teaching of reading, he has mastered the rudiments of English grammar—that is, his word order and simple tenses are mastered in a fairly standard pattern. He is now ready to translate written symbols into the spoken language.

Here he must learn a number of new and confusing rules. First, he must be selective about remembering what an object is in different positions. A chair remains a chair, whether the child sees it upright on the floor, lying down, from the left side or the right side. A car remains a car whether it moves across the field of vision from right to left or from left to right. However, in reading, a *p* rotated on its axis becomes a *q*, or rotated on its bulge becomes a *d*, and a *d* rotated on its axis becomes a *b*. Unlike the chair, then, which always retains its identity as a chair regardless of its position, the symbols of the alphabet have quite different meanings if they are permitted to move out of a specific position.

In the same way, the direction of reading must be maintained by custom or convention in one direction— from left to right. If this direction is not maintained, the meaning of a combination of code symbols for sound becomes hopelessly confused. Thus "dog" becomes "god," and if the constant direction is not maintained throughout the word, there is still a great possibility of confusion. A "bugle" can become a "bulge," and "sign" becomes "sing," which produce quite different meanings.

As if these laws, which every young student must master, were not complicated enough, the code signs themselves are differentiated by the most miniscule differences. An experienced reader can see immediately why beginning readers are printed in large clear type. Think objectively about the minor differences and the greater similarities of the letters *c* and *e*, of *q* and *p*. The clues sometimes are very slight, like the dot over the *i* and the *j* to separate them from *l* and *y*.

Add to this the confusion caused by the difference in form, but not in meaning, between the capital letters and the lower-case letters. Finally, consider the additional complications that occur in assuring the young student that the written, or cursive, letters are really the same code symbols as the printed letters, even though they are often an entirely different shape. (Consider f, F, *f*, or G, g, *g*, as though for the first time, and think how confused you might be. If this example does not get through to you, I suggest you try to learn the Russian upper- and lower-case printed alphabet, and then add to it Russian cursive writing. This ought to bring home the point.) It is not surprising, therefore, that many schools use printed letters in their written work well into the third grade in order to minimize the confusion about letter and sound symbols which even very good students must encounter. And we have not even considered yet the additional burden of attaching at least one sound to each of the symbols.

This ability to differentiate the symbols of written speech, the alphabet, to attach them to the sounds they represent, and finally to put together these building blocks into increasingly complex patterns adds up to the progressively confusing business of reading. Translating the other way, from concept to sound to paper, is writing. While such a statement is self-evident to an adult who has had years of indoctrination in the subject, to a child at the beginning of his educational career it can be an exciting, fun-filled discovery or an impenetrable mystery that, in some cases, seems to defy solution.

Considering the importance of reading and writing to a child in terms of the remainder of his education and his entire future, the brouhaha over reading and writing in the public press is readily understandable. What is understood far less well is that, under any system of teaching, there are always some children who are unable to decode the complicated message easily. In some cases they will have such difficulty that they will be unfairly accused of not having the intelligence to learn, when in fact this is not the case.

What are the inhibiting factors, other than defective intelligence, that may block a child from normal progress in reading? Can the faults be corrected? Are there methods which will enable a parent to discover that a child does have educable intelligence even though he has severe reading problems? Finally, are there methods of diagnosis which will enable a school or a parent to anticipate troubles in the learning process and to approach schooling more carefully and with much greater individual attention? The answers to all these questions (except the first) are generally affirmative. The answer to the first is complicated, because there is such a variety of possibilities that reading experts until recently have simply thrown up their hands and said that there is no way to know the reasons for dyslexia in a child.

There is no constant set of causes of dyslexia. There are many possible sources of trouble ranging from simple ones like poor vision to the complex ones like learning blockages stemming from combined emotional, maturational, and neurological disturbances. Poor hearing or an inability to understand what he hears can also be a source of the trouble. A child who cannot interpret what he sees or what he is expected to decipher will have trouble. This may be called a visual perceptual problem. In the same way, the child whose interpretation of sound is such that he cannot properly attach sound to symbol will be called a "language," or auditory perceptual problem. Evaluation of both of these difficulties should be demanded as a regular part of the standard physical examination which a school system gives before it allows students to undertake any kind of classroom activity. Hidden defects are much more likely to be maturationally and educationally crippling, since they are rarely apparent. The causes are often vague, but include the possibilities of brain damage or brain dysfunction, which can be the result of heredity. Brain dysfunction stems from some untoward accident, interference, or "insult" to the unborn baby before birth or during the birth process itself.

The possibility of emotional handicaps resulting from a demanding and competitive social system should not be overlooked as a possible deterrent to learning. Somewhat later in this chapter there will be a discussion of behavior in children that is symptomatic of emotional problems.

In addition, there are the problems of poor teaching, which aggravates the retardation of learning, as well as the problems of parental indifference or a lack of enthusiasm among fellow students. All have a powerful deterrent effect.

Here, however, we are chiefly concerned with the hidden or nearly hidden adverse factors which are neither emotional nor environmental, and which are likely to provide parents and students with the frustrations of having a child who putatively has everything positive going for him— heredity, environment, and schools—and still has learning problems.

There are two major schools of thought which have arisen recently to explain why some "overprivileged" children cannot learn to read or write. One side lays the blame on "minimal brain damage"—that is, the minor disarrangements of the neural and cerebral systems of the child which produce subtle and suggestive symptoms in motor behavior and thinking activity, and which provide a deterrent to learning. To this school of thought, there is nothing shameful or even remarkable about the concept of minimal brain damage. Because of the highly complicated nature of the brain, the nervous system, and the coordination between them, and because of our poor understanding of how the brain works, it is probable that everyone has some form of brain damage to a greater or lesser degree. Most of us learn to compensate for the brain's inefficiency, but for some the brain dysfunction manifests itself in learning inefficiency.

The other side of the fence in this argument dismisses the possibility of brain damage as the prime evil, pointing out that some students who have no learning problems at all have background histories, psychological test findings, and brainwave patterns, (electroencephalograms) which are just as erratic as those of the poor learners. Instead, those who adopt this position suggest that the child who suffers from dyslexia and other forms of learning retardation has a "maturational lag"—that is, a lack of even development in the nervous system and in the coordinating processes of the various sensory branches.

Whatever science will eventually show to be the cause, it is pointless for parents to become involved in or upset about what is essentially a pedantic argument. The cause of a child's problems in learning to read is really beside the point. Rather, the parents should concentrate on finding a way to identify potential problems early, so that corrective action can be taken if needed.

Fortunately, such an approach is now possible since a test has been developed by the Meeting Street School of Providence, Rhode Island, an agency that has dealt with both the problems of diagnosing brain-damaged children and training them to overcome their handicaps, and of identifying learning disorders in normal children. Although the test has grown out of the school's experience in dealing with severely handicapped children, it was designed to be used in schools on normal children and to be administered by comparatively unsophisticated personnel to detect the "neurologically inefficient" child (one of several euphemisms which have been developed because the phrase "brain-damaged" has such alarming connotations in the minds of the average parents). Using this sophisticated approach, the small number of children with this disability can be identified properly. The Meeting Street School Screening Test (MSSST) measures cases where the findings are so minimal that to all outward appearances the child is normal except for his difficulty in learning to read or write.

The test is a simple one dealing with the child's abilities in following motor patterns (clapping hands, hopping), in visual matching, in visual memory, in listening to nonsense words and repeating them, in repeating a simple story, and in a number of other tasks related to "information processing." The results of the test can be scored and—on the basis of this test, plus classroom observation, intelligence tests, and other standard evaluative material—a reasonably accurate early prediction for a child's success in school can be made. Unfortunately, even this procedure leaves out the factor of motivation, which consistently upsets all the scales that psychologists have ever invented.

The MSSST is not a test instrument which can solve all problems, nor is it a panacea able to be used all by itself; but it has filled a gap in alerting schools, teachers, and parents that a child is prone to learning failure. Taken in conjunction with a coordinated program set up by a school system, the possibility of failure is lessened. Other deterrents to a tendency for failure might include the careful and sensitive grouping of children, specialized teaching techniques to match specific learning difficulties diagnosed by the MSSST, and, ideally, a team of educational psychologists, language specialists, pediatric neurologists, and specially trained teachers to provide comprehensive support. However, a sensitivity to the problem and an attempt to minimize the failure effect may be one of the best ways that a school system which cannot afford such an array of talent can combat the increasing number of categorical failures.

Grouping children with suspected learning difficulties as predicted by the MSSST and assigning to them teachers who seem to have special competence or interest in dealing with students who may have problems will aid immeasurably. The important point for schools and parents to consider is that there is more to successful learning than the possibilities demonstrated by the IQ, although this should not obscure the fact that, taken alone as a diagnostic and predictive testing device, the IQ evaluation has been remarkably successful in predicting success in the early grades, and the predictions hold up as the child continues through school.

(Interestingly, for those parents who are squeamish about the phrase "brain-injured," the authors of the MSSST talk instead about "psychoneurological inefficiency" and about "information processing," which is, of course, what a student does in school. It is of further interest to me that, despite the technical argument between the two major schools of thought concerning the causes of reading problems, the MSSST tests measure learning disabilities regardless of whether they are produced by "maturational lag" or by "minimal brain damage"—but for parental purposes the difference is semantic and unimportant.)

The test devised by the Meeting Street School is a valuable diagnostic tool for schools and for parents— particularly for parents, because when a child fails to do on schedule those things which are expected of him in school, they feel bewildered and frightened. The child who suffers from some hidden and scarcely perceptible impediment to learning may simply be written off as "slow" or "retarded" by an inexperienced or insensitive teacher, and may well be treated as "stupid" for the remainder of his school career. The MSSST does not correct the impediments—it does not even assess intelligence in the same way that the usual IQ test does—but it does tell the parent *why* his child is having trouble in school. Further, a curriculum is currently being developed around the child's weaknesses to test the validity of "prescription teaching"—i.e., teaching toward identified strengths and weaknesses in learning ability. Until such a curriculum becomes generally available, however, parents must rely on other corrective measures more generally available in conjunction with the school, with a consulting psychologist, with the child's pediatrician, or with any agency that understands the complex problem.

The chief shortcoming of the Meeting Street School Screening Test is that, although it is quite effective for five- and six-year-olds, as yet it cannot identify weaknesses before the age of four at the very earliest because of the limitations imposed by the development of the nervous system at that age. Studies currently being undertaken by a professor at Brown University give promise that identification of problems even in infancy may be possible, but until that becomes a reality, the MSSST is not effective for children below a certain age.

Clearly, the earlier a child's potential problems can be foretold, the less eventual trouble he is likely to have in adjusting to the demands of life. Are there any telltale signs, any past bits of history, medical or personal, that are likely to tell a parent what he can expect for his child in school?

It is extremely dangerous to generalize from particulars on this matter, and even more dangerous for laymen to try to outguess the experts, but there are some situations which an intelligent parent might use as guidelines to forecast *possible* trouble. These guidelines are based on the observations and investigations of Dr. Eric Denhoff, a distinguished pediatric neurologist, and they include the following observation signals and warning signs for parents.

Low birth-weight children (four pounds or less) are likely to become problems. Difficulties do not necessarily follow this condition, but such children are more prone to trouble in school, especially if they have had associated birth complications like seizures, serious diarrhea with accompanying dehydration, breathing difficulty (respiratory distress), or high jaundice level.

Very difficult deliveries which the obstetrician may regard as potentially injurious during the birth process are likely to produce a high susceptibility to future problems.

A "stress" pregnancy, during which there were incidents in the mother which threatened the fetus, such as a chronic disease like diabetes, unusual bleeding, toxemia, is likely to produce a proclivity to future problems.

As the infant emerges into childhood and takes on a personality of his own, there are observable physical landmarks and bits of medical history that can give clues to the observant parent. In addition to infant jaundice, low birthweight, respiratory distress, and Rh disease, parents of children up to the age of four should take into account frequent infections, especially ear infections in the early years when the child is learning to differentiate sounds. The colicky baby who finds it "hard to thrive" (in Dr. Denhoff's phrase) is likely to emerge as a high-energy child who exhibits enormously excessive motor activity. This high level of activity, when matched with a short attention span in which the toddler shoots from one activity to another with dizzying rapidity, produces a child with low learning efficiency. When he learns to talk, this child is likely to be highly verbal but physically clumsy. He may have trouble learning to read, since the pattern just described is common among children afflicted with problems of hand-to-eye coordination.

The opposite of this pattern is the passive child, who is often slow to talk. As he grows older he will not be clumsy in his activity like the hyperactive child, but, since he is handicapped in expressing himself, he may be irritable and physically aggressive because of his frustrations in communicating. Again, this child's learning process will be depressed in the language area; he will also have a predilection for spoken over written communication.

It is oversimplification to suppose that a child will necessarily be either one type or another, since nature usually combines problems in varying degrees. The two distinct types that have been described often overlap, and the worst aspects of both can be manifested in one child. In such a case the child almost certainly will be classified as a "slow learner" or "retarded," even though his intelligence is at the normal or even the high normal level.

Unfortunately, the child's true intelligence will be hard to determine in schools, because most schools are set up to give their various forms of testing on a mass basis; very few school systems can afford to test an entire student population with individually administered intelligence tests.

This mass testing of students is certain to result in some cases of major errors of measurement which the children and parents may have to suffer with for a long while. At best, if the child overcomes the conditions which make his good intelligence appear less good on a mass-administered test and becomes a good student in school, he is then classified as "overachiever."

In the same way, any label attached to your child in grade school as a result of his testing experience may well become his label throughout the rest of his school career, if it is not contradicted by other evidence of the same sort. Since I plan to cover the business of testing in Chapter VIII, there is no need now to go too deeply into this problem, except to say there are means by which a "rescue" can be made. What are they, who makes them, and at whose insistence?

The tests available for assuring you that no serious error in evaluation has been made about your child are individually administered tests which investigate reasoning power and levels of information in different areas, but without the need for a quick motor response These tests are administered individually, as I have said, by experienced psychologists, whose expertise includes the ability to make a sensitive reaction to the child tested, who can guess when there is more than appears at first glance, and who can pursue the matter to find out more. The tests used are varied, and will depend on the discretion of the testor, but among the most successful have been the Wechsler Intelligence Scale for Children (WISC).

Who decides that mass testing is doing an injustice to the child, and who feels that a child is better than his school record, despite uniformly bad report cards? More often than not, according to Dr. Denhoff, it is the parents. This surprises me because I have felt that parents are always hypersensitive about their children's lack of success; they might be expected to be less than candid about a lack of intelligence, apparent or real. However, according to Dr. Denhoff, it is the warm and sensitive parent who can see the child and his responses out of the frustrating atmosphere of the classroom and who can say, "I don't care what the school says, he *is* better than he seems."

Yet, for all the parents who have the knack for guessing right, there are probably as many more who are unwilling to accept the truth—that theirs is a child so crippled by maturational, physical, or emotional dysfunctions (or a combination of these) that there is no hope for his living up to the expectations of the family in terms of education and career in the current structure of things. This is naturally a bitter pill for any parent.

In mentioning emotional malfunction, it is important to realize that emotional and physical problems often go hand in hand. On the other hand, emotional problems alone can sometimes produce effects similar to and often indistinguishable from those of physical dysfunction. There is often a curious circularity involving physical and emotional problems. In turn, a severe environmental emotional problem (broken home, drinking parents, the absence of any kind of security in the face of great demands) can cause a child to appear far less able than he is. Reading problems, for example, can sometimes be explained in no other way than as emotional blockages. Hyperkinesia (another term for the overactive child who may be in constant motion, have a limited attention span, and be a learning and

disciplinary problem in the classroom) may result either
from brain damage or from considerable emotional
difficulties.

In the emotional area, the means of demarcation are just
as fuzzy as those in the area of physical malfunction, but it
is just as necessary to learn to detect them. Again, the young
child who has severe emotional problems becomes quickly
obvious early in his academic career. He may be disruptive
or nonreceptive; he may be in constant motion or aggressive and pugnacious to the point where he alienates his
teachers and his follow pupils.

Unfortunately, it is emotional problems that parents
are least likely to understand, because they so often involve
the parents themselves. The parent who is emotionally
disturbed, or whose habits or attitudes are so extreme as to
cause emotional disturbance in his child, is not likely to
recognize or admit the nature of the problem.

More subtle, and even less easy to explain or to prevent,
are the pressures of expectation which overshadow all the
relationships between child and parent in the middle-class
environment. Charles Downes, headmaster of the York
School in California, put it this way:

> The games people play infect education, and we have
> young men in our school who are scared to death, not of
> us, but of their parents. Their parents won't let them
> alone; they won't let them become people. Instead, they
> are supposed to become a mirror of what their fathers
> never had, or what will impress Momma's bridge party.

This view of destructive parental ambitions is held by
many. As one educational consultant said: "Once, the ideal
was to be a good parent; now it is to produce successful
children."

The same concern for education which provides the
attitudes and atmosphere at home that are likely to make for
a good student can also produce a neurotic child. Many
parents openly apply pressure, demand good academic
results, talk about the need for success, and get results in

school; the results may show up in the form of success in high school or in college. Other parents may say less but, by their example and the simple fact of their existence, provide a considerable form of pressure. In either case, for the child who is able, physically and emotionally, to respond to the challenge, there is no immediate conflict. However, for the child whose physical equipment makes it difficult for him to provide the kind of success and achievement he knows his parents demand, there is a terrible feeling of inadequacy and failure.

Thus some cases of educational failures can be attributed entirely to emotional rather than physical handicaps. Emotional blockages can produce students who cannot learn to read; emotionally caused hyperactivity can make it impossible for a student to concentrate, or even sit still long enough to become an effective member of the classroom; and personality problems can so alienate teachers, especially those who are not sensitive to problems of this sort in children, that any possibility of the rapport which is important to learning, especially in the very young, is lost entirely.

Physical and emotional handicaps tend to follow similar patterns in many ways: those that are most severe show up almost immediately in the school situation. Children with what might be called, somewhat confusingly, "heavy minimal brain damage" will have trouble in learning to read and in mastering the fundamentals of a primary education. Children with serious but not readily apparent emotional problems will have similar difficulties.

Once the child has successfully undertaken primary school in a fashion which seems roughly related to his ability, is it safe to assume that all danger of educational failure is past? It would be reassuring to say that it was, but at about the seventh-grade level there is another period of sorting out which can be particularly baffling to parents who have assumed their children were well under way. Simply, the reasons are that while the most badly affected children are clearly distinguishable at the beginning of their school experience, those whose handicaps are minimal do not begin to show up as school problems until about the seventh grade when the strain of a new set of pressures generally converge at this time.

First, the changes of adolescence begin to occur. Second, most school systems begin at this time to use a team of teachers—that is, teachers who specialize in one or two subjects—so that the student has not one, but several teachers, and the potential security he may have enjoyed by having to cope with only one teacher (which he could just manage) has been shattered by the necessity of learning to adjust to several different patterns of personality, teaching method, and so on. Third, the courses themselves begin to be more complex at this grade level. A child can rely less on his memory and must be able to accomplish more academic tasks in less time; he probably has to read more and faster than he has before. All of these things tend to precipitate a school crisis for the child who is marginally handicapped, either emotionally or physically.

When a child who has been a passable student suddenly gets into trouble, the parents are usually bewildered and helpless. Since any physical damage that might be termed marginal is nearly impossible to spot without diagnostic testing of the same general type used on younger children, there is not much a parent can do except go to his pediatrician. It is sensible to go armed with objective observations about the child: has he had difficulties (perhaps hardly worth mentioning) in catching a ball, determining right from left? Does he have any peculiarities of pronunciation which have almost become family jokes, but which may indicate that, at some crucial time in the past, he heard words and the sounds that make them incorrectly? Is his handwriting poorer than might be expected, and does he tend to invert letter or number combinations in writing them down?

Often parents have lived so long with a child that they

have become used to the idiosyncrasies which may be indicative of minimal brain dysfunction. The child who is sufficiently bright or motivated may well weather the first years of school, but then break down as teachers change each period and the work becomes more complicated. The list of possible clues given above is by no means complete, nor does the fact that any one child may show some of these indicators mean he has a crippling dysfunction. But the sensitive parent will observe and turn to the family pediatrician, to an educational psychologist, to a pediatric neurologist, or to whatever resources the community has. Since this is a comparatively new concept of reasons for academic failure, not all pediatricians and not all school systems are sensitized to problems of this sort unless they are immediately apparent. Some parents will have to forge ahead to find out answers about their children, and in so doing they run the risk of being labeled as "aggressive" or "pushing." It is very hard to know where to draw the line between when to refuse to take a negative answer and when to relax and accept the judgment of those who seem to be able to make objective judgments. Again, it is the intuitive, "good" parent who is able to draw that line, but no one has ever been able to teach intuition.

Just as the marginal physical handicap may show up around the seventh grade, the emotional weakness may also show up at this time for many of the same reasons, and for the additional reason of growing sexual maturity, which is likely to unsettle the most settled of students.

What does the alert parent look for here? Generally, "escape" might be the theme of the emotional danger signals. The child who begins at this period to complain about fatigue, or who uses this as an excuse for nonperformance, may be showing one of the classic symptoms of withdrawal. Obviously, anyone may feel tired, but a constant repetition of this as an excuse without any supporting reasons should be noted.

Other symptoms in the same vein—such as doodling,

daydreaming, and other signs of withdrawal from the obligations of day-to-day living—are, of course, likely to show up in any child occasionally; but, again, when there seems to be constant repetition without any apparent cause, parents should take cautious alarm.

Still another danger signal is the sudden change in friends. The child who feels overly pressured by his environment and who wants some kind of relief will turn to friends whose standards are not so demanding as those he has been held to. A child, like any human, seeks success. If success is too hard to get or seems impossible to attain in one setting, he then will try to measure himself by standards which are not so high. Since his parents are not likely to change their expectations for him, he must then find a group with which he is more comfortable, where the standards are not so high, or where they are different enough so that he has a better chance for success.

It is at this period that great changes occur; some children will take themselves in hand and become models of what they and their parents want. Others, as I have said, will start at this time to establish an escape route from failure. Increasingly, drugs are appearing at this juncture of a student's life, which is dismaying to schools and parents, but not surprising as a double means of escaping reality and providing an "in" with a different, lower-standard group.

One specialist in disturbed children told me: "In the lower income or social levels, the kid who is escaping from pressure will steal cars. In the middle classes, he is more likely to get poor grades or threaten to drop out, both of which are just as heinous to success-demanding parents as car stealing. The point is that both kids are crying for help . . . they are asking for release from an overpressured environment."

What do parents do in this situation. First, they must ask themselves some hard questions—have they directly or by implication put too much pressure on a child who cannot produce to the level of their expectations? Unfortunately, parents are not likely to see themselves as the ogres. A friend whose husband went to Amherst told me: "Bill keeps telling everyone that he's not pressing the boy to think about Amherst, but he never talks about anything else when colleges are mentioned."

Probably the best thing for a parent to do when the danger signals occur is to take stock of himself and have a quiet talk with the child's pediatrician, school counselor, and anyone else who seems to have the confidence of the child. Almost every student has an older person he talks to, and the question is how to find the confidant.

Once the causes are known and talked about on both sides, perhaps both parent and child can come to some understanding of how to proceed. Help in this kind of problem can come from the school counselor, psychologist, the family pediatrician, or, if it seems necessary, a consulting psychologist specializing in adolescent problems or a psychiatrist. The result may be a scaled-down expectation for the future by parents and children; but if it works, the results will be to exchange failure in grandiose ambitions with success in a slightly more limited area and this seems a small price to pay.

The parents who have children with no apparent problems at this age may well be thankful, since the major critical points are somewhere around grade seven. The next step is high school, where the academic challenge and complexity are even greater, and some children will falter under this burden as well. The next major point of indecision and despair is in college, chiefly, I suspect, when the children realize that they are going to have to commit themselves in one direction for the rest of their lives. But in the seventh grade that agony still lies over the horizon.

III

The High School

THE ALUMNUS ON THE phone was a high-powered business executive who had just been moved from St. Louis to Atlanta. He was looking for a house, he explained to me, but, before he settled on one, he wanted to know which high school in Atlanta I thought was best; he would buy a house in that district.

A corollary question which he did not bring up was whether he should put his children in private schools instead of public. Really, this question is one of geography and tradition. If the alumnus had moved from Atlanta to Baltimore or Philadelphia, he almost certainly would have asked about private schools, because of the educational tradition of those cities.

Questions like this are hard to answer because a great deal of what happens to a student in high school depends on the student, the friends he (or she) has, the luck they have with teachers, the home environment, their native ability, and finally, the teachers, courses, and equipment available.

The best high schools in the country can produce terrible students. Not surprisingly, the converse is also true: even the worst high school can produce a good student. Among the most brilliant undergraduates I have known at Brown, at least two have come from a nearby school system which I would rank among the state's most inept and corrupt.

If this is the case, then, is the quality of the high school not worth worrying about? Are the variables that go into establishing a high school's quality so great that it is almost impossible to establish a standard of judgment? Or is the quality of the high school really likely to have a profound effect on an individual student, and will this, in turn, affect his college admission and his subsequent success or lack of it in graduate school and beyond?

Questions like these concern every parent who thinks about education for his children, but the answers are not easy to come by because of the immense number of variables in the situation.

What every ambitious parent ideally would like is a high school that will take a child at about age fourteen (which many parents, and I include myself, consider to be the nadir of human development), discipline him to study without being told, teach him manners, morals, civic responsibility, give him academic training which will enable him to enter any college in the country he might want to consider, teach him proficiency in sports, and to respect his elders. If the student is a girl, the list is much the same, but it is possible that the parents would also like her to learn to cook and to make her own clothes.

No such high school exists; if it does, there are no houses for sale in that suburb. However, there are specific criteria that can be applied to schools in an area which will give an indication of how good the school *could* be if all the variables go the right way.

The important points to look at in evaluating a school system are the citizen attitudes, expenditures per pupil, condition of the school buildings, and recent record of the graduates. Other items to consider are the age of the suburb or section of the city, its immediate prospects of rising or declining as a desirable place to live, and finally the religious or ethnic makeup of the neighborhood.

If you think this sounds as though you must have a graduate degree in sociology before you can decide where to move or whether your high school is a good one or not, you are right. I don't mean to say that you have to make a scientific survey, but these are among the factors which affect the quality of schools in a neighborhood, most of which are known or felt intuitively anyway.

It is remarkable but true that not all rich suburbs have the same attitudes toward education. It might seem reasonable to assume that they have, but the difference in school systems nearly side by side in a suburban complex like Chicago (known as "Chicagoland" to the readers of the *Tribune,* "the world's greatest newspaper") shows how large these differences can be. If outward appearances are any indication, the town of Evanston, even though it has its share of slums and is old enough to be decaying somewhat, still maintains a young and lively school system which must su ely rank as one of the best in the country simply in terms of innovative features which the schools have employed. The fact that the citizens of this town have elected to keep the school young and healthy is proof enough of a citizen attitude which produces good schools. The opposite condition is equally easy to identify—the school system that suffers from a lack of citizen support probably is overcrowded and recent school bond issues have been voted down.

The sad truth of the matter is that a good school system and good educational opportunity cost money, so that expenditure is another quick index of the excellence of a system. Thus, a mediocre high school in the northeast spends about $750 per year per pupil. The high schools that can be considered superb now are spending somewhat over $1,200 per year per pupil. It is assumed, of course, that both school systems are getting their money's worth.

The actual condition of the buildings themselves are often a clue to what is going on inside. In new neighborhoods this method is more difficult to use and less revealing because school architects have learned to use materials which are virtually indestructable. But in an old town, the degree to which the buildings have been brought up-to-date is revealing. Oak Park, a suburb of Chicago so venerable that shingle houses designed by Frank Lloyd Wright in his earliest period are sprinkled throughout the residential area, has an equally ancient high school building which is centrally located. While the building is the same on the outside as it was decades ago, the interior is in a constant state of revision and modernization. (Under a grant from the government and with the assistance of private industry, Oak Park is experimenting with an information retrieval center which could set the pattern for all our schools in the future—if we can afford it.)

Perhaps the most interesting aspect of old suburbs like Oak Park or Evanston, which have a traditionally great concern for education and constantly renew themselves, is the cost. Both towns are old and therefore not liable to sudden expansion; there are no vacant lots on which to put houses, and so the population remains comparatively stable. As building prices continue to advance inexorably at the rate of $1^1/_2$ percent a month, the high cost of education in a new suburb centers around building, equipping, and staffing new schools. In the old suburbs, an established system is set up, and the chief expense and concern is keeping the buildings, equipment, and teachers at the high level they have already reached, which is less expensive than starting from scratch.

The recent record of graduates, including *where* the products of the high school went to college, is another indicator, although not an infallible one, of the quality of a high school. It will reflect parental attitudes and, to a certain extent, how effective the teaching is—assuming that the most selective colleges know the high schools. In some cases, colleges know the high schools too well; a highly competitive high school may well produce efficient but cut throat scholars, of which the college has no need. This is a different problem, however, which will be dealt with later.

A friend called me the other day from the most prosperous suburb of her city. The League of Women Voters, she announced, was studying the high school in her town and had come upon the distribution of College Board scores for the senior class. Was this information available from other schools and would it tell her committee anything about the quality of the schools in Hawthorne, where her children are in school?

It is available. Almost every suburban high school today publishes its profile, describing the community the school is in, median income, job status of the money-earners, rapidity of growth, and general inclinations (tactfully stated) about educational attitudes. The students are grouped according to their ability in standardized tests and, depending on the complexity or sophistication of the profile, according to where the graduates of the school went to college and roughly where they stood in class.

As my League of Women Voters friend realized, one profile by itself is not indicative, but a comparison of profiles from other suburbs of the city or with comparable suburbs in other cities should prove very revealing.

The reason for publishing a school's profile is, of course, to provide college admission officers with a better idea of the academic competition the candidates from that school have encountered—which is particularly important when students choose colleges outside their high school's range of reputation. The profile can be useful as well to other high schools in evaluating records of students whose parents are "corporate gypsies" moved relentlessly from place to place by their employers. (A college could achieve a quite respectable statistical geographical distribution by simply publishing the corporation movements of fathers of students. It also works in reverse; thus a lifelong Californian who enters an eastern college shows up on the register next year from New Jersey, scarcely an oddity.)

Other factors in picking the right school include a consideration of whether that section of the city is on the way up or down. Actually, this is putting the cart before the horse, since the quality of schools has kept many suburbs, like Evanston and Oak Park, healthy and desirable places to live long after they should have crumbled. This is so partly because, as I suggested before, the cost of maintaining quality education is less than that of building and developing a new school system. Hence, more important than the age or direction of the suburb is the viability of the school. Is it being modernized? Are new courses, techniques, experiments, and plans keeping it and its surroundings young and healthy?

The answers to almost all the questions about how good a school or a school community is can be traced to the direct question: How genuinely interested are the residents in education? More often than not, this question can be answered by looking into the ethnic or religious makeup of a community, as well as the income and educational level of the parents.

Making generalizations about racial or ethnic groups is currently so dangerous as to be properly quite unpopular. Yet it is certainly true that if a neighborhood is dominated by a religious or ethnic group, the attitudes of that group toward education can have profound effects on the quality of public schools in the area. For example, in the east, and particularly in the northeast, the Protestant professional class is likely to believe in private schools which robs the local public schools of a great deal of leadership energy and support. In areas where there is a high percentage of Roman Catholics there is a strong trend to diocesan education or to schools run by religious teaching orders. This, too, tends to bleed off the interest and enthusiasm of a large block of citizens who would otherwise be concerned about the excellence of the public schools. In the northeast, a combination of Yankee preoccupation with private schools and Roman Catholic concern with religious schools has severely diminished the vigor of public education.

The one group who can be expected to be vitally interested in education, and public education at that, are the Jews. Unlike the two major forms of Christianity, the Jews alone venerate learning and inculcate respect for the scholar as an integral part of their religious service. Although this is doubtless a minor reason, it is historically true that the Jews, having been hounded from place to place over the centuries, have discovered that education is a nonconfiscable resource and accordingly have built a tradition of respect for the intellectual and for learning that is at variance with the usual American distrust of learned men. Inevitably, such a tradition directs a Jewish family to a good school system like a needle to a magnet, and, once there, the family will make sure the schools stay good.

The whole question of how good the schools are in a neighborhood—and this generally revolves around the question of how good the high school is—is vitally important to any family that is anxious and prepared to send its offspring as far along the multiple degree path as they can go.

Without question, formal educational patterns have become hardened, particularly in the last twenty years, and no one needs to be told that a high school diploma is now taken for granted to such an extent that it is expected that most people will have one as inevitably as they have a birth certificate. College education is rapidly approaching the birthright stage, and ambitious families head their children toward high school with no hesitation whatsoever about preparation for college.

This decision—not really a decision, but an overt declaration of a longtime ambition—can take place even earlier than high school, depending on the school system's arrangement of schools and grades. The current educational enthusiasm is for a three-year high school and a three-year "middle" school, a courageously borrowed term usually used by the private schools as part of their private terminology. Decisions about courses, languages, and other preparations for college can take place as early as the seventh grade, when Harold or Margaret can be as young as twelve or thirteen, and not usually in a frame of mind for action on the basis of which anything fruitful could be predicted for their futures.

Parenthetically, junior high (or middle school) is usually the low point of the whole educational experience. The reason for this, I suspect, is circular. Students themselves, because of physical development, are at their most restless, fractious, and self-conscious stage. Teachers, all of whom agree that this is the most challenging age to teach, find the experience so exhausting that the ambition of every junior high teacher, so I am told, is to transfer to the high school. The results, of course, are that the teachers best able to move up do so, and the less able ones remain.

Even course selection runs into the problems of this age. For example, the noted linguistics expert, Dr. Freeman Twaddell, has said that the seventh or eighth grades, when most schools begin the study of foreign languages, are precisely the wrong time to begin. Considering the student's development and self-consciousness, it becomes "literally immoral for students to make those strange noises that learning French or German demands."

Nevertheless, it is at this unpropitious stage that programs are chosen, courses are planned, and the pattern for a child's future is securely locked up. I say "securely locked," because once the college program is differentiated from the general or the commercial or the vocational course, the divergence becomes greater and greater and the possibilities of changing from the noncollege to the college program become less and less feasible. First, the preparation for succeeding courses will not be right; then the sequences of the right courses in the right grades will be off. For these and various other reasons, the set patterns will be maintained.

Assuming, therefore, that the decision, once made, has to be lived with, how does a parent decide whether his child is proper material for the college preparation program?

Unfortunately the time when this decision has to be made is about the worst time to judge a future student. Not only is your student likely to be restless, self-conscious, fad-crazy, and hard to get along with, but thirteen (plus or minus a year, depending on the maturation of the individual) is quite often a turning point in development. This shows up in interesting ways other than in school grades. For example, in my interviewing experience I have learned that thirteen is when most boys finally rebel and give up on those piano lessons that the family has been investing in so long. (By the time he is seventeen he will probably regret it, but at the time it seemed a perfect idea.) Conversely, a college applicant who plays an instrument for his own pleasure is very likely to have begun the study when he was in his early teens, and by his own request.

Another interesting observation about language at this age: a foreign-born student who arrives before he is thirteen, will arrive in college speaking nearly "perfect" American, whereas the foreign student who arrives later will probably always have an accent proclaiming his non-American origin unless he is a linguist of unusual skill.

In the same way, a boy at thirteen may take stock of himself, make strong decisions, and stick by them. In this way an honor student at Brown took a chilly look at himself in junior high school, decided he was fat and lazy, and did something about it. Subsequently he played two sports in high school, lost weight, graduated from high school and college near the top of his class, and has just completed his requirements for the Ph.D. It is obvious that the necessary secret ingredient in such a success story is ability, but fortunately this can be measured with reasonable accuracy in almost all cases.

The behavior of girls at this critical juncture is at once easier and less easy to predict. Because they mature more rapidly, the crisis or turning point is likely to come sooner. Whereas the male student may emerge as the successful late bloomer as late as the junior year of high school or even during his college career, girls declare themselves earlier. It is for this reason that women's colleges are less interested in and less likely to accept "risk" students; because the maturing cycle runs faster for girls, they reason that if a girl has not achieved the kind of maturity that produces good grades by the time she is ready to leave high school, the chances are that she will never be much of a student.

In general, however, school officials (and other women) assure me that, as a sex, women are much more diligent than men. They accept the kind of personal responsibility that goes with being a good student more easily. Perhaps even more important, women as a sex are more verbal; they talk more; they are likely to read more by natural inclination, and consequently they are more adept at communication— reading, writing, and talking—which is necessarily at the heart of the classroom experience.

It is, of course, not true that *all* girls are better students than all boys. Girls, too, become bored with school, go crazy over fads, clothes, music, and boys, and, when fractious or unwilling to cooperate, are far harder to deal with than the worst boys. What this says is that girls are more likely to be good students, but they are less likely than boys to make dramatic changes in direction.

One factor that apparently makes more of a difference than heredity, home life, or parental nagging is the group the student chooses or is adopted by. I have been impressed again and again to interview "overachievers"—boys who are making better grades than any tests would ever predict for them; and, more often than not, it turns out that they move with the academic set, that their friends are usually brighter and better students than they are, but most important of all, the group puts high approval on academic success.

The converse is equally true. A bright student who is producing far below his expected academic potential is quite likely to be in a group where grades and achievement are frowned on. And here again the stereotypes of many years ago have changed radically. At one time, it might have been safe to generalize that the athletes, the students involved in team sports, were less concerned about grades. Now they are quite likely to be found in the top academic group. By an interesting switch in standards, an athlete can now (and often does) write poetry, act in plays, paint pictures, and otherwise engage himself in the arts in a way which is really new in our culture. Only in the last few years has it been true that a bona fide athlete might write poetry with pride, and without any suggestions that he was less masculine because of it. This side of the academic revolution is all gain, although I suspect that old-line coaches are doubtful about poetic quarterbacks, even if their teammates are not.

Again, there have been some interesting reversals on the other side of the scale. Where once the literary and intellectual element could be counted on (at least in popular conception) to carry the banner of academic achievement, the "intellectuals" now can be instead a self-conscious group of bohemians who despise the "rigidity" or "conformity" that is necessary to get good grades. While this was primarily a college phenomenon a few years ago, like all collegiate cults, it has descended into the junior levels through the honest means of flattering emulation.

As a student rises through each of the several academic strata—junior high, high school, college, and perhaps even graduate school—he seems to acquire wisdom whenever he's at the top of any particular level, and to lose it whenever he's at the bottom. Thus, high school seniors are shocked at how the ninth and tenth grades in some communities are experimenting with drugs, chiefly marijuana. On the other hand, a senior at Brown recently told a group of alumni that "pot" smoking was now considered passé by the seniors in his fraternity, but they were all concerned by the amount of "pot" smoking among the freshmen.

What a parent can do to change the attitudes of a son or daughter, or the group they choose to run around with, is conjectural. In my experience, there seem to be as many students escaping from too much supervision as there are students floundering from a lack of it. In general, however, firmness and fairness backed by genuine interest and a lack of hypocrisy tend to bring results.

By "lack of hypocrisy," I am suggesting that it is very difficult to ask a son to read if neither parent ever reads more than the evening paper and the monthly bills; it is difficult to tell a daughter to be neat or punctual if her parents are not. Most difficult of all, it is hard to persuade any teenager today that alcohol is right and marijuana is wrong, particularly when the medical profession classes both as drugs, and both as potentially harmful through abuse. What I am suggesting, therefore, is that the only productive way to reform one's children is likely to be the reformation in thinking or attitudes of the parents themselves.

A good counselor at junior high or high school can be a

tremendous help if he has been able to establish rapport with your child. If not a counselor, perhaps one teacher, above all others, has had your child's ear about his frustrations, ambitions, and parental gripes. While it is not easy to go to strangers to learn about your children, it may be the most efficient way to go about it.

The counselor, too, is the first person you must turn co (if not the last) in making the long-term course choices wnich affect career plans—especially the crucial decision made in the seventh or eighth grade which will affect your child in one way or another for the rest of his life: the choice of the college preparatory curriculum or one of several others in its place.

Counselors in high schools which serve a general population as well as in those which have a preponderance of college preparatory students all complain about the unqualified boys and girls who are put into the college preparatory program simply for the prestige of being in "college prep" rather than in any other academic track.

(In adolescent slang a few years back, the populace of a school was immediately divided into two groups—the "mondos," those more interested in motorcycles than school, and the "coleege" types, clean-cut straight-arrows who wore ordinary clothes and were, at least superficially, interested in an education. The two groups never mixed, exhibited antipathy to each other, and in general reinforced the theory that academic interest and performance depend on the group one is in.)

Because a student's attitudes and associations are likely to be so seriously affected by this decision, is it not better to make the decision college preparatory and let the child fight the battle for survival? This is the reasoning of ambitious parents, and there is much to be said for it.

First, any child may rise to a challenge. If the work in the college preparatory course is harder, the challenge is obviously greater. Second, and more important, the curriculum of a high school is pyramidal, and the prerequisites of the course needed in grades eleven and twelve for admission to college are found in the lower grades. Moreover, too many school systems are hopelessly rigid about moving a student from one level of academic demand to another, even within the college preparatory program. Therefore, a decision for the college preparatory program now keeps open a wider range of opportunities, just as continuing with math, science, or foreign language will keep open more college and career opportunities for a longer time.

But what about the college preparatory student who is not qualified, who is over his head. How can one tell if this is the case? How does a school or parent make the right decision?

Ambitious middle-class parents will make the ambitious decision—the college preparatory decision—without thinking. They will ignore test scores, the past school record, the child's disciplinary record, and the recommendations of the school against a college preparatory course. And they may be right, if only because the alternatives make for rigid and hard-to-change results. What's more, all the indices *may* be wrong.

If, however, at the end of a year, whether it be the seventh or eighth grade, the picture has not changed—if the student has not risen to challenge, if his attitude is still militantly anti-school and anti-courses, if his friends are chiefly in the noncollege groups (where he feels more comfortable), and if the test scores tell the same old story—then even ambitious parents should face the reality that college is not and should not be for everyone. The alternative is then to outline an educational plan best for your child and his abilities.

The struggle of middle-class parents to live vicariously through their children and to hope for even more material or social success for them than the parents have enjoyed is a dream that dies hard, and in the process, the death throes

cause as much agony to school officials as to the parents—
not to mention the child.

The reverse, of course, is not only true, but has caused
and will cause problems until attitudes are corrected. By
that I mean that until low income families of limited
education—Negroes, Puerto Ricans, Indians, poor whites
in Appalachia or city slums—realize the power of education
to change status and to provide social mobility, many of the
"disadvantaged" will remain so. (Both of these phrases—
"disadvantaged" and "social mobility" are part of the
sociologists' jargon; the combination of them can as easily
be identified as "ambition" as any other motivating force.)

For this reason, potentially good students from limited or
deprived backgrounds arrive at the fateful decision-making
point without either the cultural push from the family that
would have made them better readers, better test-takers, or
at least more interested students, or the family thrust of
ambition that makes a student aggressively aware of any
opportunity that comes along.

While it is not really germane to a discussion of the high
school, it is again interesting to note that the kind of mental
conditioning that produces ambitious students cannot be
expected to produce good results in the form of good and
interested students if it doesn't start until the seventh grade.
Attitudes toward education go back to preschool and primary days, and the results of negative attitudes can be
detected at age-level five or six and sometimes earlier.

Small wonder, then, that, even if counselors in junior
high school try to encourage low-income students from
deprived backgrounds to ignore financial reality and train
for college, they feel that there is little likelihood of
success—i.e., they are not likely to make many converts,
and the converts that are made are likely to find the high
school college preparatory curriculum so impractical as to
be incomprehensible. Further, there is a need for reasonable middle-class financial stability so that a student in the

middle of preparing for college doesn't have to worry about how to earn his living after graduation while his best friends are tearing down and rebuilding cars in the vocational wing.

Just as the liberal arts college, which trains a student for no particular vocation, is the educational symbol of the people who have enough financial security not to be concerned about the immediate urgency of earning a living, so the college preparatory curriculum on the next lower educational level requires to be understood in similar terms. The student who seriously chooses between a high school secretarial course and the college prep course must say to herself: "I am determined to go to college even though it looks financially impossible at the moment—I am so determined that I'll take the chance of getting a job not so good as I would have if I had stayed in the secretarial program."

The answer to this kind of uncertainty may be a federal scholarship program, but the real solution lies in the reeducation of parents. The girl who worries about the consequences of not taking a secretarial course will make the decision with fewer misgivings if she has the support—if only the encouragement—of her family.

If, on the other hand, both she and her parents are so concerned about education as immediate and useful training that a nonvocational course fills them with grim forebodings of starvation, then of course she will take the secretarial course, and quite possibly another good student will have been lost to higher education.

Many of the courses that any student takes in junior high and high school are similar, whatever the goal of his program. These are the common denominators, set in most cases by law. More often than not they include English, American History, and typing as the basic staples around which both the college student and the future machinist build their curriculum. Each state sets its own minimum requirements for high school graduation, and, in addition, often adds a required course in state history.

The options to the college preparatory student are varied within the framework of the college prep program, and a high school which sends a high percentage on to college may offer a variety of courses at many different levels of difficulty, so that the degree of academic challenge can be matched almost exactly to the ability of the student.

In its simplest form, however, the ideal choice of college prep courses includes in the four years of high school: English every year; history and other social studies; courses in the sciences, including at least one laboratory science; foreign language, ancient, modern, or both; and a variety of electives which have become more or less important depending on the school, the teachers, or the inclination of the student—e.g., art, economics, music, philosophy, "humanities," "Western Civilization," auto driving, and many, many more.

In all of these there is a lack of immediate concern for practicality, and it is not surprising that the cry of college students, "Make our education relevant!" is seeping down to the high school level. While it is easy to defend mathematics and science courses as providing the necessary background for students who will study the sciences in college, it is less easy to defend the relevance of English literature or foreign languages. The reverse is, of course, true for the future humanities student who is carried kicking and screaming through a course in physics. While the high school curriculum is certainly not perfect, it does have relevance, and the fact that it is in a constant state of change is the best indication of its real relevance and of the way it has adapted quickly to the more high-powered needs of students today.

Perhaps it is because English has changed less than other courses and because it seems to be inherently less of a challenge to the student that it is so badly taught. Actually, the challenge is so great that it is scarcely ever met, and as a consequence even bright students at good colleges have reading problems, are verbally inarticulate, have inaccurate vocabularies, and write confused, but often elaborate and pedantic prose. Certainly one of the basic problems is that everyone speaks English; as one of the great experts on the language has said "By the age of four, the average human has mastered the elements of English grammar"—that is, word order, tenses, and simple constructions. Having done this, and being able to communicate on a simple straightforward level, a person is likely to feel that anything more elaborate is not only unnecessary but open to suspicion.

Thus one of the problems most English teachers face from the seventh grade up is the fact that girls tend to talk freely and boys do not. A survey quoted in *The New York Times* several years ago announced that teenage girls talk exactly twice as much as teenage boys. Verbal communication that is out of the ordinary—the use of an unusual word or an elaborate sentence structure—can raise the whole question of a boy's masculinity; only sissies talk like sissies. With this built-in resistance to contend with, it is not surprising that English teachers are frustrated in their attempts to teach control of the language. Now that some other tabus are breaking down, with football captains writing poetry and soccer stars acting in plays, perhaps masculine shyness about the spoken (and written) word will diminish.

In the meantime, English teachers have been aware of the advances in other areas—the "new" math, exciting changes in the teaching of chemistry and physics—and they have responded to them. It is difficult to reorganize the entire English language in a way which will better reflect the newest theories, so that that kind of change has so far proved impossible. Basically, English teachers felt they should stop boring their students with the study of grammar and that they can enliven the material read and discussed in class by dropping out old faithfuls and substituting new works likely to appeal to young men and women.

Just as "classical" physics is being taught throughout the country despite the invention of a new curriculum in physics, so classical English courses are still taught—students read *Silas Marner, The Mayor of Casterbridge, The Scarlet Letter,* and the *Idylls of the King.* It may also be that in some parts of this country English teachers are still making students parse sentences, identify subordinate clauses, and write simple declarative sentences. I hope so. But in many schools, particularly those which send many of their graduates off to college, and particularly those which brag about the modernity of their curriculum, the revisions of the English courses for easier consumption have almost always included the following. the virtual abandonment of the teaching of grammar, particularly for students in the "honors" or "advanced" sections; the substitution of contemporary novels for the standards that have been general fare for years; the diminution of the amount of required English composition; a vast increase in the amount of vocabulary work and other exercises directly related to the College Board tests.

While these changes have made English more up-to-date and perhaps more popular, as a general movement they have left a number of important jobs undone. This criticism is not wholly negative: the contemporary novels really do speak to their generation—and far more effectively than *The Mill on the Floss. The Catcher in the Rye, A Separate Peace, Lord of the Flies* (to mention three adolescent best sellers) are well written and have great appeal. What's more, while they are not obvious books, they are on a level of understanding and experience which students can grasp. On the other hand, a good many teachers seek to challenge their students by offering them books which are really beyond their level of experience to understand and appreciate entirely. It is fashionable among high school intellectuals right now to read authors they would not be expected to read—and it is currently fashionable among many high school students to be "intellectuals." Indicative of this is the fact that nearly everyone I interviewed had read *The Stranger* by Albert Camus; while its mood of alienation fits nicely with the high school student's picture of himself, much of Camus' philosophy will be better understood and appreciated when the student himself is older and hence more experienced.

The point is not that I object to challenging students by having them read complex literature, but rather that I feel that in reading it at the wrong time, too early, the real point and enjoyment of the book will be lost.

This is not the case with *Huckleberry Finn*, which is not just a picaresque novel, although it can be read and enjoyed as such by comparatively young students, but which is a powerful statement on human dignity and freedom, a level at which it can be explored later in college, without its being spoiled by rereading. Yet, this book is seldom used in high school.

The grammar of the English language has succumbed to the principle that the really bright student has a limited attention span and that if he is required to do anything tedious, the school has failed educationally. In consequence, students in the sections of English reserved for the bright students are usually told at the beginning of each grade: "Since you studied grammar last year, we are not going to go over dead ground. Instead, this year, we will read poetry." The result in a startling number of cases that I have known is that, unless a student has picked up the fine points of grammar by reading, intuition, or careful emulation, he may well be ignorant of some of the most elementary aspects of the mechanics of the language.

The most memorable example was a student I knew who had a terrible language problem—French remained an enigma to him throughout his formal education. In his sophomore year at college his faculty counselor recommended an excellent language tutor to try to pump some understanding of French into him. The tutor gave up, however, when she discovered that her charge, upon whom had been lavished the most expensive education that taxes and parental funds could buy, did not know what an infinitive was! Without the student's knowledge of even the basic terms of grammar, the tutor felt it was hopeless to try to describe the workings of a foreign language.

Along with grammar, experience in writing has become a sometime thing. Here the reason is quite different. In grammar, the rationale is that memorizing the rules that govern the form of the language is boring and hence bad. In writing, the rationale is much simpler. In order to give a student proper experience in writing (which is the only way to learn to write) the teacher must be ready to read and correct what is written. The energetic teacher with twenty to forty students can assign a theme a week to her students, correct them, and return them in time for the next theme if she is reasonably diligent. However, if the student load goes much higher than that, a teacher must sacrifice a good deal of her own time in order to do it well. Since teachers in most public schools have a teaching load of about 125–150 students (the ideal number is considered to be 80–100 according to the standards set by the National Council of Teachers of English), it is not surprising that a teaching ideal of at least one 500-word theme a week is not realized very often.

In interviewing students from high schools with good reputations, I was impressed by the number of them whose writing experience seemed to center around subjective tests in English or History and one or two term papers a year. Both of these are excellent practices but do not offer the frequency which is at the heart of learning to write.

The question of what is the heart of the curriculum or

what are the important courses is one which every student and parent must answer early in the game, since the increasing complexity of the courses and curricula offered in high schools are such that the opportunity to switch around from one to the other at will is limited, if not completely absent.

Therefore, the questions of which language to choose, how many math courses are desirable, whether a course in music, or art, or psychology will be acceptable as an entrance credit in college, all crowd in on the student and his parents. Given English as a constant and a necessary part of every curriculum, what else goes to make up the perfect preparation for college once the student has decided to embark on the college preparatory course?

The one subject which becomes the most decisive factor, next to English, in shaping the future student is mathematics. A student's ability in it, his enthusiasm for it, or his lack of ability or interest are important clues in the guidance game.

Briefly, the more mathematics a student has studied, the broader are his options. A student who has taken four years of math in high school can go to college and major in English Literature or Russian History, but the student who has not had enough math may very well be blocked if he decides in college that he wants to study medicine or architecture or any kind of science, including those forms of science which laymen often do not think of as being particularly scientific—psychology, geology, and, possibly, sociology or economics. The future premed who likes biology and people but who does not like mathematics and physical sciences will find that mathematics is not required for entrance to medical school—but it is the necessary background for the courses in physics and chemistry that are required.

Like all science courses in the last ten to fifteen years, the teaching of mathematics has undergone dramatic changes in method, and many of the traditional courses that parents today remember taking have disappeared. The difference in method has become very nearly a national joke, as primary grade children prattle away cheerfully about sets and subsets, which, if the parents remember at all, were dimly connected with the math they studied in college. While it has left parents baffled by their children's homework, the "new" math (because the mathematicians insist that there is really nothing new about what is being taught, but that the arrangement and presentation of the material is different, the idea of "new" math somehow annoys them—hence the quotation marks) has made for a more efficient progress through the maze of courses, so that calculus in the senior year of high school is becoming quite common, and it is an increasingly rare high school that does not offer it.

The major difficulty raised by new methods of teaching mathematics is that there is as yet little standardization in courses or method from one school system to another. Thus a student transferring from a school teaching modern math to a school teaching conventional math will probably find himself simultaneously ahead and behind his class and, accordingly, very difficult to place.

With so many families moving from one city to another, the unevenness in method raises problems which probably tend to frighten parents and students unnecessarily. While a large number of high schools offer calculus, it is not a requirement for entrance into even the most demanding college science programs; thus, although certain colleges have stated mathematics entrance requirements such as "two years of algebra, one year of plane geometry . . ." etc., the realization of the rearrangement in the teaching of mathematics has caused most colleges to make their own requirements flexible enough to accomodate the various new curricula.

The Commission on Mathematics of the College Board was established in part for this reason, and it developed a statement to cover the entrance requirements of colleges that avoid the traditional course breakdown and instead describe preparation in terms of topics of study:

> College preparatory mathematics should include topics selected from algebra, geometry (demonstrative and analytic), trigonometry, and possibly elementary calculus, and probability and statistical inference. The point of view should be in harmony with contemporary mathematical thought, and emphasis should be placed upon basic concepts and upon the principles of deductive reasoning regardless of the branch of mathematics from which the topic is chosen. Courses designed for other purposes (e.g., consumer mathematics, business mathematics, shop mathematics) are not acceptable.

Whatever the arrangement and teaching method, background in mathematics remains not only the most important aspect of flexibility but also the best indicator of interest and probability of future success in any field even remotely scientific, requiring statistics or even logic. Thus the future lawyer is apt to be good in geometry (because it is an exercise in logic) and if the future doctor does not like or is not good at mathematics, then he is in for trouble or frustration.

In the same way, science courses help a student keep a wider variety of course choices open. The common requirement of a "laboratory" science as one of the requisites for college admission is undoubtedly one of the historical hurdles which colleges raised to make sure they were getting the students most interested in learning, since these were the more rigorous subjects. Once again, teaching methods in the most traditional of these, biology, chemistry, and physics, have undergone striking reorganizations, and as with mathematics, the newer methods are not universal. But here the differences create less educational havoc because, unlike the differences in mathematics, they are not necessarily a part of a continuing sequence.

One of the most common ways that high school education has been speeded up and made more efficient during this revolution has been to move everything forward a little further. Biology, for example, traditionally a tenth-grade subject, now is often taught in the ninth grade, but presumably only to students so good that the question of whether they want to try the college program or not never comes up.

Following biology in the ninth grade with chemistry in the tenth and physics in the eleventh leaves the senior year with a science gap, or the opportunity to take a second year in biology, chemistry, or physics, which is purported to be the equivalent of a freshman course at college.

The traditional course in biology, one which starts out with the one-celled plants and animals and moves up the evolutionary scale, is still commonly taught. Quite often this is the first course in schools where an advanced or second-year biology course is offered. However a Biological Sciences Study Committee set up a variety of different approaches several years ago and launched them to see which was the most efficacious. The differences were noted in terms of the colors of the books used—you may have heard, therefore, of a student studying the Blue Version or the Green Version of Biology. It has since been reduced to a single approved version, but variations are common, depending on the test used and the ingenuity of the instructor. Briefly, most of the changes have centered around the assumption that biology is really better understood today in terms of the chemistry of the living organism than in terms of the organization of living things by their complexity, size, and whether they had shells or skeletons, nerve systems or digestive tracts. The criticism of the chemical approach was that if the student learned it as the only introduction to biology, he was not likely ever to understand the evolutionary pattern. Both are considered to be important; medical schools particularly complain that students know what chemical function an organ performs without ever knowing where it is and what its relationship is to the rest of the organism.

As an introduction to science, biology serves a valuable but often a confusing purpose. Particularly in the traditional evolutionary course, a student with a good memory can make a showing which seems to tell him that he is potentially a scientist. It is most often used by future medical students as the first hurdle. It is not necessarily a good one, simply for the fact that reasoned understanding is a better indication for success in the sciences than a good memory and a strong stomach (if you took biology in the tenth grade, you can recall the smell of formaldehyde and what a much dissected frog or cat looked like).

The second course in biology, if offered, is likely to be a senior subject and will call heavily on chemistry for understanding. If the student is looking for hints about his future, this will offer a far better indicator of possible college and postgraduate success in the sciences.

In the traditional pattern of high school science courses, biology is first, followed usually by chemistry and then by physics, if the student is undertaking the complete science offering at the highest level of academic difficulty. The pattern has remained, despite the protestations of a biology professor I know who feels, with predictable academic self-centeredness, that the new biology has now become so complicated and so dependent on the students' understanding of chemistry particularly that it should be the last of the science courses taught, not the first. This is probably the reason that the chemical approach to biology at the high school level is the second course, and does follow chemistry, whereas the traditional up-from-amoeba course is still the major introduction to the tough sciences.

Just as biology has changed its form and direction in response to revolutionary discoveries (Paul Weisz, a biologist noted for his extraordinarily successful high school and college texts in the "new" biology has said that since the discovery of DNA in the early 1950s, the subject has almost literally exploded), so has the teaching of chemistry become almost unrecognizably different in the last fifteén years. Much chemistry is still taught in the traditional way, usually described derisively as "cookbook" chemistry, but two new approaches—Chem Study and CBA (Chemical Bond Approach)—were devised by joint study committees of college and secondary school faculties.

For a great many parents, chemistry is remembered as a stable subject where ninety-two elements behaved according to a straightforward plan; there seemed little need to worry about the molecular structure or the submolecular structure, except that it did exist and it did affect what happened in the test tube. The age of the atom has changed all that: the table of elements is not a stable ninety-two, and the ring of electrons around each atom produces results which high school students of twenty-five years ago would have been bewildered to hear about.

In the new chemistry courses there has been an attempt to do more than simply talk about chemical action and reaction in physical or electrical terms. The purpose has been to recreate the scientific method, to introduce to students the concept of the quest for knowledge and the means they must develop to get answers. This is why "cookbook" is such a term of derision. The experiments in the new chemistry courses were designed to show a student why something happened rather than having him add chemicals to a beaker and emerge, with the result, no wiser about the mechanism than before.

Understandably, chemistry courses thus have been more difficult because they demand thought rather than rote memory. Another problem is that nontraditional chemistry courses produced such a different body of knowledge that the traditionally oriented College Board Achievement Tests in chemistry did not reflect what the CBA and Chem Study students had learned. Their initial response was to send out chemistry scores with explanatory slips to report that students in special chemistry programs might score as much as 100 points lower than the traditional students. Subsequently, the College Board has rewritten the test in such a way that neither students, traditional or modern, are at a disadvantage.

The degree to which a national testing agency like the College Board, on which the colleges rely heavily for objective, comparative information about candidates from all over the country, determines the content of a course is an important point to consider, and one which I think deserves discussion later on. I think it is entirely possible that if the College Board had not been responsive to the developments of the Chem Study, CBA chemistry, the BSSC (Biological Sciences Study Committee) biology, and the PSSC (Physical Sciences Study Committee) physics programs, then parents, more anxious about college admission than about their children's preparation, would have squelched the new programs. Fortunately, although there was an appreciable time lag (either because of inertia or the need to develop a reliable basis for testing), the concern of parents that the new science programs would produce lower scores on tests and hence impair college admission prospects should now be over.

On the other hand, all of the new science courses place considerably more emphasis on the *understanding* of the subject than on the memorization of the facts surrounding it. Because this puts a greater demand on the students' intelligence and because it is *often* the first such demand to be made of them, students many times react adversely; i.e., they get poor grades, or at least grades which are not so good as those they have earned in other subjects. For this reason, particularly in large high schools, the special science courses have often become "honors" courses because only "honors" students can handle them.

To have this happen to physics is to double the ante,

because physics has long been considered the most difficult of high school courses. The development of a new course in physics by the Physical Sciences Study Committee was again the result of efforts by a group of college and high school teachers who felt that a more logical preparation for college physics was needed. This was the pioneer group in science course reform, and, in implementing their new course, they went about it the right way. In addition to the composition of new texts and new experiments (many of which required either new or newly constructed demonstration experiments), members of the physical sciences teaching staffs of colleges in various communities oversaw the retraining of high school physics teachers in the new course. (Understandably, the new courses often approach the material in a highly unorthodox way, and any teacher who undertakes a new science course in chemistry, physics, or biology usually does so only after special instruction).

None of this preparation has rescued physics from its reputation as a hard course, and regrettably but not surprisingly, the national registration in high school physics is dropping, even though the high school population is rising. The reason is obvious: physics' reputation for toughness scares away students who won't risk any danger to their overall average or, more important, to their rank in class, which is a determining factor in so many admissions processes. This reluctance raises the whole question of whether the quality of courses taken can, or should, offset the resulting grades. It is an unresolved question because there are no definite answers, but discussions pro and con are worth considering and will be discussed later in this chapter.

This somewhat lengthy description of the new sciences has been made because a school's offering in science is one of the measures by which a parent can judge the excellence of his high school. While it is possible, of course, that a school can have a completely inept instructor teaching CBA chemistry, the fact that the curriculum of the high school was disrupted long enough to insert a new and different course is a healthy sign.

Before entirely leaving the subject of the sciences and their place in the high school curriculum, let me add that, for any student with scientific or even semi-scientific ambitions, biology, chemistry, and physics offer the most demanding challenges for a student and give him a chance to predict how well he might do in these areas later. For example, physics is the best indicator for success in engineering. The student who likes physics and does well in it will not be likely to have trouble. Trouble, instead, usually comes from the student who has made a curricular or professional choice and won't even listen to his own likes and dislikes; there are always premeds every year who secretly admit to hating chemistry, which is integral to the study of medicine.

What about the nonscience student, the liberal arts type who loves English, languages, and history, but hates science. Fortunately, the larger high schools have developed alternatives which are usually less "scientific"—i.e., a little easier—but can still be counted as sciences for those fussy colleges that still tabulate entrance requirements on a rigid basis.

In general these "soft" science courses—earth science, psychology, physiology—are also newcomers, designed to fill a need. Like any course in a high school they can be rigorously taught or not, depending on the teacher, but in general they tend either to become electives for the competitive students who want a little breathing space, or to provide the required science background for those who would otherwise avoid science courses.

In addition to providing the essentially nonscience student with some immediate insights into the mechanisms of some sciences (as opposed to the "new" sciences, which are really concerned with attempting to teach a student to *think* like a scientist), they also provide a valuable preview of courses that will be offered in college. Certainly much of the confusion that freshmen and sophomores traditionally have undergone is the result of not having any real idea of what many of the major fields—psychology, philosophy, economics, and so on—are really about. But in recent years many of the electives which have been added to high school curricula have the value of providing just such an introduction. It is also true that by bringing these courses into the high school, a good deal of the mystery of college is lost, and the students may react to college with boredom. However, that is a different problem.

Like most of the other disciplines taught in high school, foreign language has undergone a technological and pedagogical revolution. Before considering how this came about and how 't has changed language study, consider whether or not language study should be an integral part of your student's preparation for college and why.

First and simplest, foreign language is still an entrance requirement and a graduation requirement at virtually all of the private colleges that can be termed "competitive."* Some foreign language study is required of entrants to most medical schools, although in many cases these schools do not specify which language. A reading knowledge of at least two foreign languages is required for nearly all advanced academic degrees. In other words, on a purely practical basis, it makes sense for a student to have some foreign language study because, without it, he will be much more severely limited in his choice of degree programs, colleges, and even professions.

The second reason is more arguable, but centers around the "one world" concept and the problem of communication. Travel has probably never been so readily available,

---

*The massive liberalization of curricula in the last year makes this statement almost, but not quite, out-of-date.

so quick and cheap as it is now. In consequence more Americans than ever are walking around—and sometimes making themselves understood—in countries where English is not spoken as the native tongue. The sense of power being able to speak a language other than his own gives to a young man or woman is reward enough for having gone to the trouble of learning it, and, not surprisingly, interest in languages and in travel have gone hand in hand. This is still more the case in the East and in the large suburbs of the Midwest, but the overall growth in language study and teaching in the last ten to fifteen years has been phenomenal.

The third reason is really a corollary of the second. Language, as the distinguished linguistics-anthropologist Henry Lee Smith has said, *is* culture; the two are inseparable. Thus it is necessary to study French, to read French literature in the original, and to speak to Frenchmen *in* French in order to understand them—and the wave of travelers out of America does want to talk to and understand others, and to be able to explain America to them.

Fourth and not least, is the reason that the study of a foreign language makes your own language more understandable. As I have said, English grammar is seldom taught any more, but a student can get a good view of the machinery of English by the indirect means of studying Latin, for example. Not only does Latin have a bearing on English grammar, but it also has a considerable relationship to a good many words and phrases in English and the Romance languages. Although now "dead" and unspoken, it provides an excellent practical background for the study of any subsequent Romance language.

Not everyone agrees with this statement A Swiss engineer of my acquaintance who speaks French and German as a matter of birthright, and fluent English besides, said recently that studying Latin in high school is a waste of time. He would, however, defend firmly the need to know French, German, or English. Since language is culture, our views of it have the same prejudices that are built into the culture.

Still another negative point of view was registered during a conversation I had several summers ago. A distinguished scientist and a presidential adviser on science were talking about things which I understood only dimly, but they switched to the problem of language study. To the distinguished scientist it seemed superfluous for any American scientist in training to have to learn a new language since virtually anyone of any education now speaks English or can write in it, and therefore most of the important publications in science need no translation. The scientific advisor, as I remember, did not disagree.

There was also a time quite recently when machine translation from one language to another seemed to be the solution to any foreign language problem, making it unnecessary for students to add this burden to their education. The only problem was that even machine translation requires special skills to read, since even a computer cannot make a flowing, easily read translation.

And while it may be true that the most important information is published directly in English, there are many, too many, periodicals that are not, so that it is impossible to keep up with the flow. Therefore, the young student, particularly the one with scientific aspirations, should have a reading knowledge of at least one foreign language, almost without regard to what the requirements for his degrees will be.

This being the case, which language or languages? French and Spanish are the most commonly taught in high schools, followed (depending on local situations) by Latin, German, Russian, Ancient Greek, and in a few far-seeing (or fearful) schools, Chinese. The choice which a student or his family makes is often based on practical considerations.

For example, there is a widespread belief that Latin offers excellent background for the study of medicine or law. The Latin names of the parts of the body and the descriptions of pharmacology in medicine and the generous sprinkling of Latin terms in law have undoubtedly bolstered this belief. Since legal Latin has frozen into specialized meanings which do not necessarily translate expectedly into English, and since anatomical Latin is best memorized, the usefulness of the language in that way is doubtful. Other folk views of language are legion, and sometimes true. For example, Spanish is the easiest; Russian is the hardest. The second statement seems true from my experience, but the first is far from true. What is true is that the phonetic demands of Spanish are more straightforward than those of French, making Spanish easier to pronounce and comprehend. In its higher levels, the elaborate grammar of Spanish is complication itself, but few high school students get to that level.

In general, choice of language study is best determined by the student's interests. Thus a future scientist—including students thinking of medicine—should take French, German, or Russian. Latin is not necessarily useful, and Spanish will not be useful at all. On the other hand, liberal arts students who plan business, legal, teaching, or government careers may elect any language they choose, since any of them may subsequently be useful. It is quite likely that, as a student goes into a specialized field, he may discover that another language is necessary. A favorite student of mine at Brown was majoring in Russian language and literature. Since much of the critical work on Russian literature in the nineteenth century was written in French, it became essential that he learn to read French, which he did with a college level reading course not concerned with the phonetics of the language. He was quickly able to read French as easily as English, but his command of the spoken language had to be heard to be believed; why his trip through France did not produce mayhem proves that the French can be much more generous about the use of their language than they are usually given credit for.

However, as a result of the electronics explosion which has made the tape recorder and hence the language laboratory possible, the ability to speak and comprehend a foreign language is a consideration in choosing which language to study. Language laboratories are built around gleaming banks of tape machines into which are tied individual listening booths; selection mechanisms which permit an individual to choose any of several hundred tapes; and a monitoring system so that the student can listen to tapes, respond in the language, and then hear his own efforts; and finally a supermonitoring system which allows the instructor to hear what is going on in any of the listening booths. All of these things were grafted onto a system which the language-school king, Berlitz, developed in which the student is spoken to in simple but understandable terms in the foreign language he is learning, and is expected to answer in the same tongue, without ever making the direct translation from one language to another.

Word order, grammar, inflection, and vocabulary are all acquired by the student in this way. With the addition of electronic devices this method essentially became the Audio-Lingual Method (ALM) of teaching languages—and, while it has not wholly supplanted the more traditional methods, it permits a degree of fluency and linguistic authenticity which is hard to achieve in the older way.

A veteran French teacher of some thirty years' experience told me that, at the end of one year of ALM French, his students had the fluency of third-year students under the old style, and an accent and inflection which were usually not possible at all. The tapes which the students mimic are, of course, made by native speakers of the language.

This teaching system is not without its shortcomings. I

have heard it criticized for not being able to deal with the intricacies of advanced grammar, and very good students often find that parroting inane conversations about the grocery store, when they want to use their new skills to read Sartre in the original, is very dull. As a consequence some schools have compromised between the old and the new, but in any case, the emphasis on aural comprehension and oral composition is here to stay and should be considered by the student in choosing a language to study.

Skill in this area is not easy to determine. One useful approach to this problem is the cafeteria style course offering a quick introduction to three languages, usually in the seventh grade, permitting the student a chance to choose whichever one he finds easiest, most stimulating, or most interesting. Language study in the primary grades (and a number of school systems have been experimenting in this area), offers an opportunity to learn about a student's language ability or disability early enough so that it does not have to mar the high school record which is so important in college admission. (Another point which has been made before, but is still valid, is that language study undertaken before adolescence is likely to be much better received because students are still young enough not to be self-conscious about making strange noises and the concomitant necessity of screwing their faces into unfamiliar patterns in order to make them. In the primary grades, foreign language can be fun; in junior high school it is likely to be simply embarrassing.)

There are a few other useful points to be considered by the student interested in language. Tone-deaf children make poor French students; students with reading problems are likely to have particular difficulty with any foreign language. These are problems without solutions, which means that parents of students with foreign language problems must understand the special nature of the problems and be sympathetic and encouraging. Some language problems, however, are more easily solved. For example, a primary school girl with particular reading problems was making no progress in her special classes. Finally the teacher discovered that Sarah was also taking Hebrew lessons three times a week. Since the essence of the child's problem was that of moving her eyes from left to right and reading letters and words in that order, her Hebrew lessons were countermanding this training. The parents, who had not considered religious training to be in conflict with secular training, realized the problem immediately when confronted with it; Hebrew lessons were stopped.

In general, regardless of the specific problems, interest is the greatest key. The student who hates Latin and thinks he might do well in German should be allowed to try; it is far better to switch from one language to another than to produce a consistently poor language record.

Like the sciences and the languages, the social sciences have changed in the last few years, but not so radically. New courses have been introduced, but they are usually at the elective level, not a necessary part of the high school curricular plan—courses like economics, psychology, and, increasingly, community and urban problems. (The question of whether psychology is a "real" science or a social science is not easily solved. At the high school level, more would vote it a place in the social sciences.) The American History course, which is usually required by state law for a high school diploma, sometimes emerges as Problems of Democracy, or Problems of American Democracy, sometimes in the usual guise, and often, in the college-oriented high schools, as Advanced Placement American History. The entire concept of advanced placement in history and other subjects is one which very much concerns the college bound student and it will be discussed in some detail later in this chapter.

History teachers have kept up the "relevance" of their subject most easily of the nonscientific subjects by adding not just harder and more complicated courses, but by spreading the traditional scope of high school courses beyond the traditional European and American history. Although these are still central to the core of history taught in high school, Russian and Asian history have been added to many school curricula for the same good reasons that Russian and Chinese language teaching has become more prevalent. In response to more urgent pressures, schools all over the country are now adding African or Afro-American history courses to the list of possible social studies electives.

The worth of a history course, whether required or elective, is in the quality of the teaching. Badly taught, it relies on memory and rote regurgitation of facts. Properly taught, it can introduce high school students into the discipline of history as they will find it in college and make them cognizant of the need to evaluate all sides of a question before drawing conclusions. Generally, high school history is descriptive more than analytical, but this too is changing. The American History course at Phillips Academy in Andover, Massachusetts, is largely a study of constitutional law, and it is so justly famous and tough that for many years the most selective colleges accepted students with a failure in history at Andover, and those students subsequently went on to pass American History in college with flying colors.

The important point about history is that it offers the nonscience student the greatest challenge of the high school years; the subject is complex and demanding, but comprehension and appreciation do not depend on experience and emotional maturity to the same extent as they do in literature. Further, the process of gathering information, drawing it together, and writing about it offers the best kind of preparation for the college experience and is in itself an educational experience of great worth. It is not surprising, therefore, that many electives in history have sprung up, and that the advanced placement course in history is the most popular (with the possible exception of calculus) of all those offered. To the student, a history course can offer the best preview of college experience, and his success and enthusiasm for it (*if* it is well taught) are good indicators of what is likely to happen in college.

What are advanced placement courses and what is their place in the current high school curriculum? In 1952 a group of high-powered secondary schools and colleges met to discuss the problem of overpreparation—i.e., that students from very good schools often found themselves in freshmen curricula that were too rigid to escape and pitched too low for either academic challenge or enjoyment. Because the colleges were aiming their beginning courses at the low end of their entering group, in order to bring all the students up to a common level of academic experience, the courses were dull or disappointing for the very well prepared student. A typical response was that the student found the work so easy that he assumed, wrongly, that he could pick up the thread at any time, and enjoy himself in the meanwhile. Too late, the overprepared student often discovered that he had been passed by and that he could not now catch up.

(A student from one of these high-powered academies came to me early in his freshman year quite concerned about his fellow freshmen. "These high school kids are really too dumb to be at Brown," he explained to me earnestly. I urged him to make a list of names so that we could find out if his allegations were true. Unfortunately, he flunked out at the end of the first semester.)

In 1952 the group of colleges and schools joined together in agreement about a higher level of college preparation. A few selected schools would teach courses at the "college" level, and a few selected (and selective) colleges would accept these courses on the same basis as though they had been taken in college; that is, credit would be granted for those courses toward meeting degree requirements for graduation. In this way the "overprepared" student could bypass the elementary courses that would bore him and go right into more challenging courses at a higher level.

This was the original premise of the Advanced Placement Program and it has remained basically the same since then. Shortly after its founding, the College Board took over the job of examining these overprepared students in a standard way, and the number of high schools offering advanced courses and the number of colleges accepting them has grown enormously.

The tinkering with preparation goes on. Currently a group of great private schools is again concerned with the combination of their ability to offer high level courses and the increasing probability that a student from their school will enter graduate school after college. Consequently they are investigating the idea of adding the first two college years to their curricula and keeping the student body through the sophomore year in college, thereby allowing some colleges, in turn, to concentrate on the more sophisticated student, taking him through the last undergraduate years and continuing into graduate work of various kinds. Although the idea presents enormous problems in terms of violating traditional patterns, it does make it possible for each institution to concentrate on what it does best: the school to teach and the university to concentrate chiefly on students who are graduate-school bound. In its way, it is no more radical than the Advanced Placement Program, and may become as widely accepted.

It is obvious by the very nature of these advanced placement courses that these will be academically more demanding. They were, as a matter of fact, one of the earliest attempts to break through the "democratic" barrier to offer brighter students more interesting work. Particularly after the publication of the Conant report in 1957, "honors," "enriched," "fast track," and other courses aimed at the superior student (including, of course, the special science courses) came in to increase his challenge, to make his education more interesting, and, because the courses were more difficult, perhaps to lower his grades.

This last hideous thought came into full flower as college competition increased and students and parents became overly conscious about how good a student's grades had to be in order to get him into certain colleges. If they had to be at a certain level, would the college (more specifically the admission office) realize that advanced placement history was a more difficult course than ordinary American history and, accordingly, that Sally's grade in it might be a shade lower? These questions, which must have started with the inception of the advanced placement program (I mercifully cannot remember), have continued.

The answer is not entirely satisfactory to parents, students, or even schools. To the question: Do you consider the difference in difficulty of an honors, enriched, or advanced placement course in looking at grades? the answer is yes, but . . .

A counter question is likely to arise. Does the school itself recognize the difference in the level of difficulty by giving extra weight to these courses in determining overall averages and class rank. The best high schools I know do take these factors into account, sometimes by a simple coefficient which curves an average in superior classes upward, or more frequently by an elaborate schedule of equivalents which gives different levels of the same course slightly different values. The New Trier High Schools come to mind. They have four or five different levels of competition for most of their college level courses, and the resultant mathematical work undoubtedly requires the services of a computer, but it does a most serviceable job of equalizing competitional differences.

Schools that don't take these differences into account are defeating their own purposes. It is unfair to tell a college that Lincoln High School's honor program is difficult and the grades in it mean much more if the school itself is unwilling to back up its assumption by rewarding the students in its honor program. Otherwise, the school is asking colleges to make assumptions about it that it is unwilling to make itself, which, though flattering, is not realistic or fair to its students.

Before a student goes into an honors program, he has every right to know what effect it will have on his education and his admission to college.

Ideally, of course, enriched programs provide more challenge and keep the intellectually superior student alive and interested. Many of these programs were developed after the Conant report discovered that the bright student was the least cared for in many of our schools, and that good brains often went lazy from lack of work because courses were gauged to the middle or lower end of a class. One of the advances brought about by the Conant report is that it sufficiently put to rest the form of educational idiocy that maintained that it is "undemocratic" to separate students according to ability—a view which has had considerable currency and is responsible for many of the bright students being bored into academic antagonism.

However, enriched programs for the bright student are not an unmixed blessing. The first point I have covered before—the danger that in challenging students, the material used will be emotionally and experientially beyond their understanding. The second danger is probably more prevalent than the first: teachers may think that bright students should be able to cover more work than in fact they can. I asked a friend, who was the director of admission at a famous college, about a high school in his city which had set up a college preparatory high school flagrantly undemocratic in its standards—an IQ of 125 and a grade average of 85 were required for students to get in and stay in. His response: "I'll feel better about the school if the teachers don't think that twice as much challenge means twice as much work. Those kids need imagination applied to their problem—not more busy work."

Without question, too much "busy work" in high school must account in part for the lack of academic fervor in college, the restlessness with courses, curricula, and the system in general. The constant pressure of competition is also a source of fatigue which is accelerated and intensified by honors courses.

In putting together all the bright students, the challenge is increased, and so is the competition, since virtually every teacher grades on a curve of distribution which exists in his own mind. Because of the prestige, and because of the haunting fear (and justified) that if they are not in an honors course, some admission officer will wonder why they are not, the brighter students pour themselves into honors and enriched programs and struggle for the best grades, which in turn produce the best chances for college admission.

Grades alone are the best predictors for success in college, better than College Board or ACT (American College Testing program) tests by themselves, and, in no small part, they depend on the competition against which the grades were earned. In a small school that does not send many students to college, a high rank in class may not mean anything, but in a large suburban high school where many want to go to competitive colleges and only a comparative few will be chosen, the ability to rise to the top of a large class is very significant; the degree of significance and the degree of competition go hand in hand. In some highly competitive schools, class rank, while maintained in the office for college and counseling use, is considered confidential. Places are won or lost by minute changes in the decimal part of an average, and the constant concern about grades, averages, and class standing is an exhausting experience for the student.

The colleges have experienced the same phenomenon as

they became, against their will, preparatory schools for the graduate and professional schools. Competition for grades, class rank, and subsequent admission to schools after college was what students had hoped to escape in college. At the same time, such competition undoubtedly has a depressing effect on a student's academic activity; i.e., he is more likely to write the safe answer which he thinks will get the good grade than the offbeat idea which has just popped into his head, and the result according to my friends on the faculty, is deadly.

The current response is to take the emphasis off grades so that the student can devote himself wholeheartedly to the joy of learning and let the grades take care of themselves. Some colleges have done this for a long time—Bennington and Reed, for example. However, at Bennington the grades are recorded; they are simply not made public to any agency but the graduate school to which the student applies. More recently, other more conservative institutions have followed suit, and now some number of a student's courses can be "pass-fail"—that is, no specific mark is assigned, and the student either passes the course (at the D-level or higher) or he fails it.

Many medical schools have operated on this basis for years in an attempt to cut down on the vicious competition for grades which lead to choice internships. At Yale Medical School no grades are assigned for the first two years and the first major test is the administration of the National Board Examinations. Up to that point assessment is made on a personal basis, and the overall assumption is that a medical student good enough to get into Yale should be expected to survive and flourish. They do.

It is not surprising, therefore, that high school students should look above them and see what means they might take to relieve their own pressure-filled lives. In the selective independent schools and in the highly competitive high schools of the selective-through-the-high-cost-of-real-estate suburbs, there has been a growing feeling that some measures should be taken to ease the strain of competition, or at least to recognize and combat its more corrosive effects.

One of the most interesting experiments in this area centers around the date of notification for admission of highly selective colleges—April 15. This is the high point of the senior year for many students, and schools have discovered that much of what happens afterward is anticlimatic, no matter how much they or the colleges guard against the post-decision slump. (Many colleges make their acceptances subject to completing the senior year of high school "successfully," which usually means no serious slump in grades. Colleges can and do invoke this threat to rescind the acceptances of a few hapless students each year.)

The independent school answer was to end the senior year at the end of the second term—about March 15—at which point the students go home for spring vacation. At that point the schools, enjoying fully their "independent" status, have taught all that they think is necessary in the first two terms. The last term is then turned over to the student for an independent study project, work and study, or a combination. Pomfret School in Connecticut sends students off-campus to work in the cities on projects involving urban or civic problems. A report is required at the end of the term, before graduation. Another variation on this plan has been instituted by the Providence Country Day School. In the last term each senior has a number of course options for the first four weeks. Students in good academic standing may then go into an "apprenticeship" program, sampling an area in which they have a strong vocational interest. Recent seniors have worked in hospitals and banks, with social agencies and veterinarians. At the end of the year each student writes a report of his experiences under the supervision of a faculty member, and also makes an oral report to the school, in which the human relationships (worker-boss) of his experience are stressed.

The high schools, locked by law into their curriculum and the number of days of instruction cannot do this, but they are experimenting with various other possible solutions to the problem of pressure.

One of the first was the attempt to abandon class rank in school reports to colleges. Some selective population high schools have announced for years that class rank means nothing because the students there are so strong and get such good grades that there is no proper way to differentiate between them on that basis. Usually, however, such a statement is accompanied by a profile of the high school which shows the distribution of grades by quintiles or quartiles. It then becomes the problem of the college, if it does not wish to force the issue with the school, to average out a student's grades and place him appropriately.

Many schools, in an attempt to escape from the false exactitude of precise class rank, prefer to mark in quintiles or deciles. Thus the report to the college will read that Sheila stands not twelfth in a class of 150, but in the first decile of her class. Whether or not Margaret, who is the valedictorian gets any better treatment than "first decile" depends on the teacher writing her recommendation.

Another device to reduce tension is the "pass-fail" course, an obvious borrowing from the college grading reforms and highly sensible if used correctly. Ideally, "pass-fail" should be used to permit a student to study a course which interests him or which he feels he should know something about, but of which he is scared. Art and music students rarely show any enthusiasm or abilities in physics (a dangerous generalization!) but pass-fail would permit Bill, an artist, or Nancy, a poet, to take physics for information, squeak through the course, and not have to take the consequences of a marginal grade. But pass-fail is not the way for future doctors or engineers to take physics and any college would and should look askance at any premed who did this. Pass-fail, then, is fine for courses which are not central to the student's preparation for college, and, treated in that way, raises no questions by admission committees.

However, the latest trend will raise quite a storm, if it becomes prevalent: complete abandonment of all grades in favor of a pass-fail system. One major eastern boarding school has already adopted this system, and undoubtedly more will follow. It is more likely to be suggested in an independent school because of the traditionally lower grading system and the school's assertion that its population is so select that competition within the group has little or no meaning. Put another way, most famous name schools feel that virtually any of their graduates can survive the academic competition at any college in America and that personal qualities, not grades, should determine the difference in selection by the colleges.

The English public schools, probably for different reasons, have used nearly this system for years. A student's work is commented on by his teacher, improvement or determination noted, and whether the work is satisfactory or not. However, when it comes to applying to the universities, there is a national examination in various subjects, and only students passing these at certain set levels can be expected to enter college.

This will undoubtedly be the outcome in this country. College admission will come to depend entirely on an evaluation of the College Board scores simply because the admission process at most American colleges now must rely on certain mechanical and objective criteria since the volume cannot be handled in any other way. Small colleges like Hanover could read and evaluate the eight hundred or more applications they receive each year, but could Northwestern possibly read and evaluate the approximately four thousand applications they receive if they had to read

48,000 teacher reports which talked about a student's progress, whether he passed or failed, and then try to rank-order the students on the basis of these reports? (The figure 48,000 is arrived at by assuming that each of four thousand applicants took four courses for each of three years in high school; each applicant has, therefore, a minimum of twelve teacher reports for a grand total of 48,000.) The answer is patently clear: the college under these conditions has no choice but to rely on such standardized tests as the ACT or the College Board. (Since part of the ACT reporting procedures depends on grades in courses, their reports might have to be drastically reorganized if the move against grades becomes widespread.)

Heavy reliance on standardized test scores alone would create a reaction on the part of nearly everyone—students, parents, schools, and colleges, each for varying reasons. Students feel such a method makes selection too mechanical; parents feel that more attention should be paid to a student's year-long performance as opposed to what he can do in three hours; schools will protest that their courses are tailor-made and do not conform to what is tested; colleges, running full circle, feel like the students, that selection on the basis of scores is too mechanical. However, a study by Dean K. Whitla of Harvard of the selection practices of forty-three major colleges showed that, all things being equal, a college selected its students more nearly on the basis of College Board scores than any other criterion.

Does this mean that there would be no difference in the future if high schools dropped grades since colleges (or many of them) make selections mechanically by scores? Not at all. The study did not suggest that all cases were decided by scores, but that scores were the most powerful consideration; the quality of the high school record and the personal qualities of the student are still important and are used to confirm or deny what the test scores reveal. However, at present, I know of no highly competitive colleges that *automatically* eliminate a student on the basis of poor scores or that automatically accept because of good scores.

(An interesting sidelight on how fine the differentiations can get in a highly competitive college is shown by the publication to a select few colleges of the raw scores on the Level 2 Mathematics test of the College Board. The top score on the College Board scale is 800 but this is not necessarily a "perfect" score, since it is determined by a raw score. On a recent test, for example, a raw score of 47 was perfect, but a score of 38 still entitled the test-taker to an 800, which is considered to be a student's crowning achievement and generates much applause and comment in his school. However, the prevalence of 800s in the math area led the College Board to give certain colleges the raw scores so that an applicant can be more closely examined to see whether he has earned a "high" 800 or a "low" 800. In certain cases, the difference could mean acceptance or rejection.)

As horrifying as this sounds, we must realize that artificial cutoffs would probably have to be established if grades were abandoned, so that the committees could narrow the field down to a manageable number.

In the meanwhile, what about your high school, if it were to become a pioneer in the abandonment of grades? What would happen to the application of your child competing against traditional high schools? There is no absolute answer, but there is a considerable possibility that with the greater difficulties of reading and analyzing a gradeless dossier in comparison to the conventional grade forms, the admission committee members will turn in exasperation to the scores—and if they are good, wade through the rest. If they are not, the readers may go no further. In view of the amount of reading and analysis that must be done in far too short a period of time, this is not unreasonable.

Further, in what might seem to a paranoid admission officer (and their tendency to paranoia seems equally reasonable to me) a deliberate attempt to confuse and slow down the process of selection, guidance teachers and the other purveyors of information from high schools are limiting the degree to which they will assist a college in making a judgment on an applicant. The traditional degree of "push" that the guidance teacher used to give a student has now disappeared in a shuffle of concern about the validity of the school's right to make judgment. The counselor often feels that his position is not to judge, that judgment and guidance are incompatible responsibilities, and that the counseling relationship would be ruined if a student knows he is being judged.

The unfortunate but realistic assumption behind this reasoning is that every student is anxious about the future, and particularly about college, and that if the threat of a good college recommendation hangs in the balance, then Joe and Mary are not likely to expose their real characters and personalities to the guidance counselors and hence no rapport can be established. The real reason, I feel, for this abdication from responsibility is that teachers shrink from making judgment that might hurt a student's future chances for success (for the best possible reason: all teachers really feel that virtually everyone has the potentiality for great success—that's why they are teachers). A second, less laudable reason is that less than enthusiastic recommendations may cause a repercussion from the parents that the teacher wants to avoid if possible.

A comparatively small number of high schools handled this question in a highly satisfactory way. Their records read: "It is against the policy of this school to give a principal's or counselor's recommendation; the recommendation is derived from teacher's comments." Not really a compromise, this is the most sensible kind of recommendation, since few guidance teachers and virtually no principals are able to know a student well enough to make an absolute recommendation, but instead have to draw on the anecdotal reports of teachers for their conclusions.

What about the high school recommendation when such is made? Is it effective, and do college admission committees pay attention to it? Absolutely! In a recent study done at Brown University the counselor's degree of enthusiasm for a student's success at Brown was discovered to be the most accurate predictor of academic success, higher than College Board aptitude or achievement scores or class rank. In other words, the counselor's evaluation of how well a student can expect to do in a specific college is highly valid; the good counselor can and should direct her students to colleges where they can do their best work, and should also discourage colleges from accepting students who cannot be successful at that college.

It is here that the difference between the public schools and the independent schools becomes most apparent. Independent schools are highly concerned with how well their products do in college. Too often, the public school is chiefly concerned with keeping peace or not "intruding" on the privacy of a student by giving him negative recommendations. Conversely, the private school parent is for some reason more likely to accede to reason from his student's counselor than he would if the student were in public school. Doubtless it has to do with the cost of advice; cheap advice from public school officials is held to be worth what it costs, but advice that costs from $1,000 to $4,500 a year must be worth a good deal.

Does this mean that the best counseling is found in independent schools? Not necessarily, but the odds are in favor of it. Many public high schools have superb counselors who know their students or can find out about them. Many private schools have ineffectual counselors, but the lower ratio of students to counselors and the greater intimacy of a private school are likely to produce better counseling in the long run.

The public school student has put up with larger classes, a smaller share of the facilities, a less available faculty and counseling staff, and as a result probably has developed a greater toughness and independence than his private school brother.

What happens to the products of these two different systems is predictable on the basis of the foregoing descriptions: all other factors being equal, the record of public school students in college has been better than that of private school students. This finding is based on studies made at colleges where there are large enough samples of both to make valid studies. It is hardly reassuring to a parent who has spent a great deal of money, in addition to his school taxes, to make sure his children are the best prepared for life or college or whatever it is he is concerned about their facing.

This being the case, and since the colleges respond to this knowledge with no essential differentiation in their admission practices except for College Board Verbal aptitude scores, then why bother with the expense of private education? Given these statements, what justification has the private school to offer parents and students?

To assume that each private school is concerned only with college entrance and that the independent school parent is motivated by snobbery is to indulge in considerable oversimplification of motives. Certainly schools are worried about their graduate's record of entrance to and success in college; and certainly many parents use private schools as a means of conspicuous consumption of money; but the complete picture can and should be more complicated than that.

A parent should consider private schools if he feels after investigation or experience that the public schools are not good. The independent school (the schools themselves prefer the term "independent" as less snobbish than "private") may provide religious instruction which the public schools may not teach, offer athletic development to boys and girls who would not otherwise be able to get it from the sporadic gym classes at most schools, provide small classes where the shy and the reluctant can and are expected to be heard, offer extra help in the areas where a student is having particular trouble, offer extra challenge for the student who is so good that he has run through the traditional offerings. Above and beyond all this, the headmaster or headmistress of the independent school can use the institution totally as a learning machine in areas where the public schools have given up long ago—morals, the appreciation of beauty, manners, and attitudes.

The picture that emerges, then, is of an expensive institution which permits the children of the prosperous an opportunity to correct local educational ills or be given help to overcome special problems which might overcome them in the laissez-faire jungle of the public school.

This picture is more or less accurate but outdated. For many years the independent schools have felt the need to make their resources available to more than just the rich, but in many cases they went about the job of giving scholarship help in an inefficient way, quite often giving it to anyone who felt the need for financial assistance. One famous old academy simply asked the parents of a student who had been accepted to pay what they could rather than to meet a standard requirement of contribution.

The increasing trend to financial democratization made a scholarship system like that of the colleges a necessity, and an arm of the College Scholarship Service now performs the same function for the secondary schools. Parents pay not on impulse but according to the standards set up by this national agency, which uses the same complicated analysis of income, financial responsibilities, savings, and debts that is used to determine college scholarships at most of the major institutions of the country. Similarly, virtually all of the important independent secondary schools now subscribe to this service.

At the same time most of these schools have made a sincere and strenuous effort to increase the amount and availability of scholarship funds. For example, Lawrenceville School reported about ten years ago that only 7 percent of their students were on scholarship; now, under the capable leadership of Bruce McClellan, the student body has been seriously modified if not transformed, and the 25 percent of the students on scholarships from all sorts of backgrounds has made the school immeasurably healthier. Other schools have been at the same game even longer. With their enormous endowments, Andover and Exeter now keep their tuition comparatively low, but at the same time manage scholarship percentages at about a third of the student body.

In many ways, these schools are exceptions because they are unusually well endowed and equipped. But many of the small, even marginal, day schools may have better answers for your children than the local schools. This should be an individual decision for each child—and not a matter of giving one child an advantage at the expense of the other. To sum up the private-public argument, which usually generates a great deal of emotional response about parochialism, democracy, snobbery, and the rest, the real question is what is best for the individual child, rather than which of two systems is better. The thoughtful parent should weigh both sides of the question. If the answer is independent schools, investigation is in order, even though money seems to be the ultimate obstacle. It would be fatuous to suggest that the scholarship efforts of private schools have enabled them to take care of all who apply, but certainly there are scholarships available now that were not available ten to fifteen years ago, and it would be foolish not to make the request. Remember, however, that under the system developed by the Secondary School Scholarship Service, some contribution based on income is expected from every parent; the school cannot be expected to support the entire burden.

One final word of caution. Many parents, in considering education for their children, automatically assume that one system, private or public, is better than another, and make the move without considering the student. Having seen far too many studetts whose academic careers have been stunted by this sort of uprooting, my own rule of thumb is: if your student is happy and productive at a school, let him be. Any change at all is not necessarily a change for the better; any school where a student is happy and where he is working up to expectations is a good school for him, regardless of what the critics may say, and is probably providing him with valuable momentum for the next step.

IV

Guidance and Career Planning

THE OTHER DAY A FRIEND and a classmate of mine in college came to my office to talk about his son, a sophomore in college. As ammunition he brought with him a Kuder Preference Test profile which indicated that Danny was chiefly interested in the economic, social, and religious areas, and, to father's distress (he is a successful businessman), the social and religious areas were stronger than the economic.

His problem, as he told it to me, was that his son had come to him for advice on a college major. Looking at the test scores, neither father nor son could draw any conclusions—that is, conclusions which were agreeable with what they thought was best for the boy.

I pointed out to my friend that he probably would have a very similar Kuder profile—that, although a successful businessman, he was also deeply involved in social and welfare organizations and a devout churchman. "Why can't Danny follow your pattern?" It was a new idea to him. "But if he followed the social or religious bent in his studies, what would it do for him, what should he do? What kind of graduate school will he go to?"

To explain to this concerned father that specific training is not the only way to prepare for a job, and that graduate school (or even college!) is not inevitable, was very difficult.

This story calls attention to the fact that one major complication in career planning is parental delight in tests like the Kuder, which at their best are pretty good predictors and at worst are only a mirror of what the student sees in himself at that moment. But, because the test is calibrated, and because it is scientifically prepared, parents and students hang on to the results with grim insistence, despite the protestations of the test-makers who modestly indicate that they are not perfect.

Occasionally the tests themselves get confused. A young widow I know dutifully had her three children tested extensively so that she could make the most appropriate plans for them. Two emerged from exhaustive testing with the label "Too-many-aptitude-person"—a flattering and tactful way for the tests to admit that it didn't know what to recommend for these children.

All of this forms the prelude for our discussion of the decisions about education which more and more are being assumed automatically, or which are being forced on all of us by the rapidly increasing complexity of the world and the need for trained men to run it.

The decision as to whether or not a boy or girl goes to college is not made in the senior year of high school, but rather in the seventh grade, which is one of the problems which stands seriously in the way of providing education for the underprivileged. In other words, if parental ambition and foresight did not look ahead six years, it is difficult, although not impossible, to change the direction the student has been pushed in, chiefly because the background information needed by the time a student gets to college is enormous, but acquired so gradually that in many cases the students aren't even aware of it. Thus, a young black student at a famous New England college said: "My freshman year was hell. In discussion sections other students would casually make references like the *Odyssey.* I didn't know what the *Odyssey* was, but I certainly wasn't going to admit it."

Although I think that college is a less desirable experience for *everyone* than is generally believed, it is totally fruitless to suggest that businesses might set up apprenticeship programs as they did in the last century, so that the practical minded of the world could learn by doing, while those genuinely interested in scholarship could pursue their academic studies under less crowded and less hectic conditions. It is not at all practical to consider the possibility of establishing such programs in the foreseeable future, since virtually everyone who has any hand in setting the standards for hiring and promoting, feels the college diploma is the *sine qua non.* This is too bad because, if the putative "need" for college could be effectively downgraded, the colleges would not have to cope with the students who are there because they think they should be, because they haven't been allowed by their parents to consider any other course of action, or simply as an entrée to a job with a respectable corporation.

There is a good deal of validity in asking for the baccalaureate diploma as the first credential in considering a new employee, especially one who has had no previous work experience; the college diploma proves, or should prove, that the student was intelligent enough and diligent enough to learn what he had to in order to meet certain standards. The reasonable implication that a future employer draws from this is that the student will be able to learn the intricacies of any job he might be offered well enough to be effective.

It is interesting that various studies which have been

conducted on how well academic success predicts success in business sometimes contradict each other. A study made by the Western Electric Corporation showed that the better the grades in college, the better and faster the advancement, even allowing for differences in grades between "hard" colleges and "easy" colleges. A twenty-fifth reunion report on a Dartmouth class some years ago showed that twenty-five years after graduation the Phi Betes were earning appreciably more than the "letter sweater" winners. A similar survey of the twenty-fifth reunion of the Brown class of 1942 showed a direct correspondence between grades in college and salaries. Those with the best academic records were also those with the highest salaries twenty-five years later, and as the college grades went down the scale, so did the incomes.

On the other hand, there is constant but incomplete reference (particularly by alumni convinced that admission officers are dedicated to the discovery and admission of Phi Beta Kappa recipients to the exclusion of everyone else—especially those who might produce a winning football team) to studies which show that the men who do well after graduation are the doers in college—athletes, class politicians, etc. It is certainly true that there are college students earning the outmoded "gentleman's C" who will be more interested and able in the practical world than they are in academic environs.

My own view is that the best analysis of the situation is to be found in a recently completed study at Brown on the success of students after they leave college. This study shows a direct correlation between the degree of academic success and the subsequent advancement in a variety of fields. Of particular interest to those who worry about the future leader was the analysis of the successful businessman as one who got good grades despite the fact that he was not particularly academically oriented. Described another way, the successful businessman is a person who, as a college student, was able to see his academic courses as problems to be solved efficiently—which he did without becoming so involved in scholarship and academic success that he considered his education as a goal itself, rather than as the means to an end.

For practical reasons, therefore, it seems sensible for business and industry to ask their applicants for a college diploma as the first step in their training process. But then, they don't have to worry about providing it.

If the college experience, by teaching processes of thought rather than specific information, becomes the basic training course for the future executives of business firms, why not postpone going to college until the student has reached a point of maturity where he understands himself, his motives, and the purposes of his education? Further, in considering college as a preparation for the future, what difference will it make to the young man or woman what college he or she goes to? Will it really affect chances for original employment and subsequent promotion, or is this another ungrounded fear of parents about education?

For girls there is seldom any problem about the smooth succession from high school to college. In the first place, girls are usually more dutiful students and more mature (or at least steadier) in their outlooks than men of the same age. More important, since women are not subject to the draft, there is no pressure to enter college immediately after high school except that it is the conventional pattern of education.

For men the story is quite different. First, the pressures of the draft force them into continuing the educational pattern between high school and college without a break. Even more important is the general belief that one has to study subjects in college that directly prepare him to make a living, and, therefore, the choice of subjects itself is vital. Understandably, this vocational set causes a considerable crisis in boys who, in terms of maturity and experience, are not up to making what they think will be final choices.

For these reasons, I feel strongly that many male high

school graduates should enjoy (or endure) a moratorium of one to two years before entering college, during which time they should either work off their wanderlust by traveling or get experience by working in a field they think might be an eventual choice of occupation. In both cases, boys would gain the maturity, insight, and experience which would make their college experience more understandable and more enjoyable.

Parenthetically, very few students are in college for the love of learning, although that concept has enjoyed considerable vogue in the last few years, particularly in the high pressure, high-competition colleges where the "joy of learning" is spoken of in the same way that a saint might speak of his mystical and supernatural experiences. By the time most students have begun to understand why they are in college and decide to enjoy it as an experience other than social, they are seniors and ready to leave. It is for this reason that I suggest postponing entrance to college for a year; maturity more than any other factor brings a real understanding of the needs and purposes of education.

The chief reason for the hurry, of course, is parental anxiousness, which, coupled with a natural desire to get the whole expensive business over with as soon as possible, argues that any delay is likely to prevent their son from going to college. It is also parental pressure, far more than any other factor, that is in back of the concern about the prestige of the college their child attends.

As income or ambition rises, the preoccupation with college as a label or as an entrée into business or preferential social circles rises proportionately. This is reflected not only in everyday conversation, particularly of men and women whose children are of college age, but also in all the novels which mirror middle-class life. John Marquand understood upper middle-class status symbols as thoroughly as any viewer of the American scene, and he summed up the preoccupation with college backgrounds neatly in this

bit of dialogue from *Sincerely Willis Wade:* Professor
Hodges of Harvard has just been introduced to Willis.

> "Did you ever take my introductory course, Mr. Wade?"
> "No sir," Willis answered, "I went to Boston Univer-
> sity."
> "Dear, dear," Mr. Hodges said, "I attended the Univer-
> sity of Chicago myself once, but I finally contrived to live
> it down. Don't you think so, Martha?"
> "No, Homer," Mrs. Hodges said, "you've never lived
> down anything."

John O'Hara is another author whose constant preoccupation with his character's colleges almost rivals his
enthusiasm for their sexual activity.

In the face of this kind of encouragement, it is not
surprising that parents push their children directly or
indirectly into the most prestigious colleges. Naturally,
most parents will not admit to yearning for prestige for its
own sake, but they can, and do, talk unabashedly about
educational excellence. Since this alternate description is
used so often to describe the socially desirable colleges in a
way that cannot be criticized, all concerned suffer a form of
brainwashing and believe the statements as made. Thus,
the faculties of these institutions are often disappointed
that their students are not zealously academic, but instead
are bright and dutiful members of the middle classes,
preparing for a useful life in the middle classes. This does
not mean that these students are not really interested in
academic excellence, but it does mean that many of them
see their experience as part of a necessary training process
and not as an adventure in scholarship.

In the face of these prejudices and myths, how does a
parent sensibly assist his child in the selection of a college?
The chief criteria to be considered, it seems to me, are
these: size, distance, expense, admissability, and "rightness."

Size is self-explanatory (as are many of the others). The question is, can your student survive and thrive in a large institution? If he (or she) is mature, outgoing, self-reliant, and self-confident, the answer is probably yes. Particularly in big universities, the fraternity or sorority assumes considerable importance because it permits the student to associate himself with a smaller, a more "digestible" group of people. Therefore, if you are considering a large university, think about your child's ability to cope with large classes; a bureaucratic administration, a higher degree of impersonality. All these are balanced against a broader experience—which could well be more socially educational than the experience to be found at a small college—the broader range of courses and facilities, and finally, the opportunity to compete at almost any level of academic competition he chooses to.

Distance need be no problem, particularly if parents and the student want public, municipal, or some other local form of education. A sizeable percentage of the undergraduate population of America lives at home or is attending college within a 200-mile radius of home. Conversely, very few colleges and universities can be said to have truly national representation in their student body. The student who is willing to go a long distance to college is, by nature, more adventurous and outgoing, more mature and self-reliant; or he should be. The student who goes away great distances to college, not from his own wishes, but because his parents yearn for the greater prestige in distance will almost certainly have troubles in college. Similarly, the student who chooses to go far away from home in order to escape a family situation will discover that the problem tends to travel with him.

Expense: The cost of education has gone up so fast in the last fifteen years that there is no real need to comment on what educational costs are doing to college choices; it is obvious that there is an increasing trend to public institutions. It should be understood, however, that the private colleges have made (and are making) a desperate effort to provide scholarship funds so that the huge cost differences between public and private institutions can be bridged, if not leveled. Thanks to the College Scholarship Service and the scholarship arm of the American College Testing Corporation, an evaluation of financial need based on a confidential statement filed by the parents enables colleges to make awards which balance the budget.

In effect, the formulae of the scholarship services make an estimate of a family's financial strength and assess it a certain amount for the education of the student. This assessment is based on a vastly complicated formula (administered, of course, by computer) which takes into account family income, number of dependents, other children in college, years to go before retirement, savings, aged relatives who may be living with the parents, the amount of equity in the parents' home, and a number of other variables. The college then uses the assessment, adds to it an amount which seems reasonable for the student to earn during the school year and the summer, and subtracts the result from the total cost of attending the college—including living expenses and travel. Thus a moderate income family might find that it was expected to spend less to support a child at an expensive private college than it would cost to support him at the state university.

If the private college decides to make an award, it will probably do so in the form of a "package"—that is, a combination of the different forms in which financial aid is offered, including scholarship, loan, and employment.

Scholarship is financial assistance that need not be repaid, and is often called "gift aid."

Loans, depending on the source of the funds, are low-cost and long-term. The initial resistance of many families to financing a college education through loans has broken down rapidly and millions of dollars a year are now lent to students. According to financial aid officers, the investment is apparently a good one, because most student loans are being repaid ahead of schedule.

Student employment is an age-old and honorable college tradition. There is often a prejudice against giving a student a job in his freshman year, for fear that the pressures of academic demands plus the time required by the job will be too much. Actually, if the amount of time the job takes is not too great (twelve hours a week is considered reasonable), the enforced scheduling which a job imposes on a freshman is very beneficial. One of the most difficult adjustment problems that any college freshman faces is that he must lay out his own day; colleges are placing fewer and fewer restrictions on their students, who must learn to organize their own lives. Athletics, employment, and other regular activity, if not carried to an extreme, can be most helpful to the student, particularly in the freshman year.

In considering expenses, parents should keep in mind that, in addition to the loan funds which are usually available through the college, there is now a system of state and federal loan guarantee and interest subsidies which enable parents and students to borrow from local banks for educational purposes, much of the cost of interest and administration being absorbed by the federal government. This means that even a prosperous family that has not made extensive preparations for the expense of college in terms of savings can still afford the greater expense of a private institution if they are willing to spread the payments out over a number of years.

In 1969 the sudden rise in interest rates threatened the whole system of underwritten loans to students. Because the subsidy paid by the government still made the income from loans to students less than from any other type of loan, banks became very reluctant to make these loans. Recent federal legislation has eased this situation by paying banks an interest subsidy on educational loans, making them more attractive to the banks. At the same time, the government itself is going out of the student loan business and expects the interest subsidy to enable private banks to provide the needed money. The chief objection to this plan is that the interest subsidy is available only to families whose annual income is under $10,000, which has caused a number of educators to worry about the effect this will have on college choice patterns. Parents who are too rich for scholarships but too poor to pay for their children's education out of income may decide that borrowing money at very high interest rates (because they are not eligible for federal subsidy) is too great a price to pay for the increasingly expensive private colleges, and will be forced into public institutions. Private colleges are worried that they will not be able to fill their classes, and state institutions are afraid they will be swamped.

Again, parenthetically, the full burden of the cost of education need not and, I think, should not fall on the parents. Loans can be made out to students (if countersigned by parents when the students are younger than twenty-one) and can be considered by them to be their future responsibility. As I mentioned earlier, employment opportunities for recent college graduates are so good at the moment that education loans, for the most part, are being paid ahead of schedule.

One final method of meeting college expenses should not be forgotten—the installment plan. Both colleges and commercial organizations offer plans whereby the parent can divide the year's bill into nine parts to be paid during the academic year, or into twelve monthly payments. This is a great assistance for those who can pay the bill out of income, but not in a lump sum.

Nothing in the foreseeable future will reduce the cost of education, and the cost gap between public and private institutions will continue to grow, despite various mechanisms which can ease the financial blow. The real question remains: is the difference worth the money? Only the purchaser can know, and it may not be until fifteen years after his graduation that he can assess just how valuable it was.

Admissability: Each year the high-school principal talks to the parents of his students about how many "first choice" colleges his students were able to get into. The immediate impression presented by the principal's statement is that a lot of students were able to go to the colleges they wanted to. Actually, "first choice" or, even more sterile, "the college of your choice" is not the college the student really wants to go to, but rather that college which he feels he can get into. Thus, in an interview at Old Siwash, the interviewer is often baffled (if he is inexperienced) when a staggeringly honest young man says during the course of the interview: "Old Siwash is my first choice—I'd really like to go to Colgate, but I don't think I can get in."

This is what I mean by "admissability"—the judgment on the part of the candidate of his chances to be admitted. In general, guidance teachers tend to be pessimistic about college admission; parents tend to be aggressively hopeful; and students, who live with the problem every day and know which colleges have shot down which valedictorians in years past, are inclined to be coldly and accurately realistic.

For this reason, in choosing a college, parents should consider the realities of the situation. If Old Siwash has everything that Harold wants and needs in a college and if, in addition, it is a college to which he can safely aspire, then it should be on Harold's list. Perhaps there also should be one or two long shots—colleges, like Colgate, that he would dearly love but doesn't expect to make. Almost every bouquet of admission applications includes one or two such, and it probably should. "A man's reach should exceed his grasp, or what's a heaven for?"

"Rightness": When Harold decided that Colgate or Old

Siwash was precisely the place he wanted to spend four years and upward of fifteen thousand dollars, it was probably a purely chemical response to the architecture, a girl he saw on campus, brainwashing from birth, or the fact that it was raining when he saw Hamilton, but the sun was shining on Old Siwash. Students meticulously send for and read catalogues, investigate curricula, ask searching questions about the student-faculty ratio, and then make final decisions on the basis of where the sun was shining.

What is more, I am not sure this is bad. Harold and his many sisters and brothers will change enormously in the next four years, and in ways which neither Harold nor his parents can imagine. It thus becomes impractical and probably impossible to choose the college which will anticipate all the possibilities of growth and development. In Germany students change from university to university on the basis of their changing interests, but transfers are rare and are actively discouraged in this country. Therefore, the campus on which the student feels the most rapport, the one on which he thinks he will be the happiest and most successful in his pursuit of education, will indeed provide the setting for the most advantageous investment of all that time and money.

With the factors of size, expense, distance, admissability, and "rightness" taken into consideration, what is the answer—a private college or public? It is more than likely that "size and expense" have already determined the answer this question, but what are the differences in admissability?

The picture has changed markedly in the last few years, and what is just beginning to be apparent now may well presage major changes in American education in the next twenty to thirty years. The state university is moving up, in terms of every kind of prestige, at the expense of the private college.

This has been so chiefly in the Middle and Far West

where the great state universities have always been high in prestige, but the private colleges have also held their own and have had a good and steady stream of customers. Now, however, there begin to be signs that the cost of private education is causing students and parents to think twice about its worth. The result is that the state universities are becoming difficult to get into and are developing the separate but definable prestige of exclusivity.

Of course, not all the state universities are equally easy to get into, and there are levels of prestige for the state institutions of each state. Thus, the University of Illinois requires more excellence from its entrants in terms of standardized test scores and rank in high school class than does the Southern Illinois University at Carbondale, and hence becomes more prestigious and desirable because it is harder to get into.

From the exterior, the private colleges appear to be still enjoying the fruits of the educational revolution, but there are danger signs. The financial collapse of the gigantic University of Pittsburgh was a warning that anyone could hear. The consolidation of Case Institute and Western Reserve University into one university was a marriage of economic necessity between two not entirely compatible partners. The forced absorption of Temple University into the complex of the state colleges of Pennsylvania was again evidence that all is not well on the balance sheets of private educational institutions.

The smaller colleges of the Midwest have not been immune to these influences, and the complaint is usually the same: "Although we can find as many girls as we want, we are having difficulty maintaining the number and the academic quality of our men." Perhaps this means that in the Midwest the importance of an Eastern prestige college is greater for men than for women, or simply that midwestern families do not send their daughters away. Alternatively though, perhaps families are more likely to pay high tuition for girls, while the boys go off, independently and much more cheaply, to the state university.

The question of expense, even with larger scholarship budgets and extensive loan programs, has come into considerable importance and is mentioned more and more frequently by the guidance teachers as the reason for the accelerating interest in the state universities.

This is not surprising, but even more ominous for the future of the independent college is the thesis of Humphrey Doermann, one-time Director of Admissions for Harvard College. In a book called *Cross Currents in College Admission,* Mr. Doermann points out that intelligence and sufficient income to pay private college bills are limiting factors. In other words, the more selective a college gets, the higher the level of intelligence and achievement it will require, and the fewer students there will be with these qualifications. The same is true of income. As college costs go up, the number of families who can pay private college bills gets smaller and smaller as the size of the bill mounts. Now, if you combine these two factors and look for families whose children are both bright and hard-working *and* who can afford the luxury of a private college (since 60 percent of those who enter must pay their own way—"paying guests" is Mr. Doermann's term), the available pool gets smaller and smaller. Small wonder, then, that some of the private colleges are beginning to feel a slackening in admission pressure, which will certainly make for a decline in the admission standards, and which might, therefore, bring about considerable damage to private institutional prestige.

Chiefly, this erosion of the private college has gone on outside the East, where the private college has reigned supreme for three centuries and its walls show no visible signs of collapse. Yet even in the East there is a good deal of shuffling going on, which is probably symptomatic of troubles.

One of the chief examples is the move to coeducation. While it is certainly not true that college boys have only recently discovered girls and vice versa, it is true that in recent years the colleges devoted to a single sex, particularly if geographically isolated from large sources of supply of the opposite sex, have had disappointingly lean years when the greatest part of education has enjoyed a boom. Certainly, only a major force could cause such bastions of tradition as Vassar and Yale to abandon age-old tradition of "separate but better" in favor of coeducation. Yet, whether they like it or not, they and many others have succumbed to the pressures, or lack of them, from applicants.

For admission competition is not and cannot be manufactured by a college to generate prestige or an aura of exclusivity that is spurious. Competition to college is generated because more students apply for entrance than can be accommodated and some have to be turned away.

In the public colleges, this can be accomplished by setting up rigid cutoff dates for applications, by raising the minimum grade point average requirement or the minimum acceptable entrance examination score. The surplus is then spilled to the next lower (in competition, prestige, or standards) state institution or to the state or community junior college.

The private institutions, on the other hand, treat high competition for admission in a different, subjective way. Thus, while the state institution asks for and rigidly requires a certain academic average in high school, a minimum test score, or a minimum rank in class which is set by law and cannot be altered, the private selective college is permitted by its independence to take whatever kind of student it fancies.

(The contrasts are often bewildering, but usually interesting. A friend in Florida told me of a boy in his high school who had truly remarkable ability in math and science. He was, however, so little interested in history that he failed the American History course required for his diploma. Result: The University of Florida was unable to accept him because he had no high school diploma, but MIT, being a private institution, was under no such stricture. Needless to say, the boy studied there.)

These differences between private and public schools in admission policy and attitudes may considerably affect the decision which you and your student make about the type of place he will apply to. Private colleges now bracket the field, attracting and serving the best students as well as, the lopsided, the special, or the problem student who doesn't fit into the neat but rigid mold which the public system has been forced to erect.*

It becomes apparent in talking with public university admission officers that the rigidity of the admission standards is a blessing since it means that politicians cannot circumvent the standards in behalf of a politically connected candidate. Readmission—that is, admission for the student who has entered but has flunked out and now wants to return—is not generally covered by statute, and hence the political finagling that can be done occurs more often at this level. Thus lunchtime conversations with deans at major state universities are apt to be liberally sprinkled with the names of senators, judges, and speakers of the house, all of whom seem to have nephews applying for readmission.

The director of admission of a state institution exerts little or no influence on his academic community because he has no leeway to work within: *all* candidates who meet certain rigid standards are admitted; none are admitted who fall below the arbitrary line. The private college admission director, particularly of the less selective college at the

---

*In the rapidly changing field of higher education, the rules are shifting dramatically. How many institutions will try and continue "open admission" is open to endless conjecture.

lower end of the scale, is out looking for customers, while at the same time emanating as much of an air of selectivity as he can. To attract students he must rely on traditional connections (e.g., religious), the generally smaller size, the putative prestige of the private college, and (most important) a particular curricular specialty of the house, and/or the interest and teaching ability of the faculty.

This last is, in my opinion, the key to the future for the private college and what makes me say that currently there probably is better and more interesting *teaching* going on in the small and in many cases marginal colleges than there is anywhere else in the country. It is the key to the future because, if private education is to survive at all, it must provide something that cannot be had in public education, something that makes it worth one to two thousand dollars or more a year for the cost of education. The quality of teaching and the degree of individual attention are the only areas of real competition. Only a handful of private colleges can offer a challenge to the superb libraries and other physical facilities of the public universities—and this handful, the truly competitive, private, prestige universities, have in many cases achieved this competitive position by steadily enlarging every operation, from the size of the entering class to the number of students in each seminar in order to achieve more economical operation.

What is more, in the rush for funds needed for survival, the importance of a faculty member depends increasingly on his ability to produce papers, perform research, or publish books which will attract government or foundation support; his classroom teaching may also be good, but it is financially secondary, and bad teaching will be overlooked if the faculty member is productive enough in garnering grants. This attitude of the college toward teaching is one of the underlying reasons for some of today's student unrest: an unusually fine teacher who fails to be a "productive" scholar is dismissed, while faculty members distinguished only for their ability to get into print, not for teaching, get tenure.

Why, then, is quality of teaching and interest in the undergraduate likely to be better in the not-so-prestigious smaller private colleges? Because it is the chief attraction these places have to offer. Whether it is enough depends on the importance which a student and his parents put on individual attention.

Unfortunately, it is quite difficult to decide whether a college is telling the truth or simply indulging in wistful hyperbole about the quality of its teaching. Good teaching is like honesty. Everyone is for it in principle, but it is sometimes not expedient. When a conscientious student and his parents follow up the catalogue statements with inquiries of their own, the truth of the matter comes out: that a lot of good teaching depends on student response, just as student response depends on the quality of the teaching.

If this circular piece of reasoning makes no sense, perhaps an example will. A young friend, after a brilliant undergraduate and graduate career at Brown and Harvard respectively, decided to teach at a fine small college in the Midwest, partly because he was really interested in teaching, but mostly because he wanted out of the "Ivy League publish-or-perish rat race." He is naturally a good teacher, and has in addition superb training; he should, therefore, be able to get the maximum response from his students. He finds many of his students unresponsive, and is likely to put the blame on them. If the unresponsiveness continues, in the space of some years, he may conclude that teaching is a hopeless battle and simply offer the same course year after year without worrying whether it provides the challenge and stimulus he originally intended.

However, as Thomas Edison said, "people would rather do almost anything than think," and students, oddly enough, are no exception. What faculty often do not remember or realize is that students often understand only dimly why they are in college and what is supposed to happen there. For that reason they are curiously, even understandably, resistant to the process. The good teacher realizes this and is willing to work despite the expectation that he will have perhaps only one or two students in each class who respond in an ideal way.

This is a fact of pedagogic life which many young teachers either have not realized or feel they can change. Often, of course, they blame the makeup of the college for not producing more genuinely scholarly students, but even at the most selective colleges there are still far too few such students to satisfy the young scholar who feels his classes should contain nothing but eager disciples.

The immediate question comes up: if teaching is the real key to a "successful" college experience, why do the small colleges not turn out a high number of "scholars"—i.e., candidates for the Ph.D.—each year?

The answer brings us back to the circular question of whether students produce good teachers or teachers produce good students. The answer is both; some students are inspired by their professors to the point of emulation, but conversely there are some situations where the teaching has little to do with the academic productivity—where the students set the pace, not the teachers. Such a place is the City University of New York which reputedly generates more Ph.D. candidates than any other college in this country. Rather than the excellence of teaching (although their faculty has a deservedly strong reputation), it is the force of economics that produces this rush to scholarship because there is no better way for an intelligent and hardworking boy from a poor family to make himself affluent and respectable than to take the Ph.D. and teach in a college. The field of education, which at one time was almost the exclusive property of the middle class, has been invaded by the ambitious who see college teaching (virtually impossible without the Ph.D.) as the quickest way to a comfortable and generally pleasant condition of employment.

Academic "productivity" at a college where the clientele, in large part, are already middle-class is likely to be less great. That is, the number of Ph.D.s—the chief measure by which a faculty can gauge its teaching success—will not be so great proportionately. The reason for this is that education offers no special opportunities for advancement to the middle-class student unless he has a natural flair for scholarship. Hence, the usual "dull" middle-class student simply is not interested in education in the intense way that his lower-class brother is. Instead, he is concerned about law or business as the means by which he will move up. Medicine was once in the same category, but has become, like education, a quick and certain way to prestige and financial security. Not surprisingly, therefore, most students who can stay with the demands of a premedical program are anxious for prestige and security at almost any cost.

With that curious circularity which sociologists notice from time to time, the upper and lower ends of the social scale often behave with great similarity. Education no longer provides a haven for rich dilettantes as it once did, but now serves as a proving ground for the student who is so rich and secure that he has to try to prove himself in any area where effort and ability, not money, make the difference.

So, in choosing between private colleges and public, you can look at the record which each makes and discount it to a certain extent, at least as a measure of faculty excellence. Poor teachers with eager students may produce more impressive results than fine teachers with intelligent but "unhungry" students. The real factor to consider is "rightness."

The colleges, private and public, see the admission problem quite differently. The public institution sees its task as manning the gates against the flood and, by mechanical means, producing students of sufficiently good quality to keep the faculty reasonably happy. The private colleges, and particularly those with sufficient admission pressure to pick and choose from their applicant group, are attempting to create a deliberately diverse group whose interaction will itself be educational.

Their choices are often difficult to understand until it is realized that the ability to do good, even excellent academic work is not the chief basis for selection. This is particularly difficult for parents of good students to understand, because to choose students for a college on any other basis than the ability to produce a good college academic record seems to be pointless and, moreover, a negation of what the college is all about. This kind of selection can only be done when there are so many potential scholars in the applicant group that the group has to be considered as all equal in scholarship, so that personality, background, interests, and potential become the basis for choosing one student rather than another.

Quite another problem is that, by compressing into one class all the best scholars who might apply, one raises the rate of academic competition to the cutthroat level. There is a natural reshuffling as all good students are poured into a new class, and inevitably someone has to be at the bottom. For a student who has always been on top before, this can be a shattering and frustrating experience. In reaction, he may drive himself harder, may quit and retire from the competition, or simply may turn sour with his frustration.

These complications were surely in mind when the most highly selective colleges began their turnabout in the mid-1950s. The small group of famous, old colleges, chiefly in the Northeast (led by Harvard and the clairvoyance of Dean Bender), turned down hard-nosed grinds and took football players and lopsided artists. Dean Fred Glimp saw the problem as one of finding students who had enough personal strengths to survive the shock of being outcompeted—students whose presence would contribute to "a happy bottom quarter."

Does this mean that the scholarly colleges are not interested in scholars? Not at all. But it does mean that the admission policy is designed to humanize the potential scholar by providing him with the maximum variety of influences. Inevitably, of course, some of the stabilizing "bottom quarter" in every class will fool the predictors and become infected with the scholarly life. Since scholarship is in the air, this should not be a complete surprise. "I find myself caught up in the academic competition and I never expected I would," said a sophomore at Brown whose academic enthusiasm had been cursory through high school, and whose greatest drive had been in athletics. Competition is the key word, and his drive to be competitive is in the process of changing direction, and the chances are that he will shortly be a better student but less good as an athlete.

Although the prestige colleges (the Ivy League and the "potted Ivies" of Amherst, Wesleyan, Bowdoin, Williams, *et al.*) do not produce as many scholars proportionately as many other colleges (Swarthmore, City University of New York, and Chicago, for example), the production of academics there is still significant. Many a child sent off to a prestige college to "make contact" and put the final gloss on his chances for success in business baffles and frustrates his family by electing to teach, after first going to graduate school in archeology, or by choosing some other course of action that seems equally exotic and useless to a parent.

For the parent who has urged his children to do well in school, the movement of a good college student into graduate school (rather than professional school) should be a logical progression, not only in the academic scale, but even in terms of parental ambition. The scholar has never stood higher in America than he stands now, an adviser to governments, respected in his community and, most important to many, so greatly in demand that his services are well paid for. While there is a great deal of scrambling and politicking to be done by the young scholar to assure himself of tenure at an institution, once he has become safely established, nothing less than a spectacular and public form of perversion can shake him loose from a secure position as a tenured member of the faculty.

Getting tenure can be difficult. Depending on the institution, it is earned through publication, scholarly excellence, adroit maneuvering, contributions to the educational community, or good teaching. The amount and the tenor of the politics behind the scenes is always a shock to a young and idealistic scholar, but he quickly learns the truth of Henry Wriston's observation: "For subtlety and savagery, there is no world like the academic."

To what extent can success be predicted for the would-be scholar? It is, of course, as difficult to predict as it is for any field, but energy and single-mindedness are quite important, probably more so than brilliance or imagination. The latter, of course, will distinguish the brightest lights in any field, but the ability to turn one's attention to a small area of inquiry and hold it there until the subject has been investigated exhaustively is one of the requirements for scholarship, although not necessarily the leading requirement. The reason for this is that the Ph.D. must provide an original contribution to knowledge, and with the proliferation of theses, the amount of unmined material is diminishing rapidly. This is what caused Barnaby Keeney to say: "A good Ph.D. thesis is the definitive edition of a play that should never have been produced in the first place; a bad thesis is a word count of the same play."

All of which is to say that the process of earning the union card to the pleasures and prerequisites of college teaching involves a great deal of drudgery and tedium; hence energy and stamina play an important part. The student who is intrigued by the idea of college teaching but whose depth of interest goes no further than casual interest will probably drop out at the master's level and go into some other kind of training.

The effect of the draft ruling that secondary school teachers are exempt (or are deferrable) while they are teaching will be interesting to see in the long run. Certainly it has propelled a number of students who were not particularly interested in teaching into it, if only briefly. Although teachers in secondary education are moving into the ranks of the better paid workers in our society, they are still considerably below the level of college teachers. Here, however, the prime consideration should center around the student's interest in people, his ability to be concerned about arousing the interest or enthusiasm of his charges, his willingness to get major satisfaction from dealing with younger, less sophisticated minds, and, in public education, his willingness to put up with a great deal of bureaucratic procedure as a regular part of the job.

In the private liberal art colleges, students who elect to go into teaching almost never choose public schools, at least not at first. The obvious reason is that they are "unqualified," which means they don't have the requisite courses in education to meet state licensing requirements. However, the reasons go deeper: in the independent school, the teacher is freer to use what texts and methods he thinks are appropriate; there is no official curriculum to be followed and, as long as students learn, the objective has been accomplished.

Private school teachers pay for their freedom in lower salaries and probably less formalized "protection" of unions. For a brief and self-illuminating experience, teaching in a private or public school is quite valuable. A young friend, a recent graduate of Brown who essayed teaching as an unabashed form of legal draft evasion, announced his intention to quit. "Its been fun, I've learned more about physics teaching it than I ever learned in college, and I've learned a lot about myself, but I'm not a teacher." Armed with this information, he went into the army and thence into business.

Secondary school teaching as a guidance tool is very useful. Even without the threat of the draft, I would recommend it for the many college students who come through four years of college study having acquired some knowledge, some skills, and no real understanding of how they are to be used. Secondary school teaching, both for men and for women, allows a student time to digest what he has learned, to realize how necessary (and how exacting) the art of communication can be, and permits them to earn money at the same time.

In the case of the boarding school teacher, the situation is more sharply defined; it gives greater rewards and imposes greater restrictions. In return for no privacy, and an eighteen-hour-a-day schedule, the young teacher gets room and board, a generous vacation schedule, and most of his salary (what is there to spend it on?) for travel or self-indulgence on the holidays. A few practical-minded souls of my acquaintance have even saved enough capital this way for the down payment on a house.

Any time "lost" while teaching need not really be worried about since the value of the experience comes simultaneously with the realization that teaching is not your field—usually in two to three years. This time might well be considered as the cost of the guidance the experience gave.

Conversely, it is always interesting in talking with teachers to discover how many had originally tried other fields and had come to teaching.

The question of preparation and fitness for the professions is discussed in Chapter VI. Without going into the individual requirements for the professions, it is enough to say that all are not commonly entered by way of college and graduate schools and that the formal educational requirements for any of the professions are growing steadily more formidable. Where it was at one time possible to read law, to apprentice yourself to an architect, to acquire accounting by the process of learning from your employer before taking validating professional examinations, this no longer seems feasible. Business was probably the last to go, so that although it is certainly possible that with the right connections a young man can train with a securities firm, for example, without a college diploma, the odds are increasingly against it. The reasons for it can be seen in the changing curricula of the business schools themselves. The famous "case" method, where business school students learned business by solving the problems of sample cases is being encroached on by the analytical, mathematical attack on business problems. The computer and its ability to take into account an almost limitless number of variables is increasingly important, and the new businessman must be able to understand mathematics and the language of the computers. The opportunity for the shrewd businessman who operates on his own intuition and appraisal of the facts, with or without a college education, will diminish but probably not disappear, and so the gap closes.

If this means that college, or more properly, post high school education is inevitable, is the timing crucial? Can some of the final parts of education be postponed?

I will again say yes. Not only should college be attempted in the most mature frame of mind possible, but graduate school should ideally be the final training undertaken by a student who knows himself and his abilities, and what he should do with them.

This often means that time out, before, during, or after college makes great sense. Parents are always afraid that any pause in the educational process will result in a permanent stop, that the student will get sidetracked and not continue. This view probably reflects not only parental anxiety but parental distaste for education; they are sure that the students must dislike the training as much as they would dislike the idea of returning to the grind of a student. What parents do not realize is that the students have been so conditioned to believe in education that, when they do pause, there is not the same sense of uneasiness their parents feel. This is chiefly, I believe, the result of long conditioning; even when weary of learning and anxious for a respite or a change, they are not likely to break off the process entirely. Instead, they are saying "I need more maturity," which can at once be an excuse for poor academic performance and a mandate to take the first plane to Europe. After a period away from the academic grind, most are ready to resume the process.

(This is not universally true, I realize. Despite all of our extensive conditioning on the need for education, there are still plenty of students who drop out along the way. My guess is that there has been forewarning to parents that this student might not finish. The student who causes the most violent parental reaction is the one who has always been a good student and who suddenly announces that he is ready for a break. For some reason, this sort of student, who has every intention of continuing his education, seems to have parents who are ready to believe the worst of his intentions.)

Somehow, parents themselves must learn that education is better savored than gulped, and that it produces better results when it is tailored to the mature and full grown man or woman than when it is shaped to a student whose talents are amorphous and as yet so undeveloped as to be unknown to him. If parents could understand the need for time and maturity in the whole process of education, they would undoubtedly approach it in a more relaxed manner.

And so would the students.

And the whole process would be improved thereby.

V

What Happens in College

PROBABLY THE MOST OVER-rated experience in the world is not the honeymoon, but the freshman year in college. Almost all of those eager young faces register disappointment early or late in the freshman year, which is as painful because of its surprise as anything else. After all, for the student who had planned it, college was the culmination and triumph of work and maturation. For those ambitious enough or gifted enough to aim for the most selective, the prestige college was to be the real reward for always being prepared for class discussion and never failing to complete the Latin homework. For students who either themselves were not so lofty in aim or whose parents pushed less hard, college still remained a *beau ideal* of freedom, the last open spot in one's life where there was freedom and maturity intermingled, where you were both old enough to do what you wanted and away from your family so that you really could do it. Employment, families, responsibilities, mortgage payments, and the whole familiar pattern of the "rat race" were far enough away to be either not quite believable or not quite respectable. It was a time of towering altruism unclouded by the realities of responsibility or compromise.

On the academic side, college always has been held out to students as a vastly "different" experience. In their attempts to bring about the right state of mind for college, high school teachers do not always explain just what the differences are, but they are insistent that it is different. Curiously enough, I think that most teachers tend to remember and talk about the few courses (probably in their senior year or possibly in graduate school) where seminars demanded careful reading and lively discussion. There is another school of preparation that urges the student to be ready for the lecture—to be able to take down what the lecturer says, as nearly verbatim as possible. In any case, the teacher conveys the excitement and challenge of this form of teaching and warns the students that "they will be on their own" and hence they "had better be prepared academically for the challenge."

What actually happens? There are no figures on the subject, and it is not likely that there ever will be because disappointment with the freshman year of college is something which should not be admitted, even to oneself; but it is certainly my strong impression that at present the great majority of students are profoundly disappointed, depressed, or let down by college.

A friend of mine related that he had visited his own alma mater, where he took pains to see a freshman, the son of family friends.

"How do you like it?" he asked, confident of an affirmative reply.

"Well," said the freshman cautiously, "you've probably heard from my mother that I like it. After all, when she asks me I only have two choices—I like it or I don't. I said I like it, because if I say I don't like it, I've got problems."

In this careful way, he was protecting himself, his family,

and his college from a negative commitment on his part. What is interesting in these countless cases is not so much the caution as the reasons for the lack of spontaneous enthusiasm. What went wrong to sour the image of college as the perfect experience, and is this perhaps the earliest glimmer of student unrest that seems to grow as the college experience progresses?

In the twelve years from 1957 to 1969, the number if not the percentage of graduating high school students entering a four year college has increased sharply from 556,239 to 1,074,000; from 37 percent to 39 percent of high school graduates. Along with these sharp increases have been equally heavy increases in the cost of all education, but particularly of private education. For the most part, the private colleges are the most selective colleges, but as the cost of many private colleges has accelerated, many of their potential customers have felt obliged to consider the public colleges. The result has been an evening out process in the competition for admission—although a handful of private selective colleges have become increasingly selective, the cost factor which forced a switch in allegiance from private to public in many families has increased competition for admission to the prestige state universities, particularly in the Midwest, bringing them closer to the level required previously by the private colleges. To put it another way, more students than ever are feeling the pinch of competition as they scramble for the places on the upper end of the educational scale; where this kind of scramble used to be the exclusive province of the students who were aiming at the selective colleges, it has now spread to a wider base. Although forcing students to live up to their academic limit seems laudable, it cannot fail to have certain side effects which are clearly visible from time to time on the campus.

The major components of this scramble can be sorted out as follows: (1) an increase in the intensity of high school preparation; (2) an increase in the length of time it now takes to get through education—or an increase in the total amount of education thought necessary; and (3) a readjustment in the level of academic and personal competition necessary when going from school to college.

According to Adam Smith, the father of modern economics, when a lot of people want something and the supply is limited, the price goes up. This is exactly what has happened in the colleges; the price not only in dollars, but in the effort required, has gone up as the competition has increased. In some high schools competition develops into a fierce struggle for grades and a good rank in class. In other high schools, the curriculum has been revamped so that the courses are more challenging, more difficult, or simply more in line with current thought in that area. This is the case with the revised chemistry curricula, CBA or Chem Study, which have revamped the study of chemistry until it is unintelligible to anyone who has been out of high school fifteen years. The same has been notoriously true of mathematics, which has so changed in its machinery of operation that parents are actually warned not to try to help their children lest all concerned be hopelessly confused.

All of these advances, although helping to increase the competition and the sense of pressure, have behind them the real purpose of moving into secondary school those skills and understandings of science that are essential if it is to be studied at all in college. But it is in English and the other subjects where understanding is dependent on maturity that I feel we are building in problems of adjustment to the college scene. In emulating the sciences, English has increased its challenge not so much by increasing the teaching skills or by spending more time on the writing and speaking of proper English, as by moving into the curriculum books which most students are not really capable of understanding because they deal with problems and emotions which the students only know about from hearsay or have not yet experienced at all. Thus the student may be able to follow the outline of the story without ever appreciating what made the book worth reading. For an insufficiently mature reader *Anna Karenina* becomes a straightforward and not very attractive story of marital infidelity; the sweep and nuance of the emotions involved are not likely to be appreciated by a teenage reader. More important, a too early reading is likely to ruin the book forever in the mind of the reader.

In many years of interviewing, I have yet to meet a high school senior who thought that *Pride and Prejudice* was anything but a monumental bore, yet it is inflicted on thousands who might enjoy its delicate but devastating humor at twenty-five, but certainly not at seventeen.

Catching the spirit of competition, students applying to colleges appear for their interviews with an ostentatious array of distinguished works ready for discussion.

While I am willing to believe that there certainly are students in the world who are capable of and interested in books of far greater complexity than some of their peers, I have the unhappy and slightly cynical feeling that a great deal of such reading is window dressing, merely a part of the college scramble.

It is not remarkable to have an applicant "admit," when talking about his pleasure reading, to reading Proust, Kierkegaard, Marx, or Hegel. After hearing a list of this sort, I am tempted to ask whether these are read in the original or only in translation. Unfortunately for my powers of detection, my knowledge of Hegel or Kant is anything but minute, and I cannot pursue the possibility of bluff—which I think a great many applicants have already guessed was the case. (One of my colleagues, a fluent linguist, turns on a student who says he is competent in French, and speaks rapidly to him in that language. The result, I am sorry to say, is often catastrophic; few high school linguists are sufficiently fluent to withstand this kind of barrage.)

Nevertheless, the careful preparation of background,

including exotic reading, "interesting" jobs, unusual activities, extensive travel is all a part of the game which the student playing for the highest stakes—admission to the really selective colleges—is willing to play.

But what happens as a result of all this flurry to get into college? The result is almost inevitably going to be disappointment and shock, both academic and personal.

Disappointment because colleges and universities have in many cases not done as much curricular homework as the high schools have; courses and course patterns have changed chiefly in that classes are larger, allowing for fewer individual differences in or special attentions to the student. This does not mean that in the sciences the courses have not been modernized and that in the social sciences new courses have not been introduced, but, as faculties, course offerings, and numbers of students have all increased, the inertia has made it increasingly difficult to make major revisions in the way colleges educate their students. The resultant letdown is probably greatest in the public universities, where sheer size and impersonality in itself comes as a shock.

But probably the rudest awakening, even in the public institutions which have a much broader base of ability in their students, is the sudden realization of how many bright and capable people there are. The successful student, particularly if he has been able to do well enough to get into a selective college, has come to have a good opinion of his abilities as a student. What is more, except in a handful of high schools across the country, he was able to achieve this good record without a great deal of academic effort. It is not uncommon to talk with applicants who are in the most advanced courses their high school offers and are spending a total of an hour and a half each night preparing themselves for the next day.

When such a student reaches a college where all of his fellows are of similar ability, the entire competitive scale is

severely shaken up and the students redistribute themselves. The work load and the demand on the student's time
are greatly increased, but the damage is chiefly to the
student's ego. If at all sensitive and realistic, he becomes
acutely (and sometimes gloomily) aware of his limitations.

In the public institutions that can and do select on the
basis of academic achievement, this same syndrome repeats
itself, but with less devastating effect. However, even here
the measures taken by some state universities to provide
honors programs to entice brighter students will have the
same effect as the most selective colleges. Michigan State
University, for example, has been on a vigorous campaign
to attract the best minds in the country to its honors
program—whether the students live in Michigan or not.
The result is that more National Merit Finalists enter
Michigan State than any other college in the country.
Imagine the rude awakening of a student there who had
thought heretofore that he was unusually bright!

Second on the list of disappointments is the depersonal-
ization, not just in the handling of the students' affairs but
in the classroom experience as well. The influx of numbers
has made computers, numbers, and punch cards inevitable.
Consider the problems from the administrator's point of
view. At one large state university in the Midwest, the
freshman class recently was 2,500 more students than
expected. A freshman class of 2,500 would be difficult
enough to process, feed, house, and arrange courses for, but
to be deluged suddenly with an additional number of this
magnitude epitomizes the administrative headaches that
can develop.

But apart from the weight of numbers, the demand for
faculty services and the race for prestige appointments have
put teaching and relationships with students at the very
bottom of a long ladder of priorities. The pattern is too
familiar to recite at any length, but it is most painfully
familiar to students: in order to progress it is necessary to

advertise yourself, and this is done, not by teaching, but by publications or by public consultation.

Because they are expected to be in favor of teaching in the same way that most candidates for public office are expected to be in favor of motherhood and the American flag, a great deal is said about the dedication of a faculty to teaching, usually by the dean or president when addressing alumni or faculty. To support this, there has developed a rationale that teaching and research go hand in hand; that unless teaching is refreshed by the discovery of new material and new points of view, it quickly becomes stale.

This is, of course, more than merely a rationalization; it is certainly true, and any college lecturer who is still using the same notes for even more than one year is not doing right by his students. But the way the line is drawn between teaching and research, the prestige given to research and the lack of reward for good teaching quickly point out to the young instructor which way he should turn.

Thus one young friend of mine, who is interested in students, willing to talk to them and hear their problems, has been chided repeatedly by the senior members of his department. "I hope you charge for therapy" he reported the chairman saying in reference to his willingness to talk to students.

The supreme manifestation of the sharp line between research and teaching can be seen in the case of the distinguished professor of a famous university who lives two hundred miles from the university's campus, to which he makes one trip a week, staying overnight to cover the few classes he teaches. Obviously he is a distinguished man in his field and, regrettably, a superb teacher. But to say this man is really on the faculty of the university in terms of availability to students (graduate or undergraduate) or even in terms of his ability to participate in the life of the university as a faculty member is absurd. Yet this is his supreme reward for excellence in his field. Not surprisingly, many undergraduates feel cheated when they measure what they are able to get from faculty against what they had hoped to get.

This is not to say that all faculty today are against teaching or are poor teachers. Many are not only respectable scholars but brilliant teachers; just as many, in reverse, are quite decent as teachers even though brilliant scholars. But certainly, as even the smallest colleges have grown and many of the large have exploded, the traditional picture of the college teacher has disappeared. The new replacement, while interested in students, is also interested in furthering his career, which means not an interest in students and teaching, but in government contracts, consulting for industry, writing books, and giving lectures outside the university. The result is that one young faculty member told me that every hour he gave students was an extra hour of work for him at some other part of the day; his affairs were so numerous and complicated that his day could have been full without students, and only his interest in them made him take the time. What is true of this man is certainly true of many others of the new breed of college educators; the old concept of the leisurely tranquility of the Ivory Tower is gone—at least for the moment.

The curious part of the new academic situation is that it has grown out of the increased speed and pressures for education. The postwar baby boom, continued prosperity which makes it possible for an ever wider group to consider higher education, strong government assistance to broaden the group even further by guaranteeing loans for educational purposes and providing Educational Opportunity Grants to colleges for students at or near the poverty levels, and the increased feeling among employers that a bachelor's degree is the minimum educational standard for any managerial training have caused the explosion, have made teachers scarce and hence more expensive, and thus have made colleges and universities desperate in their scramble for government and industrial subsidies. These, in turn, are based on some outside observer's view of the worthiness of the institution, which depends in no small measure on how well known the faculty members are.

To suggest that the drive for education has killed education is oversimplification, but it certainly has been changed drastically in the process. The restlessness of students once they get to college suggests that all the changes are not good ones, but the rank and file of college faculty, having arrived at unexpected prosperity and security through the system, are less likely to criticize.

Some years ago a government agency performed studies on willing subjects concerning sleep deprivation. The victims were kept awake for days at a time to determine physiological results and to test the effect of sleep deprivation on efficiency in performing physical and mental tasks. The results were surprising, because they seemed to show that a human can survive without sleep for rather long periods of time. Efficiency is impaired, but not seriously. The chief by-product is the irritability of the subjects, which increases as the waking period extends, and the fact that there is a tendency to hallucinate after a long time without sleep. My memory of this extensive experiment may be inexact, but these are the results as I recall them.

In the sense that male college students are trapped in a situation in which they are continuously subject to stimuli and from which, because of the draft and social pressures, they are not allowed the respite of withdrawal, there is a striking parallel between the experiment and the reactions of students to their college environment.

As the academic pressures have increased to a point which few parents can appreciate, simply because it did not exist in their day, there is a wholly understandable reaction to avoid the pressure, to respond with an irritability like that caused by sleeplessness, and, in general, to question the validity of the entire system.

Thus the high school student who has been wrought to fever pitch about the joys and challenges of college life discovers his goal is disappointing. College entrance in itself had become a goal; but he discovers not so much that he has arrived at a goal as that he has simply exchanged one pressure situation for another, that he is struggling not to finish college, but to do well enough in college, in many cases, to go on to graduate school.

When he realizes this, the slacking off, the letdown that occurred immediately after entering college, is likely to disappear, but the sense of disappointment and frustration does not.

Before the beginning of the heavy activities in Vietnam and the concomitant drain by our draft system, it was not uncommon to have a student drop out of college for a year, not because of academic failure, but because of simple fatigue—although this was almost invariably viewed with alarm by parents, particularly by mothers who immoderately envisaged the departure of their child from the ranks of the middle class by abandoning education, and hence respectability.

More often than not, what happened was wholly salutary: the student worked, loafed, loved, or traveled, and returned to college refreshed, older, more experienced, and more willing to put up with pressures. In the case of one student I knew well, his short reserve turn in the Marines, his tiresome job cleaning soap vats, and his marriage to an attractive girl all were more responsible for his success after returning to Brown and for his subsequent good record at business school than all of his parents' nagging and groundless fears when he left college. But all this changed when the manpower drain of the draft made college the only safe place to be.

A dean I know has made a remarkably humane statement on academic dismissal from college. "It is not a punishment," he says, "rather we are saying to the student, you are not progressing toward your goal at the rate we think you should. Why not take some time off from your studies to reorganize your values and your thinking?" This kind of attitude coincides exactly with what many students, even many in good standing, have decided is the right course of action when their college career seems to be hopelessly askew and all the obvious goals seem somehow to be the wrong ones. But, with the advent of Vietnam, the dean's wisdom in dismissing a student for his own good becomes punitive whether he sees it so or not, because a student not in college is no longer a student and hence draftable.

By the same token, the student who wants to take time off for his own revaluation and intellectual refreshment is blocked from doing so. The result is a trapped feeling, a sense of frustration. It is not surprising that there should be eruptions on the campus as a direct result of these frustrations.

Why these things happen as they do is a mystery: why does a student who has always made the right academic moves suddenly get tired, confused, irritable, or irresponsible? The most compact and pat answer is the identity crisis. This psychiatric catchphrase has become so much a part of the language that on many campuses it is referred to as the "I.C."—and it is assumed that everyone has one. Since parents went through high school and college without a recognizable identity crisis, why should there suddenly be a rash of them? What special problems have generated a wholly new emotional fault in today's children?

Naturally, it is not new; only the name which the popularization of psychiatry has made available to every amateur psychoanalyst is new. The problem of the crisis itself is more a sequela of age, of breaking away from parents, of being exposed to new ideas and points of view, and probably most important, of being made suddenly and painfully aware that full-fledged involvement in the world is just ahead and one had better be ready for it.

In previous years it had never taken the unsettling forms it has on campuses currently because the combination of events had never been quite the same. At any other time when reality severely obtruded on the student consciousness there had not been such a tremendous preoccupation with the need for education together with concomitant pressures on the student in the course of getting that education. In earlier days a student got drunk, dropped out of college for financial reasons (a highly acceptable reason until recently—now the ready availability of student loans means this reason is valid for fewer and fewer students), and floundered around in various ways. Parents, then as always, were inflicting their wills on their children, urging them into courses of action which were vicariously pleasing to them, but generally only in the case of the premeds were parental pressure and academic pressure brought together. For these small numbers, there were probably "identity crises" in years gone by, but it had not reached the endemic proportions that high parental aspirations, social pressures, high academic pressures, and no escape have produced for this current generation of students.

A psychiatrist who is a friend of mine recalled with what I assume is the amused cynicism typical of his calling, the succeeding waves of student enthusiasms and revolutions—civil rights, sex, drugs, and student involvement in running the affairs of the institution. According to him, each of these has run in a two-year cycle, after which the excitement and the burning preoccupation with it die down. Thus, in turn, the students went off on freedom rides to the South, carried banners in the revolution of sex and morals, argued violently for the right to take whichever drug was fashionable at the moment, and most recently stormed the bastions of curricula, administrations, and faculty. What the next phase will be the psychiatrist did not venture; but it is true that each of these phases has flared up and burned down, quite often with results, and quite often without.

Martin Luther King, Jr., not being aware of my friend's theory, blamed Vietnam for killing the excitement about the civil rights movement among students, and perhaps he was right.

A headmaster of my acquaintance feels that students of today are essentially puritanical, and that in the sexual revolution more has been talked about than executed. Perhaps we need a new Kinsey Report to verify this, because neither sex nor promiscuity was invented by this generation of students, and perhaps we are in no different position than before. However, on reading the thoughts of the headmaster concerning the new puritanism, a young graduate responded to the contrary: "It has been my experience that the new freedom of the female (i.e., the pill) has made her much more aggressive . . . and at the same time less inhibited. It's much less difficult to convince her about the advantages of making love."

There is good deal less frenzy about drugs on campus, and in a sense, this is because of the student "good sense" in handling them. In the first excitement about hallucinogens, the horror stories of the uses and abuses of LSD were rampant. After the first flush, it became apparent that a student generation new to this kind of sensation had tried it and had found it too flamboyant or simply too unusual for their tastes. As a consequence, there was a spate of popularity and afterwards a marked decline in the use of drugs like LSD.

In part, this was attributed to the news that LSD split chromosomes (everything, from aspirin to coffee apparently splits chromosomes), that there was danger of instant return to the hallucinated state without warning, and finally, of course, the reports of permanent psychic disorders which resulted from taking LSD—a permanently "bad trip".

While that student generation wearied of the novelty of LSD and were somewhat frightened of it, there was another group behind them for whom the existence and use of these drugs is a fact of life. For them, drugs have become as quietly, but as firmly entrenched in he student culture as alcohol, and their use is strongly reminiscent of the intelligent use of alcohol by an older generation.

The novelty is gone, and with it the apprehension about the unknown qualities and tendencies of the drug which itself tends to produce bad trips. Users, realizing that their senses are not to be trusted while under the influence, sensibly take the drug in the company of a sympathetic friend who refrains. The friend is not refraining because of "straightness," but because he understands the process thoroughly, and expects the same kind of monitoring job to be done for him in the future.

On this basis, many students seem to be able to take a trip a week (more is considered to be as bad taste and as much a form of irresponsibility as drinking too much) without any demonstrable physiological or psychological ill effects. While there is still much to be learned about the physiological and psychological after effects of marijuana and LSD, the scare reports of severe damage, particularly psychological, may be just that; to date there is no hard medical evidence to the contrary.

If this sounds like a veneer of rationalization about a situation which gives many parents and college administrators concern, it must be remembered that habitual users feel that through continuing use, they have proven the falseness of their elders' fears. Two major dangers bulk under the surface of LSD use: the lack of extensive investigation of the long-term effects on users, and the danger of getting impure or adulterated stuff. This last is particularly true. For obvious reasons, pushers are likely to "cut" the drug with addictive heroin, or to cut the quality of LSD by mixing it with or substituting for it other cheaper or less desirable hallucinogens—like the one which tends to produce the nightmare reactions called "death trips."

These considerations seem to have little effect on confirmed users, any more than evidence of cirrhosis of the liver slows down many drinkers. That happens to the other guy; the happy fallacy of youth is its indestructability.

However, out of this group of habitual users of hallucinogens has come the first indications of disenchantment—not from the break-and-run former users who have recounted their history in suicide notes but from those who find the drug "boring."

One habitual user reported to his college adviser that, among his friends, the number taking trips was down by a significant amount—simply because, after a while, there are no new "revelations" which can be engendered by the drug. Another deterrent is the length of time for a trip—about eight hours. This really is too large a chunk of wasted time to be practicable for any student who has reasonable pretensions to academic interest. His latent sense of duty combined with the lack of novelty of his trip often produces the reaction: "Now that I'm three hours into this, what do I do now?" The answer is wait until the end, but the time involved seems less and less to be worth it.

Until quite recently, other forms of drug taking were comparatively rare, at least in the college and college preparatory circles. "Speed" (amphetamines), hashish, and mescaline, to name the most prominent of the recently emerged drugs, have become more prevalent at the expense of marijuana. One conjecture of the reason for this switch is that the current government drive to tighten up on the sources of supply has forced the going price of "pot" up sharply, and the comment among students that "good grass is getting hard to find" is heard fairly openly.

The greatest danger of this drive, undertaken for entirely proper reasons, is that, as marijuana becomes harder to get, a number of young thrill seekers will be forced, in effect, into the use of other drugs which are potentially more harmful but easier to manufacture and thus easier to get.

Of these, the most frightening is "speed," amphetamine, which can be manufactured, according to an authoritative friend of mine, by a "not too sophisticated chemist in his bathroom." Originally developed as a chemical "lift" for patients who are mentally depressed, the current use is as an intense exhilarant. When the dose wears off (and the extent of the drug's effect can be guessed at by the fact that the narcotic dose is one hundred times the size of the therapeutic dose), the user is left physically exhausted. Constant use is so demanding on the physical machinery of the body that a genuine speed freak has a life expectancy of about three years, according to the most recent observations. Even among in-group students, the phrase "speed kills" is a chilling comment on its use, and marijuana seems almost therapeutic in comparison.

Fortunately, the percentage of college students who are involved in this kind of self-destructive drug use is still comparatively small, although there is evidence that it is growing. For many students, however, the chief drug experimentation that occurs in college is with alcohol, which still has a warm place in the hearts, minds, and stomachs of many.

Patterns of behavior differ greatly depending on the campus. I was amused recently in discussing the use of drugs with two undergraduates to hear that at one campus, considered quite conservative by most students and parents alike, beer was out and marijuana was in. His companion, an undergraduate of a famously liberal institution where the use of marijuana has been scarcely a novelty for some years, told me with a grin that the new wave of students was drinking beer again.

One of the most interesting phenomena of recent student attitudes is the rise in acceptability and use of marijuana by the college population. As this college generation graduates and becomes young adults, it will be interesting to see what affect, if any, their college enthusiasm for "pot" will have on their subsequent behavior—will they abandon marijuana for Scotch, or will pressures for the acceptance of this drug eventually build up to the point of legal capitulation, resulting in final legality?

On the basis of what seems to be known about marijuana, it seems likely that eventual legalization is probable; but in the meanwhile it is illegal, and the penalties for having it, for using it, and particularly for selling it are frighteningly severe. If college students have had enough basic sense to abandon forms of drugs that frighten them for one reason or another, why do large numbers of students (not quite a majority, but close to it, by educated guess) defy the law and run the risk of almost permanent punishment (in terms of a court record which would almost certainly permanently militate against several professional careers) to indulge themselves?

Any attempt to outline the reasons for mass activity that is not backed up by considerable investigation is likely to produce specious results. The reports I have seen don't really probe into the causes of interest in pot except the obvious one that "everyone is doing it." A number of unsubstantiated theories have occurred to me, and they seem to make as much sense as anything else.

First, the pressures of college are omnipresent; there is always competition for grades, work which is lurking in the background of the student's conscience and consciousness, and finally the perpetual specter of the unknown, the nagging question of "how will my talents develop?" Temporary escape from this situation is as necessary for students as it is for businessmen, and they react similarly: athletics or drugs for one, and golf or martinis for the other.

Second, scholarship is increasingly a highly individual, personal, and lonely pursuit. Introspection and understanding of complex material become the hallmark of the student, the *sine qua non* without which he cannot claim to be a student. Marijuana's special ability is that it seems to clarify the mind rather than muddle it. Music, art, ideas, all things to do with cerebration seem to be lustrously clear, understandable, and almost palpably enjoyable. It doesn't really matter that the understanding is transient, illusory, and not recapturable; the sense that the student can understand is comforting to him.

(I am reminded of the great anecdote about Oliver Wendell Holmes, Sr., who, as he went under anaesthesia for an operation, groped wildly for something. On recovering consciousness he explained that under the influence of the ether he had thoughts of such transcendent beauty and clarity that he had wanted to write them down; hence the groping for pencil and paper. So great was his enthusiasm for his lost thought he was put under again, and again groped. This time he was handed pencil and paper, scribbled rapidly on it, and sank back with a happy sigh of completion. His message read: "God, what a stench!")

The third reason is more tenuous, perhaps, but possibly presages wider use of marijuana among young adults. Not only is the specter of constant academic pressure a continual source of mental and spiritual irritation to students, but increasingly the world they are about to inherit is displayed for them and to them unrelentingly by television. While the reality of Marshall McLuhan's "Global Village" cannot be denied, it is also very hard to enjoy. The conflict between the theoretical world of academics, and the omnipresence of catastrophes brought on by human stupidity, greed, and ignorance produces a contrast which is difficult enough for a calloused adult to bear and which produces shock, revulsion, and anger in the college student. As one senior at Brown said editorially, "You've ruined my world for me."

To escape from this into a private, cosy, intimate, and understanding world is highly desirable, and since marijuana seems to be able to accomplish this, again its popularity is understandable.

Although group pot parties do happen, the maximum effectiveness apparently occurs only in the presence of genuine friends and intimates, providing a kind of group privacy and retreat. And in a world filled with violence, marijuana must attribute at least some of its appeal to its peacefulness; one thing that does not happen with pot is the release of aggressive tendencies that so often mars the use of alcohol.

Alcohol as a drug has not been abandoned by the college student. It is easier to obtain, much less dangerous (from a legal standpoint) to obtain and use illegally, and the user, when discovered, is considered to be following time-honored traditions of youthful experimentation, whereas the parents who discover their children are smoking marijuana are likely to panic completely.

The difference between the two is interesting, both from the point of view of what happens during and what happens after use of alcohol or marijuana. Users of alcohol are often destructive. As Dr. Roswell Johnson, Director of the University Health Service at Brown, has said, the post-alcohol damage in terms of fights, injuries, and physical property destruction is appalling; with marijuana, there is none of this.

Perhaps regrettably, the more conservative students stick to alcohol, and since athletes are by nature socially conservative, alcohol falls into the hands of boys who are physically aggressive by natural inclination. Thus in addition to the carnage wrought by alcoholically induced high spirits, there is likely to be a considerable amount of fighting and terrorization of the strong by the weak. Further, the kinds of people who tend to stay with alcohol and those who tend to drift toward marijuana cause a polarization in the student body which tends to harden.

The morning after is also worthy of note. The intellectual sophisticate who takes marijuana claims there is no hang-

over, and affects disdain over the "disgusting" aftereffects
of alcohol. There is, in fact, a hangover from pot, but it
follows no folk-legend pattern of the hangover seen so
often in the movies and television. Instead it takes the form
of a quiet lassitude or indifference, a kind of general but
gentle damper on activity, physical or mental.

On the other hand, although students still relax with a
kind of relentless enthusiasm by drinking, they have come
to gauge the possibilities of hangover. Thus most drinking
is done on Friday and Saturday nights by the good students
at high pressure colleges because they cannot afford to let it
interfere with the academic chores that have to be done.
Occasionally some students will cold-bloodedly assess the
possible effects. Thus one student told me, "I drink Scotch
because I've found the hangover is less lethal," and being
under almost constant pressure, he did drink heavily, but
under the terms of his own rigid control. He is not alone,
and alcohol is not outmoded. Freshmen still drink too
much at once, usually with temporarily catastrophic intes-
tinal results, and upperclassmen still drink heavily at
varying times. Again, however, the innate intelligence or
good sense of most students who drink takes over in the
long run, just as it does in the use of drugs. Thus the
incidence of real or incipient alcoholism is rare, and has
probably diminished rather than increased in the last
generation despite the sharp increases in pressures on
students and therefore in the probable reasons for drinking.

Parents who are concerned (and students who have
strong-minded parents) often ask about the prevalence of
drinking or drug taking on a campus as part of the prelimi-
nary survey of a college. The answer really makes little
difference—that is, drugs and alcohol are always available
to the venturesome student without regard to local regulations or custom. The reverse is also true; any student can
resist the temptations of these particular devils, if he wants
to.

Regional differences are very interesting at American

colleges; there is little question (although unsubstantiated by "hard" data) that colleges on the east or west coast are more likely to be "advanced" in the use of alcohol and drugs than those in the central part of the country. A further generalization is that the more demanding and sophisticated the level of education at a college, the more likelihood there will be of the perils of alcohol and drugs. A prominent expert in the field of narcotics and psychopharmacology said that the incidence of pre-college drug taking was likely to be most common in an urban, highly academic, cosmopolitan high school where the students came chiefly from suburban and/or upper middle-class backgrounds. Since this is the very population most concerned about education, it seems almost inevitable that students will come into collision with the precepts of their parents unless some previous discussions and preparations have taken place.

It is in this regard that I greatly admire the somewhat radical and thoroughly unpopular stand taken by Dr. Johnson of Brown. He holds no particular brief for either of the two most prevalent drugs found on today's campus, marijuana and alcohol, but he feels that the tide of emotional response against marijuana based on misconceptions, historical misinformation, and a kind of hysterical repugnance is actually making it much more difficult for any authority to persuade students that they should be careful about other narcotics which are inherently much more dangerous.

On the plus side, marijuana is not addictive, is not demonstrably harmful physiologically, and, based on the best information available, does not lead to involvement in more powerful drugs as a natural sequence. It does cause psychological dependence, it does impair mental efficiency, and like alcohol, it can be dangerous if used while driving or doing anything that requires careful attention. However, Dr. Johnson contends that by painting marijuana in the same colors as all the other drugs, by not differentiating between the really bad and the merely undesirable (and certainly illegal), the real point of caution is lost, and there appears to the young to be little difference between marijuana and heroin.

What the proper approach should be for parents as part of the education they plan for their children is difficult to define; but parents certainly should not panic, and they certainly should not ignore the subject. In colleges today every student is likely to be subjected to temptation by a number of potentially troublesome evils or near-evils, and both parents and children should know the truth about them.

Thus it seems to me that the sensible parent will warn his child that cigarette smoking is likely to be dangerous or debilitating in the long run; that alcohol used wisely is not bad, but can be ruinous; that marijuana is not as bad as the legends make it out to be, but its use is punishable by laws of frightening severity, and finally that promiscuous sex is likely to adversely affect the possibility of a truly satisfactory marriage. All of these sound so reasonable that they will not be instantly disregarded by the student, and might, for that very reason, be heeded.

The last concern about sex and the college student and the subsequent effects on marriage is not only difficult to document, but in terms of historical precedent and present technology, almost impossible to comment on, except in that moralistic way which has been thoroughly discounted.

Kinsey's famous investigation of *Sexual Behavior in the Human Male,* which was published in 1948, well before any of the present college students had given any thought to college, and certainly none to sex *per se,* indicated that the odds were against a girl graduating from college in a virginal state.

Since that time (when the survey probably included a number of World War II veterans who had become considerably sophisticated by their travels in the service and were perhaps more venturesome or demanding of the coeds back home), there has been a general tug of war between students and deans about rules of conduct; morality has been redefined and the result has been called a sexual revolution in which students have joyfully participated. The advent of "the pill" and its widespread use have certainly made the "gains" of the revolutionists easier to accomplish. And it would appear that complete and un-trammeled sexual freedom is now so much a reality that the chief problem is to teach your children how to protect themselves from unfortunate marriages, unwanted babies, dangerous abortions, and the problems, severe or annoying, of various kinds of venereal diseases.

All of this may be a considerable overstatement of the current situation. Since there has not been a widespread and authoritative study on the sexual habits of these college students who have all of the technical help of our age at their disposal, it is not possible to say whether there is a significant difference in undergraduate promiscuity or not. Reactions and opinions vary, usually according to the local situation. Thus one head of a college medical service said: "I envy these kids the freedom to enjoy themselves at the peak of their physical powers." On the other hand, a headmaster whose shrewdness I admire said: "We are living in the age of the new Puritan. In talking about sex, and freedom and restrictions, they are satisfied, and actual-ly shy away from the reality of the situation." In his view, if students picket the president's house for the right to have a girl in their rooms overnight, it is probably to read poetry or listen to records.

Finally, a psychiatrist who specializes in adolescents feels that casual promiscuity causes a numbing of the emotions and a sense of unfulfillment (and ultimately of guilt) which will make successful marriages more difficult, simply because the novelty, or more properly, the privacy and the sanctity of the act has lost its significance.

Whether any psychological rationalization is likely to

deter young people who are in the middle of or are about to plunge into an intense physical and emotional experience is doubtful. What does seem sensible is that the entire problem of sex and what the consequences might be should be among the things which parents and students discuss before undertaking the almost staggering amount of freedom permitted in most colleges today.

Colleges, too, realize that the greater freedom to experiment requires a deeper understanding of sexuality by students. Students, in turn, are eager to learn when they have the chance; "courses" or lectures on the subject, whether for credit or not, are vastly oversubscribed when they are offered.

The concept of self-discipline has never been more necessary, not only for academic success in college but for personal survival as well. Any parent who feels that various forms of campus excess are not the sort of thing which could affect his children is probably fooling himself.

Does this mean, then, that all students at all colleges are involved in the process of active revolt, are wallowing in the new freedom of the sexual revolution, or are experimenting with drugs and are, therefore, incipient addicts? The answer, of course, is no. While there is a revolt from values which many students feel are false and which have been jammed down their throats, the degree of involvement in the various forms of unrest is usually about 5 to 7 percent of active hard-core "resistance"; and there is another 30 to 40 percent of reasonable concurrence and sympathy, if not active participation.

The remaining 50 to 60 percent of almost any college population want nothing more than to be allowed to continue their studies and their lives with the least possible interruption. Because they are unorganized (further, because their attitudes are such that they do not organize), they are being victimized by the students who exercise radical initiative.

As a case in point, a senior at Brown came to me before

commencement to protest the fact that the ceremony commissioning officers in the Navy and Air Force had been removed from its traditional position in the commencement proceedings. As a graduating officer, he would not receive his commission at the traditional time. "I bitterly resent having my commencement spoiled by a small number of students," he said, and asked what he could do about it.

The obvious answer was that he and others who agreed with him would have to find some way to organize and present counter-pressures which the authorities of the college would recognize and respond to. No such organization was ever made, but the point is obvious: that small numbers of active groups are reshaping the campus in their own images with the tacit approval or lack of disagreement from the remainder. As a tactic, it is certainly familiar to anyone who has watched events in Germany, Czechoslovakia, Greece, or Hungary in the last forty years, but it is certainly no more palatable for that reason.

The current ideology of activism excuses much of this. When deploring the situation at Columbia and other colleges because a few were interrupting the education of the rest, I was quickly squelched by an undergraduate who is only moderately to the left: "The rest of those students do not deserve to continue because they were not participating." Apparently if the 75 percent of the Columbia campus not actively involved in locking up the deans had been in pitched battle with the original dissenters, it would have been all right.

This attitude is even more striking as an example of a compartmentalized concern so typical of college students: they can become wrought to white heat by the injustices, real or imagined, performed by others, but can rationalize away those which they cause themselves. In this form of paranoia, "the system" has chased students since they were old enough to be aware, and anything that smacks of authority is fair game in reprisals for all the anxiety and concern the system has caused them. On the one hand, the departing editor of a college daily ran an editorial blaming the older generation for "ruining my world." On the other hand, one of the most voluble of the campus radicals at Brown was still on campus the day after commencement, when he had led a walkout in the middle of the ceremonies. I expressed surprise that he was still on campus.

"I didn't know you loved the place that much," I needled.

"I'm sorry to go," was his surprising reply. "I've enjoyed every minute of the four years." We then went on to discuss cause and effect for about twenty minutes. I was surprised at his reasonableness, and he at my agreement with him that the world was in terrible shape.

So perhaps our rebel leader is typical: restless, unhappy, but essentially sound. Normality is dangerously difficult to define, but it is "normal" for any adolescent of this age to be in some form of rebellion against his parents or whatever authority represents his parents—even though the constrictions of academic demands have maintained this situation longer than would be normally natural. (Incidentally, the young adults of the college world violently object to the term "adolescent." A faculty-trustee-student committee at Brown charged with studying student life and regulation got severe resistance from the students on the committee about the use of the word.)

Who else is typical? From the exterior, from the parents' and the public's view, probably the athlete still embodies the old-fashioned virtues of short hair and restrained conduct. The reasons are fairly obvious to anyone who has watched the campus population for any length of time: athletes are willing to subject themselves to external authority and regimentation in a way which virtually precludes any kind of breaking out. Coaches, for example, are usually both authoritative and conservative, and hence few will permit long hair on a team man.

One undergraduate came to me in near tears of frustration because his long hair was the reason he had been excluded from participating in crew. "I'd let you in the boat, but the coach wouldn't let me," the freshman coach had told the boy. The choice was clear—he could cut his hair or row; he chose to stand on his principles and stayed on the dock, demonstrating to the coach that he did not really want to row very much anyway.

Perhaps the coach was right. Another young man of eccentric dress and long hair, but considerable talent, returned to campus one September, shaggy but with shorter locks. Knowing his financial problems, I said I was delighted to see him back.

"I was lucky to get a good construction job," he said, "and I made lots of money."

"Forgive me for asking, but how long was your hair while you were working?" Construction workers are not notably sympathetic to long-haired college boys.

"Oh, I cut it off," he replied easily, "I'm not a damned fool."

However, long hair and beards, once the exclusive property of the restless and disaffected, have spread considerably to other segments of society. Now, many successful coaches have stopped making an issue of hair length or beards. Even more interesting, the increase in long hair and beards among young men in the working classes reveals a remarkable softening of the general attitudes—or simply a change in styles.

Nevertheless, the understanding that it is necessary to make compromises between what one wants to do and one has to do is a basic component of maturity. In this sense, a great many of today's college students are well aware that the demands of existence are about to close in on them, and they are simply making various kinds of hay while they can. Generally, the older the student, the less outlandish his response is. Thus a headmaster friend whose school runs an alumni luncheon for its graduates in college tells me that the freshmen and sophomores in college are most likely to have beards and look disreputable; the juniors and seniors are not only more conventional looking, but they needle the younger ones with remarks like: "I went through that stage too."

One final example of the problem of defining "normality": an undergraduate whom I know quite well is aesthetic, musical, bohemian, and superb in his chosen sport. He confided to me that during the season, as a special concession to conditioning, he never smokes pot. It is difficult to know where the "normal" college boy or girl stops, and where the troublesome ones that the press, parents, and alumni worry about so much begin.

VI

The Graduate School
Rat Race

ONE OF THE MAJOR EDUCA-
tional phenomena of the last ten years is the rush to
graduate schools. The more sophisticated and academic a
student body is, the more likely it is to go to graduate or
professional schools in large numbers. The percentage of
students that plan or do go beyond the undergraduate level
is usually cited by admission officers or listed as one of the
"facts about the college," the discreet form of self-
advertising which colleges allow themselves in their catalogues and other publications.

As a counselor of undergraduates, I was struck particularly by two aspects of this rush for graduate education:
first, a sense that graduate education was inevitable and
necessary, regardless of the student's own views; and
second, the striking similarity of types that elected to go
into any one field. By their actions, their taste in courses,
their response to the whole college process, the premeds,
for example, could be separated from the future lawyers,
scholars, businessmen, or divines.

Although the second point is not an important one, it has sometimes been quite useful in counseling a student who is uncertain himself about what he wants to do, but who seems to conform to a "pattern" of postgraduate study. Naturally such personality clues are too flimsy to be the basis of any serious counseling, but I think they can be helpful in suggesting new areas of investigation that the student might not have thought of yet.

Such observed behavior has been most useful to me in simply helping me to know what a counselee is likely to do next—like Tony.

Tony was sitting in the chair by my desk arranging his courses for the coming year. As I looked over the list of courses he had handed me, I was struck by the absence of science courses.

"You're not a premed any more?" I asked.

"No, sir, I'm going to major in art. I've given up on premed." He stared at me with a somewhat sheepish grin. I grinned back at him.

"I guessed as much when you let your hair grow." We both laughed.

It was not so much that anyone taking art courses cannot go to medical school, but rather that very long hair and being premed do not go together, at least at this moment. The conservatism of the American Medical Association, so often the despair of political liberals, is amply accounted for if all of the doctors across the nation were as conservative when they were undergraduates as the premeds I have seen in my counseling. From all accounts I can gather from other colleges, my view is not distorted; they are naturally conservative.

Perhaps "careful" would be a better word, and considering the difficulties that lie in the path of the incipient physician, it is remarkable that we have as good a supply of medical candidates as we do. However, the prestige of the profession and the reasonable promise of a golden return on the academic investment are enough to keep the rolls of candidates swollen.

At entrance to college, the number of freshmen who see themselves as premedical students is probably two to three times the number that eventually applies in their senior year. They come supported by parental enthusiasm, success in high school science courses (usually biology), and, quite often, unabashed hero worship of the family doctor. They understand from the beginning that the competition will be tough, and they are either prepared to see it through if they have been strong students, or to put up the best fight possible if they have more ambition than academic ability. The knowledge that there will be twice as many candidates applying for admission to medical schools as there are places available sets the competitive scene, and the resultant struggle for the academic grades that will make admission possible is not only unpleasant to watch but rather unsettling for the observer's view of medicine and doctors.

For many premeds in college the first jolt is the tremendous increase in the need for physical rather than biological sciences as a prerequisite for medical study. The premedical student more often than not has been interested and successful in biology in high school, has tolerated math courses, and has gotten through chemistry and physics without either enthusiasm or distinction. To learn that four semester courses in chemistry are a universal requirement of medical schools along with a strong recommendation of physics and math, and that biology is required in minimal amounts—no more than two semester courses—generally is the first shock. To counteract this, many students will postpone the courses in physics or math until the last moment—providing the medical school with a visible record of their disinclination for the physical sciences.

Unfortunately, advice on preparatory courses for medical school is often given by the family physician, a man unquestionably admirable in many ways, but often behind

the times in his knowledge of present academic competition and entrance requirements. Because he has gone
through the mill, he is assumed to be an expert even though
the situation has changed drastically since his day, even
when that day might have been quite recent.

The underlying reason for the shift in emphasis has been
an explosion of knowledge in molecular biology in the last
few years and the concomitant discovery that chemistry
and physics are an integral necessity to this line of inquiry.
Increasingly, the practices of medicine will rely on a base
of scientific knowledge to a far greater extent than ever
before, and the dismaying proliferation of new information
and new techniques promises no respite in the foreseeable
future.

To illustrate, at a recent colloquium on curricular reform
in medical schools, college professors in the fields of
chemistry, biology, and physics spoke to medical school
deans about the material they were currently teaching. In
the audience were fourth year medical students who had
been invited to provide the student view in discussions. At
the end of this session, I heard one fourth year student say
to another: "I've only been out of college four years, but I
couldn't follow what they were talking about."

Understandably, in the face of this avalanche of information, the medical schools are undertaking curricular reforms in great numbers: cutting out much traditional material to make room for new, making more flexible arrange-
ments for the student who comes unusually well prepared,
and increasing the possibilities for research and entry into
academic medicine, an increasingly popular venture.

On the other hand, a conservatism in medical circles is
not limited to students. One dean at this meeting was
relating the struggle in his institution over a proposed cut
in the time to be spent by students in learning anatomy. A
curricular change committee recommended a cut of 40
percent in the time allotted. The retort of the chairman of

the anatomy department was predictable: "Of course we can cut the course down by 40 percent; we'll simply eliminate the study of the head and neck!"

Quite apart from the fact that premedical studies may turn out to be considerably different from what he expected, the premedical student will find other sources of irritation, concern, and possible frustration confronting him: students, faculty, and finances.

Because the competition for medical school is so well known, the student who plans for it must never relax, must never forget what his major goal is. It is not really clear whether he need be as single-minded as he is, but it is certainly true that a propelling mixture of fear and ambition keeps him constantly concerned, not only about his own record in academic work, but also about what other students are doing, for he will be judged comparatively. In some cases, the more naturally competitive students will arrange circumstances so that they come out on top. Thus a college senior recently wrote an article for his local paper in which he described the systematic hiding of library books on reserve for science courses just before announced examinations in those courses. Obviously, if the competitive student prevents enough students from last-minute cramming, their grades will fall and his will look good in comparison.

In one major university, it has become the custom for the faculty of science courses serving premeds to make copies of the examination papers before returning them to students. This stymies the students from erasing incorrect answers, writing in correct answers, and then returning the examination booklets to the instructor for credit and higher grades.

The list of anecdotes is almost endless, but the end result is that the successful premedical student—the one who gets into medical school—has quite often developed a chilly self-centeredness which is not consonant with the warm and generous picture of a physician which the public loves to cherish. I think it is quite possible that the attitudes developed by the high level of fierce academic competition in college may be responsible for some of the attacks currently leveled at the medical profession, such as greed and lack of personal concern, and also may be contributors to the disenchantment with the profession which seems to be current.

But fellow students are not the only source of problems for the premedical student. It might be assumed that any student so devoted to getting good grades would be welcomed by faculty members. This was probably true thirty years ago when college students were more relaxed and before such large numbers began to think in terms of graduate schools. Today the kinds of colleges and universities likely to attract premedical students are likely also to have a number of students anxious to continue to the graduate level. The faculties of these schools are then faced with a choice of encouraging students to be scholars in their own fields and to become devotees of pure science, or of encouraging them to become physicians, practitioners of applied science (and, incidentally, richer than their professors in the process); not remarkably, they will vote in favor of the future scholar. And in doing so, they may view the future physician with open or veiled scorn, attempt to lure him into the paths of righteousness by whatever means they have, or plan their courses in such a way that they are more suitable for future graduate students in biology or chemistry than for future doctors.

The faculties have considerable lures other than pure suasion to change the direction of the premedical student. In the last few years it has become virtually traditional that few graduate students, particularly in the sciences, pay for their own educational expenses. Universities, private industry, and, most of all, the government have encouraged the increase in post-baccalaureate education with generous grants and fellowships. Any college student with the energy, drive, and grades to get into medical school can undoubtedly get support for graduate work in the pure sciences—but not in medicine. The scholarship opportunities in medical schools, like the admission opportunities, are notably fewer and are hedged with doubt, uncertainty, and a high level of competition. For the student whose parents are able to pay, there is no problem; but for the student who goes to college on a marginal budget or a large scholarship, the problem of financing medical school is one additional gnawing uncertainty which adds to his feeling of insecurity.

Small wonder then that premedical students are conservative. From the time they enter college they are beset by a variety of hostile forces (or forces they see as hostile); and worrying, as most of them do in every waking hour, about their chances of success, they are not likely to undertake any activity that might be frowned on by that even more conservative body, the medical school admission committee. Therefore, when placards are carried and deans are confronted, it is doubtful that the carriers or hooters are premedical students.

Even in medical schools, though, times are changing. A recent college graduate I know well, a model of premedical conservatism, reported back to me after his first year of medical school that he had been instrumental in leading a protest against the curriculum and the quality of teaching in his world-famous institution. Similarly, there is current evidence that there are now student committees at a number of the most prestigious medical colleges pressing for more participation in decision-making, curricular matters, admission of minority groups, and other reflections of the usual undergraduate ferment. Perhaps the comparative safety of having finally made medical school enables a student who has rigidly self-disciplined his rebellious tendencies to give them free rein. In fifteen years even the

American Medical Association may have an entirely different temper.

There is no reason, however, to believe that campus radicals might not be students planning to go to law school. These are no less ambitious students, and quite often, in terms of academic achievement, they are much more successful than the premed. But in most of the other ways of identification the "pre-law" student has no curricular pattern that makes him recognizable; there cannot be a student whose courses are preparing him for law to the exclusion of everything else.

Pre-law is essentially a state of mind, a direction, an expression of expectation, an ambition; but it is not a specific set of courses. A student who plans to go to law school may major in anything he wants, the chief aim being to demonstrate a very high degree of academic competence. While it is true that some colleges will satisfy a student's need and desire for a prescribed pre-law curriculum, law schools ask for none of the specific requirements that medical schools demand. On the other hand, it is true that there are certain traditional disciplinary lines which, while not required, quite often form the continuing backbone of a student's prelegal education: history, political science, economics, and, to a great extent, English.

It is fascinating to observe some of the combinations of interest that go on to law. For example, one of the most brilliant undergraduates of my acquaintance entered college with the avowed intention of becoming a mathematician. He had placed at or near the top in the high school mathematics competition of his state; his grades were impeccable, and his College Board scores were equally reassuring. For the first two and a half years of college he took math courses until he realized that he didn't really want to devote his life to mathematics. He then switched to a major in philosophy, graduated with honors, and entered law school; his subsequent record has been notable.

At a time when students are looking at business as a kind of "rat race" they want no part of, law offers an unusual opportunity for the student with a good mind to live a prosperous and, perhaps more important, an interesting life. On the negative side, the profession is overcrowded and highly competitive. No lawyer will be able to move into the ranks of the well paid as effortlessly as even the least capable physician. But it is still true that no profession offers so much challenge to the man of intellect during the pursuit of his career as the law.

It is a curious fact (which seems almost sacrilegious to mention) that practicing physicians are quite often attacked by an unexpected boredom when they have been out of medical school eight or ten years.The underlying causes are probably best attributed to the sense of letdown that the doctor suffers in his daily practice. After years of considerable and tedious academic demands, suddenly the physician finds himself on his own where there is almost no one to question or test his actions. There is little doubt that the sudden release of pressure is welcomed at first, but the lack of genuine intellectual challenge is often stultifying.

The fact that this does not happen in law may be that profession's greatest drawing card. Lawyers, in my experience, start a love affair in law school which grows and intensifies as they continue in their profession. The study of law and the involvement with it seems to become more intriguing and fascinating each day.

A great many students who might be happy with law as a career are turned away because of the sedentary nature of the trade. Medicine appeals to many because of the presumed independence of the physician to go as he pleases. Actually, of course, the demands of the patients severely circumscribe the life of a practicing physician, but he is still very independent in the sense that he has little supervision. The lawyer's work, seen in the traditional context of forbidding law libraries and the fine print in contracts (as opposed to the flamboyance of criminal trial work which is seen so often on television, and is doubtlessly recognized as atypical), does not initially appeal to many young students.

There is little that can be done to change this image in a dramatic way, because the drama of the law is almost entirely in the mind. It is both an intellectual puzzle to be solved and an instrument for social good and change. The often heard reason for medical study, "I want to help people," might be applied equally to law since the layman is usually as helpless in the face of the law as he is against anything more medically complicated than a headache.

This simple, first-aid, aspect of law is often very important. Recently I sent a student down to see a member of a leading local law firm to get advice about a fight he was having with his landlord. The lawyer, one of the best paid in the city, called to thank me.

"I loved helping that boy," he said, "that's what law is all about, for me—and I charged him five dollars just to keep both of us honest." After that direct contact with the people that laws were made for, he doubtless returned to the equally intriguing intellectual puzzle of corporate mergers.

Essentially law is the orderly process by which man gets his business accomplished, and verbal precision is the keynote. Hence, high school students who are interested in law are likely to enjoy English and social studies; if they are intrigued by math at all, it is more likely to be plane geometry than anything else. Interest in the verbal solution of problems best characterizes both the pre-law student and the practicing lawyer.

The verbal solution of problems is the heart of all educational processes, and, although cast in a more obvious practical mold, it serves the business school student as well. Since the establishment of the Wharton School of Finance and Commerce of the University of Pennsylvania in 1881, the academic study of business has been a reality. And it is one branch of education readily understandable to many Americans who have difficulty in rationalizing the existence of fields which they find impractical.

There is certainly no doubt that business has steadily grown more complex. Executive problems, aggravated by big labor and big government, to say nothing of big business and the increasing tendency of companies to merge into larger entities, require trained specialists in management. And the financial success of business administration graduates indicates that non-liberal-arts training pays off handsomely. It is not remarkable, therefore, that postgraduate training in business administration (the original purpose of the Wharton School) has been translated to the undergraduate level, where it has flourished in numerous colleges and universities across the country.

Whether business administration is better studied at the graduate or undergraduate level is not the point at issue here, although this discussion is a heated one in many institutions. (It is interesting to note in passing that Tulane University, a most distinguished institution in the South, recently decided to reverse a previous decision to teach business on the undergraduate level. At the cost of some disruption to its enrollments, business administration has been limited to graduate study. Similar rumblings are often heard at other colleges which enjoy a reputation for fine liberal training; but, in view of the continuing popularity of the undergraduate business programs, it seems doubtful that they will be eliminated.)

In any case, the deans of business schools suggest in general that it is not educationally sound to take business administration at both the undergraduate and graduate levels. Like law, there are no real prerequisites for study, although base courses in economics are a sensible preparation. Even for the student who does not bring these, they are available to (and required of) the graduate student, although not for credit.

The most popular background preparation for the graduate study of business is engineering—which is both understandable and surprising. It is understandable because such a combination provides the technical background and management training which should be ideal for the aspirants to middle management positions in manufacturing industries. It is surprising, however, because a large number of engineers apparently do not see engineering training as the means to an obvious end; they recognize the value of the education, but they do not want a career as engineers.

Engineering as a preparation for business makes further sense because of the rapid increase in the importance of the computer in business and the resulting need to have management trainees capable in mathematics and computer science. The dramatic rise in the importance of the computer in the management of business is unquestionably going to change the entire complexion of business planning in such diversely different areas as the size of inventories or the proper routing through a factory of the goods to be finished.

For this reason, although the prerequisites for entrance to business school are still very flexible, the student who has taken some calculus and some computer programming (which is increasingly available even at the most militant of the liberal arts colleges) will find himself in a better competitive position, not only for admission but also for subsequent success in school.

What are the criteria which determine admission to graduate schools of business? They are considerably less clear-cut than medical or law school standards. In the case of the first, there are numerous specific requirements, a demand for academic excellence, and a concern for personal warmth. In the case of law schools, there is not much weight given to personal charm (although honesty and integrity are, of course, understood as requirements in admission to any institution), and the greatest weight is placed on academic excellence.

Business schools manage a blend of both: ideally they

want the best students possible who also show the ability to deal with the business world. Natural selection, however, tends to make the student more interested in business than in academics, and as a probable consequence the grade levels of entering business students are considerably lower than those of the corresponding law and medical students, even in the most competitive schools.

Although less competitive academically, the business schools are still highly selective, making their choices on the basis of a national aptitude test designed to assess the probable capabilities of the student in the same way the law and medical aptitude tests do. More to the point, business schools are genuinely interested in demonstrated qualities of leadership, personal strength, and, where possible, business acumen. An undergraduate who has held elective office or been a successful athlete is likely to be given preferential treatment. So are the students who get into summer management programs like that run by Bell Telephone, for example, where the student's managerial potential is tested under actual business conditions.

Finally, the business schools have always had a soft spot for the students who still believe in free enterprise. Two notable examples come to mind. The first was a student, Larry, who fell on the idea of combing official records for the birthdays of undergraduates, then writing to their parents to suggest that he could supply a birthday cake for their favorite son at dinner in the college dining room at a nominal cost. The idea itself is now worn out through much repetition, but when Larry initiated it, it was sufficiently compelling to provide him with much needed cash and his fellow students with birthday cakes. This piece of entrepreneurial originality was undoubtedly the prime exhibit that enabled him to get into one of America's most famous business schools. The judgment of the admission committee has proved sound over the years. Since Larry's graduation from college and business school ten years ago, he has moved rapidly up the managerial scale and now heads his own very successful company.

The other interesting example was a student of mine with a penchant for financial manipulation. His chief exhibit for admission to business school was the growth, through adroit manipulation, of some money he had saved from a summer job. It had increased by six or seven times, not in the stock market, but rather through property purchases, mortgages, and shares in small businesses. Nevertheless, Mike did not neglect the stock market, and his request to the New York Stock Exchange that they let him install a ticker-tape machine in his college room remains the highlight of my memories of him. The Stock Exchange refused him but the business school did not. Interestingly enough, Mike elected finally to enter law school as the best possible preparation for a career in business.

The ultimate form of graduate education is, of course, directed toward the advanced academic degrees that distinguish the majority of college faculty members. Originally the master's degree was the major advanced step beyond the baccalaureate, but with the advent of the German style of scholarship in this country, introduced by Johns Hopkins at its founding in 1876, the Ph.D. has become the *sine qua non,* the "union card," of American college teachers. It has in fact become so established that many graduate schools discount the master's degree almost entirely; it is assumed that nearly everyone is a doctoral candidate, and the master's degree is thrown in gratis after a year of successful residence and course work.

Although standards differ at the many universities around the country that offer the Doctor of Philosophy degree, it is the supreme pinnacle of education in America, and real efforts are made to preserve the integrity of that title despite the rapidly increasing number of scholars who are trying for it.

The figures are discouraging for anyone who considers

the rapidly tapering pyramid of the educated in the United States. The statistical chances that your child will get through college are about 50 percent, based on current figures from the Census Bureau. The chances of that same child getting a Ph.D. are startlingly lower.

The lonely splendor in which the earner of the doctoral degree sits can be better illustrated by the normal attrition that attacks the college population. Of the roughly 1,575,000 who entered college in September 1969, about half will actually receive bachelor's degrees. Of the remaining who go on to academic graduate work, less than 3 percent of the original group will eventually get their doctorates. It is not remarkable then that, on the basis of perseverance in the face of obstacles, it is the most unassailably prestigious academic degree in the country. What kind of people try for it, make it, and why?

Nothing has been more suprising to me in a career of college counseling than the unexpected things that students do. Wispy, pale, poetic types have come in to announce enlistments in the Marines. A football captain rhapsodized to me about a course in architecture so good that he could never look at a building in the same way again. I have the collected poems of a championship wrestler in my desk, and, in consequence, I have ceased to be amazed when a hard drinking fraternity rakehell wins his Ph.D. in Restoration poetry or when an athlete, so solid and implacable a lineman that he is called "Dumptruck" (and a one-time flunk-out, at that), gets the academic religion and will almost certainly get the Ph.D. and teach anthropology at the college level.

What I am trying to say is that scholarship is like religion; some of the early converts continue to be as scholarly as they always have been, but the intriguing part is the number of graduate students who, when in high school, would not have believed a prediction that they might be scholars some day.

More often than not, the answer is one man—a teacher

who, by the force of his personality or his ability to present his subject in an irresistably fascinating way, persuades a student that there could be no better way to spend his life than to devote it to history, poetry, mathematics, or whatever field he teaches.

It is for this reason that in counseling I constantly urge students to choose their courses, when they can, by the men who teach them rather than by the content of the courses alone. In fact, I have counseled students, usually without result, to ignore the subject matter and rely entirely on the ability of an inspiring teacher to make any course interesting and worthwhile.

This is anti-practical heresy, because it means a student may take courses outside his major, courses which have no discernible bearing on his training as a lawyer or banker. Even more drastic, the student may become so thoroughly enchanted that, like the examples mentioned, he may elect the ultimate impracticality, a life of teaching and scholarship.

Although this becomes an increasing possibility, it is much more likely that the student who chooses courses taught by inspired teachers will simply find more that is memorable, and his pleasure in learning from a great teacher is more likely to produce good grades and a sense of accomplishment. Nothing so dulls a student's enthusiasm for learning as material that is presented in a dull manner or in which he finds no purpose.

Once the great teacher has enlisted a disciple to his cause, he can also provide the "open sesame" to graduate school, which might not be possible otherwise, particularly if there has been a conversion from academic mediocrity.

The race for graduate school has not been limited to the professional schools. The increasingly academic quality of undergraduate life has been paralleled by a great expansion in academic graduate schools throughout the country.

Admission to a graduate school for advanced scholarly

studies is usually handled in a far different way from that of the administrative admission committees which determine law and medical school entrance. The graduate school admission office is often no more than a centralized collection point for application papers where the applicants are divided according to departmental interests, and the departmental committees then judge each applicant according to his ability or his references. The second criterion is as important as the first, since personal diplomacy among scholars carries a good deal of weight.

A question of long standing among students is whether to go on to graduate study in the same university where one was an undergraduate. Some universities discourage the practice, feeling that the resultant student becomes too ingrown. Other institutions disregard the problem entirely, leaving it to the student's own discretion and direction.

The argument about the dangers of becoming ingrown usually is based on the fact that a student, by the time he has decided to make a career of scholarship, has settled on a fairly definite and possibly narrow line of inquiry. In that little area, there is not likely to be more than one professor who is an expert, and his ideas and special points of view have certainly been explained to and exploited by the student as an undergraduate. Hence, as he goes more deeply into the field, a differing point of view is educationally more sound; and different institutions, ideas, and mentors are more desirable than staying in one place.

One form of professional study that can be accomplished in a variety of ways is architecture. For the student who has a gift of design and who wants to put it to concrete use, architecture offers enormous possibilities in diverse fields, from the preservation of beauty to new techniques in structural design, from urban planning to the planning of gardens.

Perhaps because it is very much an art as well as a

science, training for architecture is available in a larger variety of legitimate ways than any other of the major professions: in combined undergraduate and graduate study, in graduate study alone, or in increasingly rare apprenticeship with a licensed architect.

It is possible to combine graduate and undergraduate study of architecture in a number of highly reputable institutions. The course of study is usually four to six years in length. The graduate architect then goes to work in a virtual apprentice status for an accredited architect in order not only to pass his state qualifying examinations but also to meet the standards of the American Institute of Architects. Those initials, AIA, after the name of an architect mean that he has met stringent standards of training for a total of eight years, including his college and postgraduate work.

It is for this reason that the broader and more flexible means of training for architecture become quite feasible; four undergraduate years plus two years of graduate school in architecture become no less feasible than a compressed four year program begun as a freshman in college, since the total time of eight years of training is required whichever way one chooses to do it.

This permits the student to study broadly in a liberal arts college all the many courses which will be of interest to him generally and also those which are important ancillary fields of knowledge for a modern architect—sociology, economics, and English—in addition to the study of design.

It is necessary, of course, to have some training in physics and mathematics. Indeed, one excellent undergraduate avenue toward architecture is civil engineering, but generally architectural schools have been more concerned with the design talent of the student, latent or demonstrated, than with specific undergraduate training. It is their expectation that the capable architect will be able to get the necessary training in engineering in architecture school; and I suspect that the truly talented architect is convinced that he can always find an engineer to translate his designs into workable reality.

Again, the advantage of a course of action which takes in both graduate and undergraduate study is the flexibility it gives the student, permitting changes of mind either way. Thus, as a premedical counselor in college, I watched over the college career of the son of a distinguished architect who either thought he was going to be a doctor or was determined that he wasn't going to be an architect. He struggled with premedical courses for three years without pleasure or notable success, but he did take some art history and studio courses as electives. Early in his senior year he succumbed to his artistic inheritance, applied to a great architectural graduate school, and was accepted.

The reverse is as often true; young men and women attracted by the efficiency and practicality of beginning their specialization early go to schools of architecture, of business administration, or other specialized schools, only to find this interest evaporating as they progress. Unfortunately, it is more difficult to "move around" in a specialized institution, and there is often more loss than gain in the total time invested in education.

Perhaps the best common example of how to acquire a specialized education in a liberal arts college today is to prepare for teaching. It is possible to take courses in education in most colleges and meet most, if not all, the specific requirements for a teacher's certificate by the time the bachelor's degree is earned. However, the master's degree is increasingly considered the barest minimum, and a fairly recent academic invention, the M.A.T., gives training in teaching and, more important, permits the student who decided on teaching late in his college career a chance to serve without having to backtrack on his education, or without sacrificing the breadth of this education.

The M.A.T., Master of Arts in Teaching, is an excellent compromise between straight postgraduate training in education and the academic demands of the Master of Arts degree in a specific subject. It requires the student to go more deeply into the academic training in his subject, but requires education courses, practice teaching, and an evaluation of his teaching techniques at the same time. The common complaints about secondary school teachers have been that either they are not educated broadly enough in their field, or, if sufficiently educated, they do not know how to teach; the M.A.T. answers both objections and has deservedly become a highly popular form of preparation.

This universal rush to graduate education has finally filled the void, and there were, at the beginning of the '70s, unmistakable signs that the trend to graduate education was about to reverse itself. The most notable indication of this was the announcement of cutbacks in the number of students to be accepted as arts and sciences graduate students at Harvard and Yale universities. Ostensibly the reason fo. decreasing the number of their doctoral candidates was money.

However, at very nearly the same time the surprising news got around that colleges and schools were not looking for teachers. Magazines reported new Ph.D.s in New York drove cabs while waiting to find the right academic opening. The chairman of the history department of a great university in the Boston area told me that his department was receiving as many as thirty letters a day from young doctorates looking for teaching jobs. A quick but unscientific survey showed that the same situation obtained in many other universities.

At the same time there seems to be a growing awareness of the need for skilled artisans—mechanics, plumbers, and the like. One mother reported to me that her son was taking his doctorate in sociology at Boston University, and her tone of voice implied that this was his idea. Virtually in the same breath she declared the need for more vocational training, but I had the strong feeling she meant it would be a good idea for other students, not hers.

Until we find some way to reward carpenters with the prestige that the advanced degree holder now has, there is little likelihood that the rush to colleges and graduate schools will stop. Meanwhile, the value of the bachelor's and increasingly, the advanced degrees will continue to suffer from the effects of overproduction.

VII

If Your Child Misses
the Boat

DESPITE ALL THE PLANNING
and anxious concern that parents lavish on their children,
the plans often go agley and young Christopher who was to
found the family fortunes by graduating from the Ivy
League had trouble graduating from high school, and
pretty Susan upset her parents by announcing that she did
not want to go to college at all. Conversely, there appear in
admission offices from time to time young men who had
given no thought to education, college, or even very much
to the future. Suddenly through some accident of fate they
decide that all of these things are very important and
should be dealt with immediately. The question that arises
is: what can be done to rectify mistakes and change
directions, and how late can it be done? If Christopher did
miserably in high school, has he ruined his chances for
education forever? If Susan doesn't want to go to college
because she really wants to get a job and be independent,
does this mean she shouldn't have any more education, or if
she should, what kind? And poor Giovanni, who took the

vocational course in high school—what happens now that he has discovered he has a brain and yearns to use it?

In an educational system as complicated as ours, the wastage is enormous. The number of dropouts from school, of flunk-outs from college, of students who were steered by ignorance or accident into the wrong programs for them are bound to be high. As a result of increasing pressures to get everyone educated to the level of his own ability, our system of education is showing a much greater willingness to lean down to pick up the pieces than ever before.

The most flexible of the educational inventions in recent years is the junior college, a uniquely American stopgap institution that could only flourish in a system that feels that the majority of the citizens, almost without regard to ability, can be educated if they want to be.

The junior colleges perform three major functions. First, they offer advanced training to high school graduates in areas which are not strictly the province of the college— that is, in skills that are technical but not essentially academic (as an electronics technician, for example). Second, they offer terminal college experience for the student whose ability or interest does not warrant the four year college experience. Third, and finally, for the student whose academic strength and preparation has been questioned by the four year colleges, they offer a chance for scholastic redemption. All of this means, of course, that the admission standards of a junior college are much more flexible, that in many cases there are no usual admission standards except perhaps the high school diploma. Depending on the junior college, this, too, can be circumvented.

Although invented in the East, the State of California has raised the junior college to a great level of availability, architecture, and usefulness. The campuses of these junior colleges dot the state and form the connecting link between the high schools and the state colleges. The University of California has, like most state universities, rigid rules governing admission which center around a B average in high school or a complicated formula which deals with College Board Achievement Tests without regard to the record. Unlike most state systems, California does not have a series of colleges in descending order of academic difficulty or admission standards; each of the many campuses is considered separate but equal, and students choose one over the other on the basis of departmental strengths, geography, or proximity. For the student without the B average there are the junior colleges, and these are generously placed, beautifully designed, inexpensive, hospitable, and eclectic in their outlooks. Their programs can be divided very simply into two categories: terminal and "up or out."

The two year terminal program was undoubtedly the real reason for the establishment of the junior college—to provide extra technical or special education for the student who needed more than high school could offer but who, academically or financially, could not take the rigors of the four year institution.

In the East the whole concept of junior colleges has been slower to catch on, probably because of the implied intellectual or financial insult. A student who was serious about going to a college but didn't make the grade might consider going to a prep school for a year, or working and going to evening classes. The junior colleges available for many years in the East were really "junior" colleges, but thought of in a different way. And they were mostly private: Katharine Gibbs for a girl who wanted to learn secretarial skills in a school-like atmosphere; the Wentworth Institute in Boston or Franklin Institute in Philadelphia that taught specific technical skills. Although there were a number of reputable and successful two year colleges for women in the East—again, private and quite respectable—the concept of the two year liberal arts college for men was resisted and not really taken seriously.

Quite possibly the public-versus-private institution struggle for preeminence has had some bearing on the whole question of junior colleges. In the East the private college was the arbiter of educational policy and the leader of the field. The democratic principle that everyone is entitled to education was somewhat late in coming to the East. New York State exported its college students by the thousands without giving a serious thought to a state university system of its own until about twenty years ago. State universities (or colleges) had little standing, particularly in the Northeast, until after World War II, and even today these are overshadowed in general prestige by the ancient private giants of education.

But in California prosperity and migration caused the building of the most remarkable public system of education the world has ever seen, and the development of the concept that everyone is entitled to more education than just high school. Although the California system led the way in terms of numbers, all-inclusiveness, and elegance of execution (some of the best institutional architecture in the United States is to be found in various branches of the University of California), other state and municipal systems have reached similar conclusions and have made the junior college and the community college an integral part of American life and expectation. (For example, in any family series on television, when the oldest child goes off to college, it is obviously in the same town where the family lives—convenient for the series' continuity, but so commonplace in most of the country as to require no special explanation.)

It is not surprising, then, that the conservative East, reluctant even to give public universities the respect which they had seized in the West, has succumbed to the idea of the junior college—of course, not without a struggle. There is still a good deal of opprobrium attached to going to junior college in the East. Rhode Island Junior College, for example, has the nickname REJECT, built from its initials and the underlying reason for many of its students' being there.

Does the junior college (especially the community junior college) really perform its function of providing nearby, inexpensive, continuing education for the student who would have difficulty in meeting even the modest tuition fees and other expenses at most state universities; of providing some advanced training of a semi-academic nature; of providing the late bloomer with an academic second chance?

There is no question that the community college does serve its purpose. It is not glamorous; it is often a building across the street from the high school, the high school building itself at night, or an educational building which some more prosperous institution has just abandoned. But it does provide continuity and opportunity.

The nature of junior college courses has raised some questions about their purpose. Despite the original technical purpose, they have in many instances developed as havens for the creative and performing arts. This may be because so many state universities offer such a wide variety of technical courses that it would be hard to imagine a form of training which was not academic enough for their curriculum. Hence, many of the prospective customers for the junior colleges were drained off to the state university. Second, "creative" people are most likely to be those unwilling to be confined by standard curricula either in high school or college, and hence they look for an essentially nonrestrictive oasis where their talents can blossom untrammeled. The very considerable offerings in music, drama, and art in the junior colleges of California, for example, have been defended on the grounds that the problem of leisure will be enveloping society before it is quite sure what to do with it, and these offerings are an important part of the answer.

But it is the junior college as a rescuer of middle-class

ambition, temporarily lost, that concerns many parents. Can it rescue a student whose record has gone off the rails somewhere in high school? Can a student who does well in junior college then continue to a higher degree-granting institution? Can a junior college permit a student in a noncollege high school course to make the switch to college preparation? In all of these cases of missed boats, the junior college, with the help of intelligence, hard work, and sensible counseling, can work wonders.

It is by no means an automatic process, however. Because the junior colleges quite often have open-door admission policies, the resulting attitude toward students is likely to be "we let you in—now make it if you can." It was for that reason that a friend of mine in California, whose son was a C student in high school, sent him to a private college in the state (with the flexible or liberal admission policy that the private institutions can employ and the public cannot) rather than to a junior college. "Dave wasn't ready for that kind of 'take it or leave it' education," said my friend. "He needed counseling and some personal attention—it was worth the money it cost."

Because maturity rates are uncertain and unpredictable, how to make the assessment for your own student as this father did (and Dave graduated successfully from his private California college) is a difficult question. Obviously, if money is an important factor, there can be no alternative; if the public institution cannot do it, it will not be done.

The attitude of the student is an important one to consider. The junior college, whether paternalistic and concerned about each student, or laissez-faire and unconcerned, will be of little use to the student who is not yet ready to undertake his education. But for the offspring who has not yet been a "student" and who grows up late to his educational responsibilities, the junior college can be the means of his second chance. In general, parents anxious to launch their children "properly" are more interested in this side of junior colleges than in their terminal education function.

Sometimes, of course, the change is unexpected, interior, and not motivated by anxious parents. Several months ago I had a phone call from the dean of one of our local junior colleges. He had made the discovery of his teaching career—and would I talk to Joe. I would and did: Joe turned out to be an ordinary looking young man with an accent that suggested foreign-born parents or at least a non-English speaking home life. He had taken the vocational course in high school and had done badly. He had gone to work after high school in a machine tool company and would probably have lived the life of a semi-skilled laborer except that a machine fell on him injuring his arm. His recovery, planned by the State Office of Vocational Rehabilitation, included a two year program in drafting and machine design at the junior college. Joe went docilely, discovered for the first time in his life that he could be a good student, and, emboldened by his success in technical courses, took a course in history—and went wild. He went to his instructor, the dean by chance, for lists of books to read, and took more courses in liberal arts. At the present time, after consultations between all concerned, Joe will finish his machine design course (because he did so well, and "it's always something to fall back on"), undertake more liberal arts courses until he has demonstrated his ability, and will then transfer to a liberal arts college. What will happen then is anyone's guess, but at the present time he is so infatuated with the idea of education that he plans to become a teacher.

Like the junior college experience, the addtional year of preparation, if approached in the proper frame of mind, can be the turning point in an academic career. At one time this was almost a standard procedure before entering the fa-

mous old colleges of the Northeast. Robert Lincoln, son of
the president, failed his entrance examinations at Harvard
and went to Phillips Exeter for a year of academic repairs
which were successful. In recent years the private preparatory schools have tried to limit the number of one year boys
(termed variously PGs—postgraduates—retreads, and in
Exeter's own peculiar patois, "nonreturning uppers"); but
as the cost of schooling has gone up and the pressure for
admission has diminished somewhat (particularly in some
boarding schools), the one year boy becomes an educational challenge that helps to balance the budget.

For a boy who has academic ability and who has not used
it wisely in high school, the idea of an extra year of school,
when he has looked forward to the freedom of college, is
not usually warmly received. Having once seen the school,
and having further realized that an extra year of high school
will not mean that he will be faced with the opprobrium of
joining the students in the class just below him, but will be
going to another school with other postgraduates, he may
well accede.

Not every boy does. I remember vividly a widow's son at
Brown who flunked himself out willfully and openly in one
semester (a feat in itself!), giving as the reason that his
mother had made him take an extra year at Andover and this
was his revenge. He estimated gleefully that his gesture of
defiance was costing his mother about $3,500. Needless to
say, once out, he never returned to Brown.

If parents are considering the extra year of preparation,
where should it be and what should be studied to make it
most valuable? To the first, the answer is that the further
away the student is from his old friends, old teachers, and
hence his old reputation and habits, the more likely he will
be to change. Reputations are built up over years of time,
and the boy who has suddenly awakened to a sense of
responsibility often finds that teachers refuse to take him
seriously and that his friends either can't or do not want to

believe the change taking place. Furthermore, anyone in
the painful process of reformation does not want to be
accused of the very thing he is trying to accomplish; it is
not only embarassing to be caught in the middle of self-
reformation, but also runs counter to the "cool" approach to
life, which is an important pose of the age. Parents are not
exempted from the list of people that the student should be
removed from, partly because they can be as guilty as
teachers in sticking to old judgments, and because it often
happens that it is friction within the family that has caused
a lack of productivity in the first place. It is almost a truism
that the child of divorced, separated, or quarreling parents
will have some reflection of this in his academic behavior.

This generalization is, of course, not always true, and
there are cases of delayed reaction which can only be
inferentially connected to family problems. For example,
an undergraduate I know from the deep South was the
marvel of his high school because he was the most stable
and productive person in his family. Father, an intelligent
and sensitive man, had ruined an inherited business, had
become an alcoholic, and was reduced to being a gardener
in the elegant suburb they had once lived in. Christopher
went off to college with the highest praises and expectations of his school and succumbed in college to what must
have been overpowering, but latent, emotional problems.
He is currently out of college looking for answers.

However, the important point about any school that
provides academic rehabilitation is that it is different, and
the chief advantage is in the difference, in its ability to
provide new challenges because it is different.

Once the student is situated at the new school, what does
he take—easy subjects that will boost his record, things he
is interested in so he will not revolt, or a repetition of all the
subjects he did so badly in so as to repair the gaps in his
education? Oddly enough, my recommendation would be a
mixture of all three: something easy to maintain the stu-

dent's confidence in his own ability; something he likes, because a degree of emotional satisfaction is an absolute essential of good morale, in a student or anyone else; and finally, repair work, which should be done as skillfully as possible.

More often than not, these repeated subjects are likely to be English, math or foreign language. In English, fortunately, there is little chance for repetition—twelfth grade English can be taught in countless different ways and need never be repetitious. Skill in writing is probably a more important area to work on than the number of French novels read and dissected in translation.

Foreign language always raises the problem of whether to continue wading through the irregular verbs of a language the student detests with a passion, or to start a new language. In many cases, it seems most advantageous to start over again, treating the student as though he had never heard of French before. If your student has a bad ear for spoken languages, then Latin may be an appropriate answer. Needless to say, the entrance requirements of the college in question are important to consider, although in general they are more concerned about the quality of preparation than in actual course counting. Therefore, it is unlikely that a college will have any strict views on two years each of two languages rather than three or four years of preparation of one. My personal prejudice is for sufficient preparation in one language so that college courses in the language are really on the college level—analyzing the literature of the language, for example—rather than learning the passive voice or one of several subjunctives.

In any case, the extra-year student is busy with a program that is part extension and part reparation, but, most important, he is now, as perhaps never before in his life, surrounded by other students who are eager for the same thing—admission to college. This unanimity of purpose cannot help but affect a student's attitudes toward grades, learning, studying, and a variety of necessary adjuncts of the successfully prepared college student. Virtually everyone has a competitive spirit, and seldom does a newcomer venture into this competitive atmosphere without being caught up in it.

Naturally, the schools themselves, particularly the boarding schools, have arranged students' lives for generations in such a way that there is little left to do after the strenuous activities of the day except study. The ideal boarding school program provides classes every day except Sunday, seclusion from worldly temptations (or at least a vigorous try at it), and a sports program which is nominally designed to "build strong bodies" or "a traditional sense of competition," but is really provided in order to wear the boys out to a point where they are tractable enough to be deprived of other diversions so they can study.

Of course, occasionally the system works too well, so that the student who found he was studying in prep school because he had not many alternatives, goes all to pieces in the free atmosphere of college where there are no study hours, no required attendance at classes, and essentially, no set schedule for the day. To combat this, many boarding schools are offering their seniors more options in how and where they may spend their time so that they will be better prepared for an unstructured life. But for the extra-year student—the postgraduate—the schedule and the life of the school is such a change that the difference between his previous existence as a high school boy living at home and his life at school are different enough to be impressive, however liberal the school may be.

The net effect, if you ask a student who took an extra year to get into college (and it is usually to get into a particular college that he or his parents yearned for, rather than just any college) about what he learned during that year, chances are he will not talk about math, or Spanish, or history, but will make the simple statement: "I learned how to study." In many cases they have, and in some they only think they have; but in general, it is usually a successful experiment.

The particularly interesting point is that, after the fact, after they have in many cases been dragged off for the extra year against their wishes, they like it; they think it is a good idea. What mysterious force tells a student after he has done it, that it was good for him to mature for one more year but will not provide that information in advance, I don't know; but in my experience, the approval *ex post facto* is universal.

In some cases the extra year for maturation doesn't have to be in the form of an extra year in school. Some years ago a student at a famous old academy who had applied and been accepted to Brown got involved in a form of vernal revelry which caused him to be suspended from school and his diploma held up for a year. The Committee on Admission at Brown felt that a one year moratorium was in order as well, and John was advised to work for a year. This he did, with no great enthusiasm, at a fish hatchery, and was admitted to Brown a year later. Notwithstanding the circumstances, he felt the year off and the resultant perspective he gained was "the best thing that ever happened to me."

In general, there has been the implication that the one year retread student is more likely to be a boy than a girl. This could be due to the greater conservatism of women's schools which don't like to jumble their ranks with one year students, but it is more likely to be in line with the different attitude toward the woman student's maturity. Since women are likely to mature in every way at an earlier age than men, there is less likelihood that a girl could profit from an extra year of high school in the sense that she would change from a nonstudent to a student.

I have also felt that another reason for this is that women

are more likely to be good students because of their inherent makeup as women. This is a gross generalization, but it is true that tiresome but delicate tasks involving great skill and patience have often been relegated to women in industry. In the same way, women as students are likely to be more dutiful, pay attention to details, and get good grades if that is their pattern. When they are good students, women are more likely to be genuinely scholarly, since they are less likely to be directly concerned about education as a means to making a living, as most men are. Smith girls who had transferred to Yale as undergraduates complained recently that Yale men were too "vocationally oriented" in their academic approach.

Otherwise they are likely to fall at the other end of the scale. This is not to say there is no middle ground, but the likelihood of growth as a student, or the sudden "late blooming" that is so often talked about in boys, is apparently not worth considering for girls—or in any case, it is not considered.

An amusing sidelight on one student's view of the difference was shown me when I recently interviewed a talkative, athletic boy who had views on everything including why girls were so often better students than boys. "They have so much less to do," he said; "no sports—so they study."

"For lack of anything better to do," I suggested.

"Exactly."

I was amused by his athlete's point of view—that athletics was the only activity other than study possible for girls—but nevertheless, his view may also have a certain validity. Physical activity and athletics consume an enormous amount of the concentration, energy, and conscious thought of most teenage boys; for many, the conversion to student from athlete comes only after time, or some other rude awakening force, has put athletics and education into proper perspective.

To give some idea of the expert's considered view of the possible value of the extra year, it is interesting to see that a number of colleges have set up transitional programs for economically underprivileged students admitted to their colleges.

This is an outgrowth of the civil rights movement but, more than that, it is the result of an uneasy sensation on the part of colleges who have served the solid middle class from their inception, and now feel that they should broaden the base of their population to include more students from the lower end of the income scale. Selecting students for this sort of project is a tricky process, because ideally a student needs both academic and emotional maturity to make it in college. The student from the deprived background has been deprived of, among other things, good schools, good counseling, and a knowledge and understanding of how middle-class college students live and think. Students from urban high schools, where only a small fragment go on to college, are likely, even if good students, to show up badly on standardized tests, or quite often, if they show up well on tests, to be not very good students. The question is which of these two types should one take in order to produce the best final results—i.e., a successful college career in a college that deals mostly with the products of suburban schools.

The question of tests is not the only one which plagues admission officers in making decisions of this or any sort. While it is true that there is certainly a "cultural bias" in most of the standardized tests which college-bound students take, it does not show up consistently. The term "cultural bias," of course, implies that items on the test are phrased in terms of the suburbanite's everyday life and experience, while the child of the urban poor (or the rural poor) might not even understand what the question is about, and hence will do badly. On the other hand, there are brilliant exceptions—boys and girls who have discovered books and reading and who do well on the tests anyway. Despite all the flurry about the bias, and the havoc it wreaks, no test of generally accepted reliability which also eliminates the distortion problems of cultural background has yet been established.

It is also true that even the desire to take a test and do well on it is probably a function of middle-class upbringing and attitudes about education. If a student understands how important standardized tests are, and it is made clear to him from a tender age, then he will try to do well. Quite the reverse was observed by my wife, acting as a volunteer tester in urban primary schools in South Providence. She found to her surprise that these kindergarten and first grade children responded quite differently to a test designed to determine brain damage; whereas other children had seen the test as a game, the response of these youngsters was complete indifference. In the same vein, Dr. Eric Denhoff, a distinguished pediatric neurologist has said that extreme cultural deprivation can produce responses which are virtually identical with actual brain damage.

The problem of preparing the deprived student for his college experience is especially acute for the highly selective college which is very much in the business of looking for students from depressed backgrounds.* The problem of having 90 percent of a student body highly selected and highly competitive, and then incorporating a minority 10 percent which has had generally inferior schooling and less educational sophistication is a difficult one to solve. In some instances it is done by other agencies before the student hits campus. The ABC (A Better Chance) Program, for example, makes use of the facilities of colleges for a

---

*Usually urban black students. Not much has been said and even less has been done about a number of other less vocal problem groups— American Indians, rural poor of any color, and the poor white; Puerto Ricans, Chinese, and Mexicans have been able to be heard, but the major emphasis has been on blacks to this point.

summer program for selected students in the ninth or tenth grade, and then sends them on to independent boarding schools for two to three years for college preparation, after which the student should be ready for college, where he can be judged pretty much on his own merits.

Another method is a summer or year-long intensive preparation program conducted by the college, which admits a student from a depressed background and then itself provides the necessary educational boost. The summer program is a crash indoctrination for the student who has been relatively strong and needs only a final polish. The year-long program is intended to provide an introduction and preparation for the college's own curriculum. The year program develops certain built-in problems, because the students brought in under such a setup have no clearly defined status; they are not regular students who can participate on teams for example, but they are on campus and ostensibly part of it. Their "second-class citizenship" is highly visible, and yet this group must be there if they are to become familiar with the courses, atmosphere, and competition that is extant.

It is interesting that the extra year of preparation, which has traditionally been the last ditch tool of the family well able to afford any extras that were needed, has now been adopted for the poor. Both have learned that there is a limit to the amount of repair which can be accomplished in one year and that even this is dependent on the willingness and maturity of the student.

Not very often, but frequently enough to worry about, a young man will limp through high school despite his college level ability and will resist every effort to prepare him for any kind of continuing education. After high school he works briefly and then, inevitably, is drawn into the service. By the time he has emerged from this experience, he is ready for education if he ever will be. In a sense, this is the best kind of preparation, because it has been brought forcibly home to the young man that education is the only magic that enables people to escape much of the drudgery of the world.

What happens to the student of good ability who blew his chances to go to college and then discovers he has made a terrible mistake? The answers, of course, depend on how badly mangled his previous record was, how much ability he has, and how forcefully he can present the case for his complete reformation. In general, the private college will be more sympathetic and flexible than the public one, but the breadth of public facilities now permits a degree of latitude for just about anyone.

Briefly, if the reconstructed student did not graduate from high school, he should immediately investigate the process of an equivalency diploma, granted on the basis of examination through his state department of education.

For the bright but stubborn, lazy, or unorganized student, passing the examination which leads to an equivalency certificate does not seem to be too difficult. The information required is understandably at the minimum level and is more useful as a means of satisfying a legal requirement for entrance to college than as a measure of academic preparation or personal readiness. The son of a brilliant friend of mine, who was himself brilliant but rebellious managed to get himself evicted from two private schools and his local high school before he went to work for a year. He then took the high school equivalency examination in his state and passed everything in the over 90 percent bracket. A large urban university, impressed with his examination grades, admitted him, and flunked him out in one semester. He then volunteered for the Navy, and after service has done so well in a community junior college that he will probably be admitted as a transfer student to a university of considerable prestige.

Special cases aside, how does the educational renegade who has good ability for college, but who has squandered it, persuade colleges that he is now ready to undertake an education? The underlying fear that colleges will not consider admitting anyone in this situation is what makes parents nervous about any deviation from the conventional educational track. It is certainly true that a college has to have a flexible admission policy to consider a student who dropped (or fell) out of the usual pattern. This means that either a public junior college or a private college is probably the answer, for neither of these types of schools is bound by rigid regulations on admission. (Some private colleges are too hungry to worry about regulations; some are successful enough to feel they can do anything they want to. Of course, some are worried about their public image and will not deviate from their own regulations.)

To any college he turns to, the dropout should present some evidence, not only of his academic ability, but also of his genuine interest in what goes on at a college, rather than an interest merely in a college degree. Many students fresh out of high school, who have no genuine interest in education, but want the "union card," are accepted on faith because of tests, high school records, and the unshakeable belief of any good teacher that a student can be induced to enjoy his education. The dropout, in contrast, has to prove he is hungry for it.

When interviewing a candidate in this situation, I am most curious about what he has read and what he has done with his spare time. It may not be possible to live a life of intellectual excitement in the service or while working in a factory, but it is almost always possible to get books. How many has he read, what has he read, and what does he think about what he has read?

Second in importance, and more subject to fanciful embroidering, is what the dropout does in his spare time. There is no *right* answer, and few admission officers would believe anyone who vowed that he spent his spare hours in rapturous contemplation of Greek statues, but when the mind is hungry for some kind of intellectual stimulation, the pattern of leisure activity will reflects this.

Less necessary, but still of considerable interest to an admission officer, are any extension courses or other kind of academic work the dropout has taken. In general, extension courses are usually pale imitations of the real thing; but again, what he took and how he fared can be indicative.

Finally, I have generally asked an applicant in this category to write a letter or a statement outlining his experiences, what he has done, what he has read, what he has thought about, and what he hopes to do. Any intelligent person who has been separated from education for some time and who has had experience which empasizes the need for education will have thought about the whole process and, more often than not, is well able to write convincingly about his conversion.

Although studies made at various institutions will not back me up, I am a firm believer in the interview. Statistics notwithstanding, every admission officer likes to have a face-to-face confrontation with his subject; he is more likely to believe interview reports in his office than he is the reports that come from teachers, friends, employers, or alumni; and he is more likely to put faith in his own interview report than anyone else's. Therefore, if a newly rehabilitated student can go to the admission office to state his case, he is probably in a better situation than if he cannot.

The reason is simple: admission officers, like teachers, take an essentially optimistic view of humanity, despite a veneer of cynicism about parents and other unavoidable aspects of admission. Most of all, they admire the Cinderella aspect of an intelligent boy or girl (more likely boy) who sees the light and decides he's really interested in education after all. This accounts for the continuing interest and concern over the "late bloomer"; it's the Biblical joy over the return of one lost sheep while surrounded by ninety and nine applications of the good sheep who never strayed at all.

Not all of the officers of education believe in this kind of transformation, however. I well remember a psychologist whose entire system of personality evaluation was dependent on the assumption that, once formed, attitudes about education and working hard did not change. This occasioned the acid comment by the Dean of the College at Brown who was having the "no-change" thesis explained to him: "If you're right and no one ever changes, then there's not much point in having a college."

Almost as unsettling to a parent as the child who muffs the opportunity to go on to college is the student who, safely settled in college, decides he wants to get out for awhile.

"Dropping out" is easy, and this is one place where there does not seem to be any strong distinction between boys and girls. The student simply announces to the appropriate official that he wants a leave of absence. So long as the student is in good standing, there is seldom, if ever, trouble from the college. Reentrance is usually a formality to be rearranged when convenient. If there is a scholarship involved, it is wise to check whether there is a time limit, or whether it can be dropped and picked up later. Usually there is no problem, but it is sensible to check.

What the student elects to do during the time off is of little importance except to the student. Parents will have to accept on faith that in most cases there is sufficient internal pressure which will bring Mike or Alice back to the campus, and that it is external pressures that have probably provoked the break in routine anyway.

Travel is good; work is good; service is unfashionable for obvious reasons; and growing older and getting away for awhile is the best of all. You have to be in it to understand it; otherwise, the best you can be is sympathetic and hope it will work itself out. It usually does.

For the flunk-out the choices are different and the situation is considerably more complex. First, in any college with a truly selective admission procedure, no one fails academically because he is incapable of meeting the scholastic standards. Not only is it the purpose of an admission office to eliminate those who cannot, but the faculty have finally become acclimated to the idea that selective admission produces a class of whom none should fail. Accordingly, some professors have prefaced courses by saying, "I do not expect any of you will fail my course, providing you show some reasonable effort in attendance and writing required papers." This is not permissiveness so much as it is realism; a student not capable and interested is not admitted. According to my friends in secondary schools who are able to gauge the comparative difficulty of the various colleges they send their students to, this expression of faculty confidence in the students has reached the point in some few colleges where a student has to work actively at flunking out in order to make it.

Public colleges and universities operate on a different system. Forced to admit a much wider spectrum of students in the first place, they give more students an opportunity to prove themselves after admission rather than before. The freshman year in a state university, for example, serves much the same purpose as admission selection, and the reason for failure could be inadequate preparation or ability (i.e., the state had drawn the admission line under the survival line), or, as in the case of the selective colleges, some emotional problem preventing the student from being successful.

Even with the greatest selectivity, some students who start college will find they are not up to the demands of the institution and will be invited to leave by the dean and his faculty committee. When this happens there is usually a good deal of what has come to be known as "agonizing reappraisal." The student, in failing, has set into motion academic machinery which is difficult to stop, and he will not be reinstated until his academic illnesses have been cured.

Internally, he should try to sort out the reasons for his failure. Since it is well known that few students fail for a lack of ability (and who wants to use their own stupidity as an excuse, anyway?), most of the flunk-outs freely admit that they "never learned how to study" or "never could get down to the books." For some, I am convinced, there is a real psychological barrier which does prevent them from being efficient students, or at least efficient enough to survive the academic demands of the college. As a matter of fact, I would divide academic failures quickly into the "can'ts" and "won'ts."

The "can'ts" are victims of their own lack of self-discipline. They are either unwilling to say "no" or have never learned how to. Their rooms become congregation spots for any fellow student who wants to break his studying for five minutes with a little idle chatter; they are the first ones to whom someone will turn for companionship at the movies or for a beer.

The contrast between what they know they should do and what they really accomplish is sometimes funny, sometimes pathetic. I knew a young man at Brown who paved his road to academic ruin with a list of things he had to do—books to read, papers to write, professors to see. The idea of organizing his time appealed to him and he tried to do it. Unfortunately the cure became a disease; his lists were elaborately drawn up, decorated, enlarged on, and finally in themselves became an escape. Interestingly, this was not a unique case; there have been several who escaped in the same way.

Conversely, the "won'ts" who flunk out are often very bright, and their method of leaving is quite often as complicated as their personality problems. This is in line with my own empirical observation that a first-rate mind will not permit itself to go unused, and instead often commits academic hara-kiri with a certain dash and flair.

Thus I have known boys at Brown to flunk out by reading two hundred novels in a single semester, by performing brilliantly on the stage or in a musical organization. One National Merit Scholar who came to us with the earnest recommendation of his candidacy as a Rhodes Scholar quickly became renowned on campus as the best bridge and poker player in recent student generations. Even so, he was bright enough that, as remorse set in at the end of each semester, he was able to forestall the inevitable until the middle of his sophomore year.

However, all of the foregoing examples, while intellectual in character, do not really have the flair for organized futility that some of our most brilliant flunk-outs have had. One bright young man undertook an extensive study of traffic frequencies on an expressway he could see from his dormitory room. Naturally, as the lone observer, he was forced to stay up all night, and could not leave during the day to attend classes until his observations were complete. Another variation on the same theme was a frequency listing of the records most often played on Providence radio stations. It required at least two radios, a remarkable Rube Goldberg chart, and a good deal of fairly sophisticated statistical analysis. Like the traffic pattern study, this one accomplished its purpose in one semester, after which the remaining roommate loyally continued it, and followed his companion out one semester later.

The flunking out of roommates in pairs is not remarkable, and, in an informal study of this at Brown, we came to the conclusion that, if a freshman or sophomore was in academic trouble, his roommate was also, or would be shortly. While this was not universally true, it was sufficiently valid to be called Gardner's Law (after Dean John Gardner, then at Brown).

The reasons for this are clear when you start with the

basic assumption that flunking out is a matter of mental attitude rather than capability. It also assumes that, in any two-man room combination, there will be a leader and a follower. If the strong man has the right instincts and the ability to resist temptation when it arises—or, better yet, has learned when to resist and when to give in—then there will be no trouble. It is a "good" roommate combination, and the weaker half will profit; he will be more of a scholar than he or anyone had expected him to be. If, on the other hand, the more compelling of the two is determined not to be a student, his happy-go-lucky attitude undoubtedly will be infectious; the room will begin to develop an attractiveness for anyone who seeks relaxation; the temptations and interruptions will increase and feed on themselves until they result in an academic crisis.

In larger groups of students, as in overcrowded double rooms, or with three or four to a suite of rooms, the strong survive, but do not necessarily exert the same influence over the weak as they do in a double room situation. Thus I have seen a brilliant student, who was also at times wildly gregarious, sitting oblivious to noise, music, wrestling, laughter, and general confusion in his room while placidly learning Russian irregular verbs. I remember also another student who was relaxed and popular except when studying. Then he brooked no interruptions and was curt to the point of rudeness if he was interrupted. Too many freshmen and sophomores are too concerned about being "nice guys" to empty out their rooms, or to leave a card game when it is time to do so.

If this means that roommates are so very important, should there not be more singles, or a way to match people properly to make sure that the maximum number get a "good" combination? The answer to the first part of this question is that singles for freshmen has always seemed a bad idea to me because college, in part, is learning to live with people. Further, the scholarly life is inclined to be solitary and a student who is solitary from the beginning is diminishing his opportunities for having memorable friendships in college. In George Weller's great novel of undergraduate life in the 1930's *(Not to Eat, Not for Love)* one of the characters is looking desperately for a roommate at the end of his freshman year, realizing that if he does not find one he will be living alone for the remainder of his college career. While this is perhaps exaggerated, it really does illustrate how early and quickly relationships are established, and, while many aspects of college life have changed drastically in the last thirty years, this one has only intensified.

As far as ability to choose the "right" roommate is concerned, this is a project constantly under consideration by every freshman dean's office that is really concerned about its charges. Some colleges let students choose their own roommates, allowing them to be responsible in this way for their own choices. A good many, however, try to make the best possible matches and will constantly refine the questionnaire which is sent out to incoming students about their habits ("Do you prefer a roommate who smokes or doesn't?"), their academic interests, enthusiasms, quirks ("Do you sleep with the window open or shut?"), their degree of neatness, and, in general, their level of tolerance. In the up-to-date college, these responses are matched by computer, and although checked by hand to make sure that no egregious electronic error has mated the wrong couple, the matching is not much more successful than it ever was when a colleague and I would spend two weeks of a summer with a table full of freshman folders, reading through to find suitable matches for roommate combinations.

The time it takes to find "suitable" roommates is not worth the effort, however, says one psychologist. Dr. John Finger, who has spent considerable time in research validating his personality profile questionnaire, says that the reason that roommates tend to perform in pairs is that "likes" will group together. An underachiever who finds himself in a group of students who believe in academic achievement and who practice their beliefs will want to move out. He will then search around for the other underachievers he may find in his group. This theory in effect says that students do not really change much in their attitudes during the college experience; that the high school guidance teacher is not being realistic who says fondly; "Once away from home and faced with the challenges of college life, John will respond to the challenge." Some tigers do change their stripes, many do not; and the general results make Dr. Finger discouragingly accurate. Nevertheless, I have known too many students who performed vastly better than we had ever predicted and who attributed their success to a steady roommate in the freshman year not to be taken with the Gardner theory.

How a parent can assay the quality of a roommate's steadiness on that fatal first day of freshman week, or how a parent can decide if his child is the strong or weak, dominant or subservient member of the combination is not a technique now known; or at least any attempt to do this would be too cumbersome to practice in the reception line on opening Sunday. Therefore, the only recourse the parents have is to hope and assume that the college has done a good job, and to have faith in the steadiness of their own child. It is with the others, those for whom the formula did not work, that we are concerned.

When a student flunks out of college, all of his doubts are suddenly resolved. The dangling uncertainty about courses, whether he could finish the four books required for a course in the twelve hours remaining, all these and more are resolved finally and completely, if not neatly, by academic expulsion. Once the dean has wielded the ax separating a student from his college, John or Mary is able to see clearly all of the reasons for failure and dismissal and equally easily to plan to correct the faults; they feel immediately they are ready to return.

As soon as the committee with which the dean operates has served its notice of dismissal, the classic countermove is for the student to make an appointment with the dean or to write him a letter stating the reasons for the recent academic debacle and making protestations of renewed effort. Occasionally, there are some few letters which the dean and the committee feel hold water—in cases where family problems, illness, or some other unexpected disruption has disturbed the student's academic pattern so severely that he has gone to pieces. However, this seldom works, because committees of academic standing seldom act on one poor semester; they must be convinced that a student has started a trend of academic failure which is so clear that a break in the usual cycle is needed in order to put him back in the right track. Academic dismissal, it should be clearly understood, is not a punitive measure, but a therapeutic measure; the student who is academically sick is removed to regain whatever it is that he needs to be successful.

More often than not, attitude rather than ability or background is the most important consideration for academic success. It is very unlikely that the feeling of euphoria that follows release from academic pressure is anything more than temporary. It is my experience that students who have been dismissed always want to return too soon, convinced, as long as they are outside the academic rat race, that they can survive in it.

In general, colleges wisely decide that a space of time, at least six months to a year, elapse before a student should resume his place in that academic society. Thus, if he is dismissed in February he might be readmitted in September, but the greater likelihood is that a full year of regeneration and maturing will be required before admission is granted again after petition. Policies like this automatically take care of an overoptimistic outlook on the part of the student, but even here caution is advised simply because many colleges have strong views on the double flunk-out.

That is, when a student, for whatever reason, is dismissed from a college, the odds are probably in favor of his reinstatement after a reasonable period of time. Nothing, of course, is ever promised by the deans, because uncertainty itself has therapeutic qualities which speed the cure, thus no one student or parent can be absolutely sure of reinstatement because each case is unique. But the academic community, as recent events have underscored, is a remarkably forgiving group of people, by nature disinclined to let former mistakes be held against anyone forever. Therefore, the odds are in favor of readmission *once.* However, after erring and straying once, if a student who has been readmitted commits the same academic sins again and flunks out, it is usually a fatal error; the second dismissal is permanent.

A few last observations about flunking out: the longer a student stays out, the better his chances are to be successful on his return; the later in his college career that a student is dismissed for academic reasons, the greater is the chance he will be ultimately successful. These two thoughts are based on our experience in the Dean's Office at Brown, but seem to be universal rather than institutional. The first observation is virtually self-explanatory. The second is true probably because students who are emotionally so unprepared for college that they botch the job from the beginning are likely to have more lasting or more difficult problems than those who do well enough at the beginning but then trickle down and ultimately out. My final thought in this vein is neither novel nor remarkable, but unquestionably true in my experience; the male student who has had academic troubles and who gets married almost invariably does very well indeed. Some of the most remarkable turnabouts I have ever seen have been the product of this combination; it is much more effective than counseling, fine teaching, or interesting courses.

Just often enough to make it interesting, I talk with men and women, some of them comfortably middle-aged, some quite young, who get bitten by the education bug too late to consider any of the usual processes. In some cases they dropped out of high school; in other cases their education was wildly erratic because of wars, or displacement from one country to another, or simply because of poverty. The recent drive of many colleges to recruit promising black students has brought almost as many cases of black men with incomplete or interrupted educations to the fore as there have been black high school applicants.

The burning questions for these people, once they have made the decision to become reinvolved in education are: Is it possible to pick up the threads so late? What kind of a college will have me? How do I find out more?

The first word I would offer is one of reassurance. No one in college administration, who should be there, will laugh at anyone's educational ambitions. Education is like religion to most teachers and administrators, and nothing is more exciting to anyone in it than to find another convert.

The sources of information are many. First, every local high school has a counseling staff available (on appointment, and with due regard to the fact that counselors in high schools and colleges are overworked) for consultation. It is sensible, before going to see the counselor to have in mind what the final goal is that makes education necessary. It is obvious that an established businessman who wants a college education and a degree to satisfy himself has different needs from the highly efficient office manager who suddenly decided, when her children were grown and educated, that she wanted to go to college to be qualified to teach primary school. The high school counselor, even if he has had little experience with the specific phenomenon of the late-blooming convert, can offer useful advice on where to go for testing and what colleges are likely to be receptive to a candidate with unusual or incomplete credentials.

College admission officers can be a very useful source of

information, particularly about their own institution and its requirements, but also about the means the prospective student has of learning about himself. In many cases the colleges themselves run testing offices for their own students, and are willing, for a fee which will cover the administrative costs, to administer batteries of diagnostic tests.

The whole question of tests is likely to strike terror into the heart of anyone about to reenter education, yet the fact is that, making allowances for the uncertainties of any objective test ever developed, they can tell a great deal about anyone if taken in the right spirit and interpreted properly. However, the terror is usually engendered because "I haven't been in a class for five years" and the speaker is sure that he will not be able to compete with students who go to class every day. This fear is most likely to be justified in the tests which nearly every student takes as part of the college admission process—either the College Boards, or the ACT. The Scholastic Aptitude Test of the College Entrance Examination Board is designed to test two major skills—first, a verbal ability, including reading speed and comprehension, vocabulary strengths, and, to a certain extent, the ability to evaluate abstract ideas; second, quantitative reasoning, which depends almost entirely on arithmetical and other mathematical means of problem-solving.

In measuring verbal ability in a test of this sort, the taker of the test assumes that a person returning after a long absence will be at a considerable disadvantage in competition with a student who has had daily classes in English, vocabulary word lists and drills, and all of the other forms of "preparation" which many schools supply. What the late student forgets is that verbal skill is an ability in almost constant use, and that it grows and develops with age and experience. Young boys (more often than girls) are embarrassed by any display of verbal precocity, at least in this country, and so very little premium is set on the simple ability to express oneself clearly, precisely, and gracefully. The "late" student has probably been in business, or at least in the world, trying to convey his own ideas and understand those of others. What is more, if he is really interested in education, he must have done a great deal of reading on his own. All of these will contribute considerably to verbal skills and will be reflected in any objective tests. Since verbal skills are those which are the most important for survival in college—unless, of course, the student is in an engineering or science program—a good part of the admission office evaluation would be on the verbal side of the Scholastic Aptitude Test, rather than on the math or quantitative side.

The other major college entrance test which is so widespread as to be standard is the ACT—the American College Testing program. Essentially, the chief difference between the SAT and ACT, except for the constituencies they serve and the fact that they are active rivals, is that the basic test of the ACT is divided not into two, but into four major areas, English, social studies, mathematics, and natural science, each section of which is scored and then summarized in an overall score. Whereas the SAT presumably measures raw ability in the same way as IQ tests measure ability, so the ACT measures ability with a greater emphasis on achievement—how that ability has been used. For this reason the student who has educated himself, but has taken few formal classroom courses of the standard variety, may have less luck with the ACT, except for the fact that the divisions of the test would show up strengths and weaknesses more accurately than the Scholastic Aptitude Test.

In any case, the purpose of the tests is to reassure the appropriate powers that the prospective student is genuinely capable of undertaking college work. More important, it seems to me, the student must persuade himself that what he really is interested in is the process of education, rather than the diploma. The questions, pro and con, of how genuinely interested the great bulk of current college students are in *education,* in contrast to their interest in the opportunities which the diploma makes possible, is not the point. When an ex-commercial-curriculum business woman decides that she needs an education, she owes it to herself to sample the process ahead of time, before disrupting her life by quitting her job to attend college full-time or disrupting her bank account to pay tuition for something she discovers she does not want.

Although every would-be student has to make his own decisions, whenever I am consulted on the question of going to college late or returning to college after having started a family or business, I try to refer the applicant to someone who has already gone through this process. In this way all the problems likely to come up can be aired.

About ten years ago, a successful businessman came into my office to ask about admission to Brown as an undergraduate. Here was a man of culture, intelligence, and energy who ran a number of small but successful enterprises well, but who wanted the college experience. We gave him the chance, and he was superb at it—not only as a student, but *with* the students as well. It was a struggle, though, and half way through his third year of running his businesses *and* going to Brown as an undergraduate, he had a heart attack and was forced to suspend his academic activities. Some time later I referred to Mr. Livesey a local man who wanted to give up his business to return to college so he could go to medical school. In the process of notifying our former star student that he might be asked for advice, I talked with Mrs. Livesey, who had strong views about the problems which going to college in middle age had caused her husband—and it became quite apparent that a good deal of intra-family strain had been involved. Incidentally, I suspect Mrs. Livesey got to the wife of the would-be doctor. He was never heard from again.

In order to test the genuineness of his academic interest

there are a number of things the future student can do before ever making formal inquiries. Perhaps the most important is to take a strong critical look at his own reading habits. More than any other two things, college requires a great deal of reading and writing, and the reading must be done before the writing. The aspirant must ask himself if he reads for pleasure, to what extent, and what sort of book he reads.

If he finds (and he must be really honest) that the bulk of his reading is newspapers and sport magazines, he should be wary, but not discouraged. If he finds reading of any sort to be painful, slow, or boring, then he is in potential trouble as a college student. The best prospects, of course, are those for whom reading is a major source of relaxation and satisfaction.

Not only is it important to enjoy reading (or if not "enjoy"' it, at least be willing to undertake a great deal of it), but it is also important to have read a good deal before attempting college. This is particularly true of the non-college prep student who decides later that college is what he wants. Because of the nature of their program, the students in college have a background of general knowledge that comes chiefly from reading, a familiarity with names and places that show up in class discussions, papers, tests, and so on. For the student whose background information may be sparse, an important corrective measure is to acquire reading as a habit, something to do each day. To acquire the habit, reading should be made pleasant and should involve reading books which are legitimately good as literature, but not necessarily troublesome to read. Put another way, the student can lure himself into reading more by reading the most enjoyable sort of books while acquiring the habit.

Another way to assess one's interest in or enjoyment of academic work is to sample it in the small doses offered as evening or extension classes by most colleges, and in the service, by the correspondence courses or extension courses set up by the services themselves. In general these kinds of academic offerings are somewhat watered down. They are more inclined to present the course information sugar-coated, without making any serious demands on the student. But, although a student cannot make any very valid judgments about his future success as a college student based on how well he does in extension courses, he can get the flavor of what is required, and make some fairly valid guesses about his reaction to the academic world.

If all the indicators point in the right direction—if it seems that he has the interest, the willingness to work, the means by which he can repair his background— then what next? I have emphasized the verbal or literary side of late college preparedness somewhat heavily. However, if the student wants science, engineering, premedical, or any similar fields he must have preparation in mathematics, physics, and chemistry. Again the high school counselor becomes the best source of information because courses of this sort are best taught in high school—either as adult extension or in the regular classes. The former is unquestionably easier, academically and socially, but the latter will probably produce better results and give the returnee a better idea of what kind of students he will be up against. However, let the high school counselor decide the better arrangement for remedial work.

Assuming there is willingness and ability, what specific vocational direction should the late student take? Although they are not perfect, an extensive battery of tests administered by a trained psychologist can tell a great deal about what kind of education and how much might be undertaken, but no survey of abilities can measure the motivation of the student.

An interesting case in point is young John Schaeffer, who limped through the vocational courses in high school and

found himself unhappily working in a factory. Feeling a
need for training, he applied to a local junior college for
technical training in electronics, but fell almost by accident
into some liberal arts courses in which he did so well that
his teachers urged him to switch his goals. When he came to
me to ask to take courses at Brown as a special student, I
suggested a complete battery of tests to try to straighten out
his thinking before he plunged too deeply in any one
direction. The results were most interesting; they showed a
strong interest in the social studies and the humanities, and
considerably less interest in the technical areas he was
studying. Yet in his post-testing interview, John was reluctant to abandon what seemed to him the safe and practical
training in technical studies, for the nebulous uncertainty
of liberal arts, in spite of the test results and the fact that he
was somewhat interested in liberal arts. In this same way,
many people refuse to recognize and develop their
strengths, because they feel that some other form of training or development is more desirable. In my experience,
this occurs most frequently with premedical students who
have no real interest or ability in science, but whose
families are pressing for a prestige profession. In the same
way, sons of machinists often want to be engineers. Liberal
art studies are disguised as "pre-law" or as "business" in
order to give the proper vocational slant, but, notwithstanding, a student who is being pushed into something he
doesn't understand or want will have problems of motivation.

The skilled counselor, therefore, not only must interpret
tests properly, but also must find ways to tell the client
what his abilities are and what they might be best used for,
even if they are in conflict with what the client thinks he
now wants, or what his family now wants. This is particularly true for the late starting student. If he has never been
motivated before to use his brain power, it is only the desire

to complete a course of action which is meaningful to him that will motivate him. If the motivation runs counter to his abilities, the skilled counselor has the delicate job of transferring that energy from one direction to another.

One special problem counselors run into is the student so deeply interested in the arts, or philosophy, or "important" literature that he finds the school work he is expected to do meaningless and his compatriots in school immature, shallow, materialistic, and, therefore, completely intolerable. Just the reverse of the student who does poorly in high school because he is not interested in intellectual pursuits, this student does poorly precisely because he is interested. In many ways he seems to be a symbol of the times.

In my own mind, I am not quite sure whether this is a form of adolescent restlessness, or a quite subtle form of rebellion and attention-seeking. A highly intelligent and quite reasonable father called me recently to ask that his son be a special student at Brown in philosophy courses. The boy had dropped out of his high school in the tenth grade and had been a dropout for a year. He was under the care of a psychiatrist, the father told me, who had suggested that the challenge of college courses and the stimulating competition of college students would encourage the boy back to the normal course of action. I disagreed, feeling that a highly selective college should not get itself into the business of providing therapeutic courses, lest we become the refuge of every psychiatrist on the East Coast.

The father was most reasonable and saw the validity of this argument. "I doubted you would say yes," he said, "but I was willing to ask, because the boy is obviously suffering, and I want to help him if I can."

It is difficult to say what the best course of action is for this kind of situation, which shows up frequently. My guess is that the reasons for it are unquestionably family attitudes that have been developing for fifteen years, and no one course of action is likely to change anything so established. My own authoritarian feeling is that a boy like this lacks discipline, either external or internal, and has not been willing to hold himself to standards set by others, or more importantly, those set by himself. The cure? Growing up, being made to assume some responsibilities for his own actions, and patience mixed with a willingness to say no on the part of the parents.

There are no easy answers, no one right way and one wrong way to establish educational plans or to correct mistakes. Parents want so much and know so little, but what they usually do not realize is that seldom does anyone else know more.

VIII

How to Find out More about Your Child

THERE IS SCARCELY AN AD-
mission officer alive who has not been told by a proud
mother, with fond regret, that "Sam, I'm afraid, is an
underachiever." The translation of this to the auditor who
has had experience is as clear as it is familiar. What Mrs.
Witherspoon is really saying is: "Thanks to genetics, Sam is
quite as bright as his parents, but because of our affluence,
he has never had to work."

For some reason, the possession of unused brains is
always more appealing than the "overachiever" pattern,
which combines hard work with low test scores. The
implications of "overachiever" are equally clear, and I have
always felt slightly uncomfortable in the presence of a
student who announces that he is an overachiever. He, too,
is making a well-worn statement in terms of educational
euphemisms: "I work hard, and I get good grades, but the
test scores have branded me as not very bright." What is
more, in many cases, the student has made an accurate
assessment of himself. Not infrequently I have observed

that the overachiever, the low-tester with good grades, is a hard-working, worrisome student without much sense of humor and a great concern about grades for their own sake. However, I can also say that this has not been the case often enough, so that I remain as confused about what really measures ability as any of the authors of articles who decry the use of standardized tests.

Before the turn of the twentieth century, the student who had good grades was bright and the student who did not was stupid, and the special qualifications of over- and under-achievers had not yet been invented.

Although the measurement of human differences had fascinated scientists from early in the nineteenth century, the idea of finding some way to measure intelligence did not take shape until 1905. Two Frenchmen, Alfred Binet and Théodore Simon, developed a test to determine which children should be given the advantages of education. The Stanford-Binet Intelligence Test, still in use today, is a much revised but still recognizable descendant of this pioneer effort.

Since that time, intelligence tests have proliferated greatly. The development of mass testing, of "pencil and paper" tests, was an outgrowth of World War I, when the mass influx of large numbers of untrained soldiers made it necessary to develop some way to assess how best to train them. Now every schoolchild expects to be tested for intelligence, for reading levels, for the amount of Latin or math he has learned, whether he should be a stockbroker or a carpenter, a musician or a nurse. Psychological tests tell school officials about the mental health of students and various aptitude tests are designed to predict how well a student will do in college, in law, medical, or business school; subsequently, many companies use testing devices to see how well Joe will sell beer or shoes if he is hired.

Because the tests have become so numerous and because so many of the agencies of everyday life seem to place so much importance on the ability of tests to predict how humans will behave, it is almost inevitable that there has been a reaction against them.

W. H. Whyte devoted a full chapter of *The Organization Man,* his insightful book on the social structure of big business and its employees, to the ways to beat the aptitude test given to a new or prospective member of the organization.

Indeed, by now every schoolboy has been so accustomed to tests of every sort from the first grade on that he is likely to refuse to take them seriously. A favorite indoor sport of young students is to load the vocational tests in some direction other than their own, giving absurd answers to questions simply because the direction the test is taking seems so obvious or ridiculous to them.

(The test makers indignantly deny that they are obvious in their intentions. An acquaintance of mine who has devised a personality inventory has a number of items which are signals that the taker is cheating on the test. "For example," he said in explaining the system to me, "I have a question: 'If you see a piece of paper on the street, would you pick it up?' Clearly the answer is no, because no one does. If they answer yes, they are trying to play with the test." Even five years ago I thought his assurance about how humans behaved was smug, but now that so many of us are actively concerned about litter on the streets, I wonder if he has rewritten some of the items on his test.)

Notwithstanding the reactions against tests and particularly their mass administration, they continue to be given and used, and are in fact highly useful in the majority of cases. It is obvious that school systems must rely on tests given in large numbers, to large roomfuls of students at a time; individual testing is an economic impossibility.

This should be no problem in a perfect testing situation, where the students who take the tests are fully aware of how important they are, where they have no physical or physiological disabilities which would impair performance on tests which depend on motor skill and speed for proper completion, and where their maturity is such that they are not distracted by other students or other stimuli likely to result from a roomful of students. Since this situation is unlikely to occur, mass testing, good in theory, generates numbers of exceptions which may or may not be recognized.

For these reasons, school counselors, from those who counsel the first grade on, should realize the shortcomings of tests administered on a mass basis, and be ready to acknowledge that there are some bright children who do not operate at peak efficiency in a room filled with restless students, or that the age of thirteen is very unlikely to produce a boy interested in a multiple choice examination, or that some children with quick minds have physical impairments which prevent their operating efficiently on timed tests.

These are only a few of the possibilities that form a framework within which mass testing and its results must be judged. But it is also true that too many parents, anxious for better results for their children, try to find excuses when none are needed.

All of this raises the pertinent question about the most common and the most used of the school testing instruments, the IQ test. What is the IQ, how is it derived, what does it mean, how should the school interpret it, and how much should a parent know about this score?

First of all, the IQ (intelligence quotient) test is the result of the intelligence tests which Binet and his successors have developed over the years. It is designed to test the capacity to learn, the innate ability.

Purists about the word intelligence have pointed out that there are many kinds of intelligence, and the intelligence test only measures that kind of intelligence that it was designed to measure. For example, mechanical ability is a kind of intelligence, and there are aptitude tests which will measure this. However, a student who scores quite high on this kind of test is not necessarily gifted with the kind of intelligence which he might need to be a doctor or even an engineer.

In the same way, even "straight" intelligence tests which are designed to test ability in a varied academic program are likely to be skewed according to the interests or the concerns of the designer of the test. On this basis, a test designer who felt that the primary ingredient of intelligence was verbal skill (and many of the testers do) would build a test which relied heavily on this ability. If he felt that quantitative reasoning (math) was more important, he would build a test which reflected this.

The scoring of the tests is based on a comparison of what the designers of the test originally think is a normal number of right answers for any one age group with the answers which the individual subject makes; the validity of this assumption is then tested by a complicated sampling process and statistical analysis. The child of twelve who answers all the questions it is expected a child of twelve can answer correctly is considered to have a mental age of twelve as well. Dividing the actual, chronological age of the child in question into the mental age which he has as measured by the test, results in the "intelligence quotient," or IQ. Another child of twelve who answers the questions correctly at the sixteen-year level gets a higher score— twelve divided into sixteen, which results in a number of 1.33, rather than 1.00 as in the first case. The decimal is dropped, and it becomes the familiar three figure number which so mesmerizes parents and teachers.

The statistical procedure just described was the earliest basis for the IQ. Now there are more sophisticated methods to determine it: the mean of the norming group is 100 and the standard deviations from the norming group define the degree of variation from that central point. The first definition, although considered unsophisticated by the standards of those who now construct statistical designs, is close enough to be informative without being confusing.

Although the most reliable tests have been backed by careful research and statistical analysis, it is still true that the questions which the testers feel should be answered by a twelve-year-old are not an absolute index, and even if chosen with extreme care are a possible source of error in determining IQ. For example, if the questions are harder for a twelve-year-old than they should be, a normally bright child will be able to answer fewer questions correctly at her age level, and her IQ will suffer accordingly. If they are too easy, the scores will be inflated. To offset this possibility many statistical procedures are used to test the reliability of any broadly administered test. Nevertheless, differences remain in the makeup and the direction of the various intelligence tests, and these in turn show up as score variations.

For example, at the maximum score level of five widely used group intelligence tests (Otis Quick Scoring, California Mental Maturity, Kuhlman Anderson, Lorge Thorndike, and Pintener General Ability) the scores ranged from 140 to 151, and these scores presumably represented the same segment of the population. At the middle of the test, however, the differences are negligible, ranging from 100 to 102.

This point, although minor, is worth making only to show that the IQ is not a rigid or absolute score, that it varies slightly from test to test. Moreover, although the IQ is popularly presumed to be a standard, unvarying measurement of a person's intelligence, it is quite possible to record the growth of ability (or more properly, the growth of what ability the tests measure) as a child matures. This has been most clearly and interestingly demonstrated by the experiments of Dr. Benjamin Bloom, who tested young black children brought from the stultifying atmosphere of the rural south into an urban setting. Not only was there an increase in the measured IQ of these children, but the increase was so clear that Dr. Bloom was able to predict the amount of increase with considerable accuracy.

This clearly indicates that one important aspect of intelligence as we know it is the environment in which the child is raised. The heredity versus environment argument has, of course, been fought furiously for many years, and the resulting truce has settled on a compromise: both are important, but environment seems to be particularly important in the formative period of a child's life, his preschool experiences.

The extent to which the early experiences of a child within his home and family affect his ability to learn is being studied heavily now in graduate schools of education because of the importance it has on planning education for the urban and rural poor. What is emerging is of interest to all parents, for it is becoming apparent that a great many of the abilities and attitudes that make a good student in our schools have been acquired by the student from his home environment by the time he enters school. This is certainly one of the reasons that good students are often not ruined or even adversely affected by bad schools, and conversely why good schools do not necessarily make good students.

Undoubtedly this early training will be the subject of measurement someday, and schools will be able to use it for the prediction of classroom success, but in the meantime they are still dependent on variations of Binet's tests which were designed for the same purpose.

One of the greatest dangers in using any instrument of psychological measurement is the possibility of its being misinterpreted. Test scores alone mean nothing without the proper interpretation. It is probably for this reason that IQ scores have been considered as such highly confidential information that schools did not publish them to students or parents, and circulation of this information even within the school is likely to be limited.

The original reasons for this are clear and reasonable; a

major danger of objective scoring is that the test scores will be taken as absolutes rather than indications, and that the information will be abused in various ways by parents and students.

Parents, on the other hand, quite properly want to know as much about their children as they can and will often try to get the school to give them what they consider to be rightfully theirs. School counselors, concerned about literal minded parents and how they might put the information to use, have resisted, but have been forced to work out some compromises as a result of continuing pressures.

One of these is the grading of IQ scores on an A, B, or C basis. For example, the school might describe an A student as one who has very good potential, who should be taking a demanding program, who should consider college and graduate school, and who should easily be able to meet both scholastic and extracurricular demands.

The B student might be described as "capable of college study, depending largely on the degree of his motivation. Capable, but not brilliant."

The C student falls in the middle, a "student who should probably not undertake a four year college without careful counseling. A general course in high school, with perhaps some vocational training seems the most appropriate course of action."

The D student is "slow to learn, and finds school a difficult place. Educational plans, except for continuing vocational training, should probably not go beyond the high school level."

This scale, of course, takes into account only the potential learning capacity of a student as determined by testing and says nothing about past performance, student and parental attitudes, and a variety of other forces which a skilled counselor would take into account. However, it does provide parents with information which can be useful, without at the same time giving parents the means of making minute and meaningless comparisons of Jimmy's ability versus Brenda's.

With this information, the parent can then discover for himself whether Jimmy is discharging his academic obligations in accordance with his ability and to his parents' expectations for the child's success. It is here that the hazy line has to be drawn between what parents expect of a child and what the child's ability can reasonably be expected to produce.

Parents, I have discovered through much exposure, are seldom able to make dispassionate evaluations about their own children. Quite recently a mother was explaining to me that, while her son's record in school had been less than remarkable, the boy was, in fact, quite bright.

"That is, allowing some leeway for a mother's natural prejudice," I suggested with a smile.

There was no smile in return. She leaned toward me in a manner which suggested that I had been faintly insulting and said earnestly: "Oh, that's not just my opinion. A number of his teachers have told me that Neal is very bright."

Neal was a student in a private school of uncertain financing, and his IQ was about 115, which made him intelligent and potentially college material, but certainly not "very bright." Since Neal's mother had probably been supported in her own maternal view of her son by his overly enthusiastic teachers, she cannot be blamed very much. However, it is just such maternal (or paternal) pride that makes many teachers want to avoid this area of discussion entirely, and probably not a few of a teacher's protestations about the propriety of revealing IQ scores stem from a fear of having to injure parental pride.

This is particularly true when the scores are bad and the ambitions of the family are high. Many schools have found to their dismay that parents will not believe or will not abide by the results of the tests.

And sometimes, the schools are right.

But as a veteran watcher of parents, I was interested and astonished to have a friend of mine who specializes in educational problems of children tell me that it was more often the sensitive parent (rather than the child's teacher, for example) who had correctly refused to believe the results of mass testing, or poor performance in school as a measure of his child's ability.

"The tip-off is uneveness," says this highly experienced counselor. "The child who has problems in school learning to read or write, or who seems to have difficulty in staying still long enough to learn anything is often written off by teachers as stupid. As the child encounters failure, he is likely to appear increasingly stupid to his teacher. But at home, he has learned to tell time faster than any of the other children, or he has acquired a fund of information on a subject that interests him, and his parents see that he isn't the hopeless case they have been told he is."

Understandably, if teachers see a child who has low scores on standard ability tests and who also seems to have troubles in learning, the two observations reinforce each other, and in a modern school—probably overcrowded, and geared, in any case, to mass testing and teaching—there is no real reason to expect a teacher to do otherwise than to assume the student is indeed a "poor learner."

Faced with this frustrating situation, what can a parent do to bolster his conviction that his child is better than the school thinks he is? Certainly one of the first answers is private individual testing. The first intelligence tests were designed to be administered on a one-to-one basis, and it was only the advance of science in World War I that made mass testing necessary and possible.

Interestingly enough, one of the most important individually administered intelligence tests for children is a direct descendant of the original Binet tests, modified and improved over the years. Lewis Terman, a pioneer in the development of tests in this country and on the faculty of Stanford University, brought out the first major revision in 1916, and subsequent editions of the Stanford-Binet have continued to hold their place as one of the most effective tools for the individual testing of children.

The other most widely used test is the Wechsler. This is a more flexible test than the Stanford-Binet in that it provides more diagnostic information. The Binet provides only an IQ score, whereas the Wechsler provides verbal, perform-ance, and total scores, so that it can be used for illiterates, for children (or adults) with language difficulties, and for subjects from impoverished backgrounds. Originally, the Wechsler was designed for administration to adults; the Wechsler Intelligence Scale for Children was developed subsequently. A further refinement on this has been a version of the test for preprimary children (WPPSI); which is considered by many psychologists to be better in the testing of young children than the Stanford-Binet.

Tests which perform sensitive tasks like this must be administered by skilled psychologists of a kind which few schools can afford any more than they can afford individual testing. The trained eye can sense a response behind the hesitation of the tested child, where the pencil and paper answer sheet remains blank in the face of a child's indeci-sion, confusion, or hesitation.

Generally, psychologists equipped to administer in-dividual intelligence tests are also available for other kinds of testing and counseling. They are usually listed in the classified telephone directory under "Psychologist" and quite often the professional qualifications are also listed— "Ph.D. in Clinical Psychology" or "Diplomate in Clinical Psychology." As is the case with physicians, the relation-ship between patient and practitioner is quite as important as the professional man's diploma and where he earned it. On that basis, an anxious parent who is looking for more information about his child might well ask either his pediatrician or the central guidance office of the school department for the names of psychologists they have dealt with.

It is perhaps unfair to the profession of psychologists to enter a word of caution here. Because of the extensive availability of mass testing in all our school systems, the parents who turn to psychologists are usually concerned or anxious, almost by definition. The psychologist, therefore, has been dealing with parents who, in most cases, want to be reassured that their children are not hopeless. The psychologist's report is likely to be written with this situation in mind.

This does not mean that a licensed clinical psychologist would give a parent misleading information just to avoid difficulty or to smooth over an unpleasantness. It does mean that most of the reports which I have seen have emphasized strengths and have been tactful about weaknesses. The important point to make is that the parent must understand realistically what the report is saying before going off to the school to demand that Abigail's section in English be changed to the college preparatory course.

What should a parent do who discovers he has a child whose ability is far greater than the school's measurement or the child's own academic production? If the child is doing well in school and the chief problem has been to get the school to realize that he is not an overachiever who may well be overextended in a difficult academic program, there should be little trouble. The information which the psychologist and the individual testing have provided should be enough for the guidance department of the school. Since the information which the psychologist has acquired about your child is both technical and professional, it is likely that he will want to convey the results of his testing directly to the school authorities.

But what about the child who is having trouble in school and who comes up surprisingly well on individual tests, just as parental intuition said he would? What course should a parent follow here? Although there is no single answer, the parent must realize that if his child has had difficulties in school despite good ability, he is likely to have a problem which the local school may not be able to solve. The problem may be neurological, psychological, or physiological. That is, your child may be suffering from physical impairment (faulty vision or hearing), minimal brain damage (which occurs frequently and need not show up in the familiar symptoms associated with serious brain injury), or psychological maladjustment. The testing psychologist would be able to give you some assistance in the last area, and suggest whatever seems necessary. In the case of the first two possibilities, your own pediatrician may have the answers, but probably you should have him refer you to a pediatric neurologist, a physician who specializes in the many small things that can go wrong with the growing child's intricate machinery, and which in many cases cannot be detected except by the expert observer.

Consultations with these new sets of experts may result in special schools which are geared to take care of neural and physiological blocks to learning, or in special training to overcome neuro-muscular problems, or in special counseling. All of this will be designed to enable your child to enjoy success in school, for success breeds success.

While the initial visit to the psychologist for testing may cost in the neighborhood of a hundred dollars (prices will vary according to neighborhoods, parts of the country, and the extent of testing), subsequent visits to specialists will, of course, come to a great deal more, but the successful schooling of your child is worth it. In some cases, if your child has an unusual problem, the local school system will pay his tuition at a special school for the length of time that he needs it. Again, consult with the guidance department of your school system before and after your investigations.

Any parents who begin to investigate their child's intelligence will be told by counselors that intelligence takes many forms. That which is usually tested in schools, and which results in an IQ, is the measurement of capacity to learn, particularly in an academic situation. However, as the child becomes old enough to begin to plan his own future, the other kinds of intelligence he may have become increasingly important, , and these will show up in tests of vocational guidance and selection.

Many public high schools administer these tests to their students as part of a general interest and ability inventory, which has become a standard part of the school guidance procedures. For the child or parent who wants a more specific and exhaustive examination of abilities, private, individual testing is available just as it is for intelligence testing.

Like intelligence tests, aptitude or interest inventories measure certain skills or enthusiasms, such as ability to memorize a sequence of numbers, or to look at a diagram of a piece of machinery to decide whether it will work, or what way the wheels will go. Some other forms of the same type of test will ask the subject to decide whether he would prefer most to walk in the woods, go to a concert, or see an exhibit of new inventions. The intent of the questions is clear; by establishing the preferences and intuitions of the subject, he can then be guided to a vocation which has an established pattern close to his own.

Like all testing instruments, this sounds more direct and to the point than it really is. Taken at face value, a student who is beset by indecision about what he wants to do need only take an occupational inventory to be told what he should do. And for some, it can be that simple. For example, a friend of mine took an exhaustive regimen of aptitude tests while still in college, his avowed aim at that time being medicine. The tests told him that he did not have the finger dexterity to become a surgeon, and that his most probable bent would be scientific administration.

Twenty years later that was exactly the field he found himself in.

While it is probably unusual to have a test make so precise a fit of talents, the history of these tests is very encouraging on the grounds of their predictive accuracy. An extensive study of the results of interest and vocational inventories taken by the Air Force during World War II and followed up thirteen years later showed that eventual occupations and the recommendations of the guidance tests substantially paralleled each other. What the tests were unable to predict was the degree of success in the field selected. For example, if a student takes an occupational inventory and the scores indicate strongly that he should go into medicine, that subject will not necessarily turn out a more successful doctor than another student whose scores were less definitive.

Another more recent study published by Brown University in 1970 says substantially the same thing. Dr. Everard Nicholson examined the results of the two interest inventories administered to the immediate postwar classes entering Brown from 1946 to 1948. The results of both the Occupational Interest Inventory and the Strong Vocational Inventory Blank confirmed that the score results of the freshmen tested were logically associated with the eventual occupational groups of those tested, with one exception— personnel managers.

One of the major goals of the Brown study was to measure how well the tests predicted the success of graduates after college. Again, occupational inventories were not good predictors of future success. (The best predictor of future success for Brown turned out to be high school recommendations.)

As is the case with the intelligence tests, the tests administered by your school system are mass tests. Individual interest and ability inventories on an exhaustive scale are available at testing centers in large cities, again often administered by a practicing clinical psychologist. Privately administered tests will be more precise, more expensive, and more accurate, but what is perhaps more important, they probably will be taken more seriously by the youthful subject. Individual counseling and recommendations are a part of the function of a private testing service.

An inevitable part of many students' lives today is the college entrance test. Depending on his location in the country or the kind of college he plans to go to, the college-bound student will take one of two major programs which have dominated the field for some time—the College Entrance Examination Board or the American College Testing program. Both of these are so universally known that it is probably not necessary to explain their purpose, except to explain the differences between the two.

They are competing organizations. The College Board is older and, having been founded by a group of famous old colleges in the East to standardize the entrance examinations to those colleges, it has been more oriented to the private college. (It is interesting that one of the founding colleges of the College Board, Dartmouth, did not require their examination as part of its admission requirements until about fifty years after the founding of the Board.) The College Board tests are divided into two main groups—the Scholastic Aptitude Test and the several Achievement Tests.

The Scholastic Aptitude Test is designed to measure a student's innate ability to study at the college level. It is divided into two sections, verbal and mathematical. A student's score on the first part depends on his reading and vocabulary skills; the second section tests quantitative reasoning skills.

The Achievement Tests are measures of learned knowledge in certain areas like physics, French, or European history. Whereas the Aptitude Test is a test of ability, the

Achievement Tests deal with how much a student has learned. Presumably a student with good ability and poor grades (the underachiever) will have good SAT scores, but will have comparatively poor Achievement scores. The overachiever should have the reverse pattern: good Achievement scores and a comparatively poor SAT score. In actuality, a good many students who have very good SAT scores and who do no work in school and hence get poor grades still manage to get decent achievement test scores, indicating that something is happening to the student, if only by osmosis.

The scoring of the College Board tests is so complicated that it seems to make no sense. The scale runs from 200 to 800 and 500 is the presumed midpoint for all of their tests. Actually the scale is more logical than it sounds, running in theory from 0 to 1,000. Because the incidence of scores below 200 or over 800 is very slight, the scale was cropped at either end by two hundred points.

Perhaps the most important point to understand about the College Board scoring system is that it is geared to a college-going population. That is, 500 is the midpoint on the scale and hence "average" for that population, but well above the average for the age group. It is dangerous to try to exchange one system of evaluation for another, but my guess would be that 500 on the SAT scale would be roughly equivalent to an Otis IQ of about 115. Assuming that every high school senior in America took the SAT, it is assumed that the average score would not be 500, but about 370. Anxious parents should interpret their children's scores in that light.

The American College Testing program is of much more recent vintage and was developed in response to the need of the great public universities of the Midwest for a test which could be rapidly scored and would be comparatively inexpensive to administer. Whereas the College Board tests were a combination of aptitude and achievement tests, the ACT are four tests of educational development and academic potential: Natural Science Reading, Social Science Reading, English Usage, and Mathematics Usage.

It is interesting to note that when it was first developed, the Scholastic Aptitude Test was expected to be a prime predictor of success in college, but experience proved to a great many colleges that the College Board Achievement tests were superior as predictive devices. It is perhaps for this reason that the ACT, which seems to lean quite heavily on the educational development side of testing (that is, on the achievement side), has been able to set up successful prediction equations for individual colleges based on the past experience of using ACT tests in that college. This is a remarkable piece of efficiency and only one of several ways that the ACT testing program can be of use to an institution in addition to providing a standard test score.

The scale of the ACT tests runs from 1 through 36, a scale as difficult to rationalize as the College Board's. The chief difference between the two is that the ACT scale covers a broader population, rather than just those going to college, which tends to make the scores for college-bound students somewhat inflated. Solid scores for admission to most colleges are in the low 20s.

Ranking the effectiveness of a school by using standardized tests to compare the achievements of the school's students against national norms is a game which few schools can resist, and most good suburban schools, in matching their students against the national medians, come out pretty well. This is particularly true of achievement tests in reading. National norms are set for levels of reading skill, and this is one of the standard tests schools commonly give to their children over the twelve year primary-secondary period with frequency. It is, of course, quite proper for a school to test out its comparative efficiency in teaching reading and all the other subjects. Typically, Lucinda arrives home with a report that although in the third grade, she reads at the sixth grade level or the tenth grade level. This is gratifying but not remarkable when it is considered that Lucinda has intelligent and reading parents and that she is being measured on a national scale. Probably the majority of the class in her school measured at better than the third grade level nationally.

On the other hand, if Lucinda reads at or below the grade level she is in chronologically, then her parents have real cause to look further into the situation, particularly if they have educational ambitions for her. While this is also true to a lesser degree of other achievement tests given to school children, reading tests are the most serious barometer of success or failure since the reading process so easily goes awry and proficiency in reading is so important.

Again, if there are any serious disparities between the parents' view of the child and her school record or test results, they should be discussed with the school.

So far our discussion of abilities and their measurements has centered around what happens to the school or college age child. Is it possible for adults, whose abilities might reasonably be considered hardened, to be measured? The answer, of course, is yes.

Interest and ability batteries—including psychological and attitudinal testing as well—are given frequently by business firms as a regular part of a job application procedure. Will Joe make a good district manager? Does Tom have enough aggressiveness to be a really successful salesman? In fact, the Wechsler intelligence test which is so useful for individual testing of school age children (particularly for students in their teens) was adapted from a test originally designed to measure the intelligence of adults.

One of the most interesting of adult intelligence scales is one developed by Lewis Terman as part of his study of gifted children. As his gifted children grew up, were educated, and took their place in society, Terman came to the conclusion that a great part of their ability lay in verbalizing highly abstract concepts. Out of this grew the

Concept Mastery Test, an extremely complicated, highly sophisticated vocabulary examination which is designed to be taken on an untimed basis and which measures the tested adult against lawyers, physicians, Ph.D.s, and other highly educated groups. It is rather like the weekly crossword puzzle in *The New York Times,* or Double-Crostics; if you happen to like that sort of thing, it can be a lot of fun.

Sources of these and other tests are the private testing programs set up by clinical psychologists or companies which make a specialty of psychological testing and guidance. Less expensive, and probably quite as effective, are the public programs which the Veterans Administration runs and those which are available through the public educational system—i.e., either the adult education division of your school system or the public college nearest you which specializes in education courses and training teachers. Again, the best source of information is likely to be the guidance department of your school system.

For those who enjoy taking tests such as these, a session of finding out more about yourself may be worthwhile and even fun. There is probably a cause and effect, or reward and reinforcement relationship at work here, so that most of the people I know who do well on objective tests enjoy taking them; it is a game. Conversely, those who do poorly on objective tests will dislike the whole idea of objective testing, and with good reason. If you are not good at this speciality, it becomes a handicap, because the skill, or lack of it, seems transferable to all objective tests. Thus a student who flubs his group IQ test in the seventh grade is quite as likely to flub his law boards some ten years later.

This statement is not based on any scientific studies, but rather on my observation of a number of generations of frustrated students and test takers. Whether an immunity to or an enthusiasm for objective tests can be developed is an uncertain point. However, I well remember a student whose law aptitude tests scores were high enough to cause remark when he entered Yale Law School, and his favorite pastime was *The Times* crossword. I began to recommend this form of test preparation to all those undergraduates who looked forward with great trepidation to taking law or medical boards. I have no way of knowing whether this is a system which will help the hapless test taker or not, but I know at least one other premedical adviser at a famous college who has come up with the same suggestion, and he claims success.

The real answer is probably that verbal gymnastics and exercises may help to improve the test scores because you thereby develop those abilities which the tests measure. But even if the scores do not shift much, any attempt to improve verbal ability is likely to provide dividends, because the verbal skills—reading and communicating—are so often the chief ingredients of success.

IX

The Changing Vision

"THE MASS OF MEN," WROTE
Henry David Thoreau, "lead lives of quiet desperation."
This discouraging but perceptive comment from a man
who did pretty much as he pleased throughout his life is
directed, I have always felt, to the many men who have
been shoe-horned by circumstance or some other powerful
external force into work for which they are not suited or
have no interest. An almost classic example was a legend in
the city where I grew up. A prominent citizen had wanted
to be an architect, but had been forced by his father to
assume control of the family business. He manifested his
thwarted enthusiasms for architecture and design in a remarkably beautiful house, inside and out, but suffered for his
frustrations by a continuous and painful form of eczema.

This legendary example may be overdrawn, or it may be
quite accurate, but it seems quite logical to me, from having
observed a number of generations of college students go
through the agony of curriculum and career selection, that
there is a constant struggle in the minds of most young men

between what they would really like to do and what they feel they should do. If conscience or practicality or external pressure forces submission to a decision which runs contrary to the young man's interests or abilities, he may very well find himself established with a wife, children, mortgages and unpaid-for chattels before he decides he would like to change, and at that point it is not feasible.

What the resultant toll is in broken marriages, high blood pressure, alcoholism, suicides, eczema, irritability, or failure cannot be known, but I think there is little doubt that there is a toll.

Although parents are consciously or unconsciously shaping their children's plans almost from the time they are born, it is in high school that parents really begin to worry about career choices. Perhaps it is a holdover from the not too distant days when high school graduation was something of a distinction and college only for the very few, but even today the high school junior and senior is asked for his vocational plans. According to many of the students I have interviewed, even guidance counselors, who should know better, seem annoyed or upset if a seventeen-year-old boy has no very clear idea of what he wants to do. It is at this point that the external forces begin to operate to shape his choices, and it is easy to imagine a young student fixing on a goal of the moment simply to answer the "life-goal" question, and then find he is propelled on his way toward it, almost beyond his ability to stop the process.

However, as sociologists are quick to point out, the ambitious aggressiveness of the middle-class youth is the result of constant conditioning by the parents: "When you go to college . . ." or "If you should be a doctor, you will be able to. . ." This constant inculcation into the idea of education and vocational training is necessarily a part of the training of the middle class. ("Middle-class" as a descriptive phrase has become in the last few years even more a term of opprobrium than ever before. The term "bourgeoise," so fashionable in the 1930s to describe the same attitudes, has gone completely out of style. In virtually the same way, the term "conservative" has become almost an insult on our campuses today; no one would willingly permit himself to be so described.)

However, like all inculcation and conditioning, it has to be maintained constantly until circumstances and momentum can take over where the parents and the school leave off. An interesting example of this is the sudden flash of truth I had when I was interviewing a college senior concerning his applications to medical schools. Hoping to discover something about his real interests and motivations, I asked him to tell me what he would *really* like to do—discounting parents, society, the need to make money, and any other mundane considerations.

The senior listened to the question and stared off into space for a moment: "Forgetting everything?" I nodded.

"Well, I'd play the clarinet, I guess." I knew he was a good and devoted musician, and his answer didn't surprise me. His second thought did.

"Wait," he said, "if I could really do anything I wanted without worrying about the consequences, I think I'd play basketball!"

Not all products of parental ambition and coaching reveal themselves as quickly as he did. In some cases, students will fool themselves or at least will be persuaded that following a set path toward a specific profession they are not really interested in is better than following their own instincts. For example, another undergraduate recently asked me what the minimum requirements for medical school were, since he did not want to take any more biology or chemistry than were really necessary. I pointed out that a genuine interest in science was a necessary attitude for the successful medical or premedical student, and that anyone who was trying to duck science probably should not be considering medicine as a career.

The student considered what I had said and returned: "You're probably right. I'm not sure whether I want to go to medical school or not, but it just wouldn't seem right not to have to endure the torture of another biology course—so I'll go on with it." Needless to say, an attitude like that is the product of more efficient brainwashing than any captured soldiers ever had to undergo.

What happens to doctors, lawyers, engineers whose drive or whose combination of external and internal motivation enables them to complete their training and become practicing members of the profession? I will return to this question later because it is clear that, for any man of courage and decisiveness, imprisonment in a profession he does not like is unnecessary. It is easier, of course, to stop the machinery during the course of the training itself; thus each year a number of students drop out of law school after the first few weeks, and once in a while a medical student quits after his internship.

But for all the students who are unwillingly enmeshed in the coils of parental ambitions for them, there are many more who are genuinely persuaded that they know what they want to do. To me, these are the lucky students in college. They are untroubled by the problems of uncertainty about the future, and, with a certain serenity unmarred by doubt, they move efficiently toward the goal. In general, I would characterize these students as vocationally oriented; education is the means to a specific end. If they are science students—engineers, chemists, and the like—they are not even seriously troubled by a possible choice of courses because, with a few exceptions, the curriculum has been blocked out for their undergraduate career from the beginning. For the premedical student there is some choice, but within a fairly limited range. For the future lawyer or businessman who is convinced of his future, the wide range of acceptable courses (there is no pre-law concentration; interest in going to law school makes anything studied "pre-law") can be confusing; but the agonizing uncertainty of what to study, so that it will be of the greatest use in the future or so that it may point the way to a possible profession, is not there; the decision has been made, and all that is necessary is the acquisition of enough undergraduate credits to get into law school or a graduate school of business.

Of course, undergraduate programs which are strongly directed vocationally, in business or physical education for example, offer the same comfort of a decided goal and a quick and efficient means of accomplishing it. However, the very directness and efficiency, which are so useful when the student knows what he wants, become so very confusing when he develops indecision.

The liberal arts student in a liberal arts program has, in a sense, prepared himself for the torments of indecisiveness; he knows he has yet to make up his mind and that, until he does, he must continue to search, sample, and hope that he will find some area of interest to which he might be willing to devote his life. If he is so sophisticated academically that he realizes that what he studies in college and what he elects to do for a living need not have much in common, he will suffer less, but he is still searching behind every course for the magic response. For the vocationally oriented, those whose education is aimed, rifle-like, at the goal, there is little thought, as I have said, because there need be none. On the other hand, one of the major casualties of any educational institution is the neatly anchored engineer who discovers he does not like engineering, or that he cannot do it well enough to graduate in that field. The same awakening may come to premeds, would-be scientists of all sorts, and anyone who has entered college with a specific absolute goal in mind.

These casualties rapidly fall into two groups: those who discover they are unable to meet the demands of the course they have chosen and understandably have some difficulty in reconciling what they had hoped for with what seems possible; and, those who have decided, on closer examination of the academic offerings available, that they would like to try something different. This last syndrome does not seem at all remarkable, and it is not—unless it is complicated by parental forces. Parents, I have come to believe firmly, live their children's lives vicariously to an astonishing degree, and though Sam Jr. may not be concerned that he has lost interest in engineering, Sam Sr. sees a course in engineering as economic ballast, a "trade" his boy can fall back on, and he may, therefore, raise a good deal of fuss over the switch from "practical" education to "unpractical."

One of my favorite colleagues over the years, a discerning and sensitive sociologist, who unlike most members of his discipline also wrote and spoke a remarkably articulate brand of English, always turned first, when interviewing an undergraduate, to the section of the student folder which dealt with the parents' education and background. Both his training and his experience told him that many of the problems which students develop in college arise from the parent-child conflict over what education is and what it should be. Vocational orientation among parents is strong, particularly if they are not college educated or if they have jobs which do not require a high degree of formal training. Often the parents are motivated by their view of the ladder of responsibility or prestige; thus pharmacists see medicine as the ultimate profession, laborers look up to engineers, and artisans such as bricklayers often aspire for their sons to be architects.

Where the parental prejudices are known and voiced, the pressures which build up on the student can be severe, literally to the point of destruction. Where the disappointment is indirectly expressed—that is, where parental ambitions have been so thoroughly absorbed that they are no longer recognized as such—the results are less devastating, perhaps, but produce in many cases a sense of guilt or inadequacy that is hard for the student to live with.

The worst manifestations of this in my experience are the premeds. Students who start out as engineers can usually be pacifically converted to business and occasionally to the pure liberal arts, and sometimes to medicine or another branch of science; the same is true of almost every other vocational orientation—it *can* be cured, except for medicine. What special indoctrination patterns have been developed to make this one career choice "incurable" I do not know. Probably the combination of social prestige, assured income, and the mystical quality of the doctor-patient relationship all contribute. The result can be magnificent: able students who are superbly motivated to move through difficult and increasingly complex courses of study without looking back or wondering if what they are doing is right. The problems arise from the students who have essentially misunderstood the academic demands of medicine and cannot make the grade, or who have discovered that the great amount of science now required even as an undergraduate is distasteful; whatever the reasons, the feelings of guilt and inadequacy which arise when a student changes his mind about a medical career are in no way abated.

Even the interesting fact, only occasionally revealed, that the intellectual demands for *preparation* in medicine so far exceed the intellectual demands of usual clinical practice does not soften the blow for those who fail. This fact, however, seems to indicate that perhaps some modification of medical education is needed to produce practitioners who will be happy and fulfilled by the demands of clinical medicine. Instead, things seem to be going in the direction of increasing the academic demand for preparation, which is likely to produce either restlessness, boredom, or a continuing increase in the number of physicians who elect to go into research and teaching—necessary fields, but no more necessary than clinicians.

Regardless of these considerations, however, the specter of latter-day disappointment is seldom the reason for career shifts in high school and college. Originally, as I have said, vocational directions grow out of parental concerns, but as the student grows and develops, realizes his own strengths, and discovers his own interests, the possible shape of his own future begins to appear. In the last few years the "identity crisis" has become a standard feature of undergraduate life, so much so that a number of undergraduates I know refer to it intimately but casually as the "I.C." ("You know Jim Fisher; he's in a bad way—going through his I.C.")

Although the search for identity has been portentously (and pretentiously) draped with all kinds of words like "self-discovery," "relevance," and "meaning," it seems to me that the chief crisis in a student's life is his discovery of what he is good at and how he would like to use these gifts, as opposed to what his parents think he is good at and what they think he should do. If his self-knowledge comes to him slowly or unclearly, then there is indeed a "crisis," and if the parental image clashes with the student's discovery of himself, there will also be a crisis.

A career shift, then, is not a sign of weakness, nor is career uncertainty a sign of indecision, but rather an indication of growth. The best changes come as a result of the awakening of interest in a new field or the reaffirmation that an old field of interest really is valid as an interest for life.

One of the most consistent changes that seems to occur in many students, with a regularity that has to be observed to be believed, is the switch from the sciences to the humanities and social studies. For many students, particularly boys, and most particularly bright boys, science holds a special fascination in the high school period. As a sex, boys tend to be better in quantitative areas than in verbal, just as girls tend to perform better in verbal areas and less well in math and science than their male counterparts.

Quite apart from the male identification that often goes

with science, there are doubtless many other good reasons for this tropism. First, science courses are usually taught better at the high school level than nonscience courses. Second, the courses themselves have been kept more continuously up-to-date and hence are more "relevant"—a word in frequent use to describe courses that students find interesting, just as "irrelevant" is used to describe courses which are uninteresting. Finally and I think most importantly, to the mind which is emerging into mental maturity, there is a logic, a precision, a neatness about science which appeal to the young student. As he learns more about science and begins to suspect that he can understand the mechanisms of the physical world, it excites him in the same way that a disemboweled alarm clock excites a twelve-year-old mechanic who wants to see it work, or a car mechanism excites a sixteen-year-old.

All of these factors—teachers, courses, the nature of the material itself, and the shiny equipment that more often than not figures in the laboratory work in the sciences (it does not really matter if the equipment is shiny or not; it is inherently fascinating)—bring an interest and enthusiasm in the sciences to its high point in the senior year in high school or the freshman year in college. Apparently, the better the student, the more likely he is to be interested in the sciences: a survey of the National Merit Scholarship winners showed a disproportionate number planning to study science in college, and a survey of the entering class at Harvard some years ago showed that over 50 percent were planning studies in the sciences, which is a staggeringly high figure for a liberal arts college that does not even offer a Bachelor of Science degree. Even though these figures have undoubtedly changed some in the last few years, as the number of students interested particularly in the physical sciences seems to be diminishing appreciably, other branches, now notably medicine, biology, and biochemistry, are gaining.

The switch away from the sciences, which often upsets parents who have heard their student-children talk loudly about career plans and who assumed that there would be no changes, usually comes at the end of the freshman year of college. The change can be upsetting to the student particularly if, as I have suggested before, he is a young man who is worried about studying "something practical" with which to earn a living. The motivation for the change often is not clearly expressed. Occasionally one hears such reasons as: "I wanted a theoretical course and there was too much busy work in the labs," or "I wanted a course that would deal with real problems, and there was too much theory." But the student who made this last comment then went on to major in art, which is not "practical" but does deal in real problems which he had to solve.

However, what students say and what they mean are often widely divergent. My own interpretation of the migration away from the sciences in the early college years is that college is better equipped to exploit and teach the inexact subjects and make the inexactitudes fascinating, whereas high schools teach the sciences best. As students mature emotionally they begin to appreciate how much more interesting are the inexact responses of humans to events, music, philosophy, and the other machinery of the liberal arts, than to the comparatively exact and predictable sciences. In a sense, it is a manifestation of growth and of maturity that the students have come to the realization of how much more complex and meaningful to their innermost lives is the study of the humanities and social studies.

What does this say about the scientists, the students who, as I have said, often are the happiest because they have no second thoughts and pursue their course of study with pleasure and efficiency? The unflattering conclusion I have come to is that most of the "scientists"—i.e., the science students who persist in studying a science curriculum in college without being distracted or drawn off into the "liberal" fields—are cases of arrested development. I say this quite seriously in one way and with tongue in cheek in another because, although no one could seriously question the mental development of a student who can successfully pursue the most demanding kind of academic program, it is also true that the natural development of interest in the arts, philosophy, and music is often suppressed in the successful science student, just as it is allowed to flower in the many students who try science and give it up. But most remarkable of all is that, among many science students I have known, the final flowering of interest in nonscience areas comes with unusual strength and intensity, as if it had been stored up during the time that science prevailed. The result, exaggerated of course, is that, having achieved his scientific goal, or having reached that point in his education where an interest in other areas cannot distract him, the science student blossoms forth with the biggest, most elaborate stereo set in the neighborhood and owns more books, paintings, *objets d'art* than would be thought possible. This late-satisfied hunger makes the science faculty that I have known usually far better educated than many of a liberal arts faculty because they have read extensively and know more about the humanities, for example, than the humanists know about the sciences. Before they get to this point, however, their singleness of purpose makes this development difficult to foresee.

It is interesting to consider what forces shape students into making career and curricular choices other than the sort of natural development that seems to change students into scientists and then out again. Obviously, not everyone will be affected the same way concerning science, or any of the other motivating factors, but, in analyzing what makes your student come to some of the decisions he does, it is probably useful to consider the underlying causes.

One of the strongest of these, I have found, is hero

worship. Whether girls are as subject to this form of emulatory flattery as boys I cannot say, but boys certainly do succumb and allow themselves to be shaped by its force. The hero may be the boy next door who is three or four years older, may be Father himself, or may be a teacher or some other readily accessible subject for adoration.

In counseling premedical students, I have been struck by how frequently this theme, consciously or unconsciously, repeats itself. The reasons for studying medicine are usually complex, but apparently of great interest to medical school admission committees since the question is frequently asked. Apart from the usual "interest in science" or "I want to help people," there is a surprising number of cases where the student was sick or injured at some time which was critical to him, and the successful intervention of the doctor made him the hero of the day. This reaction is so prevalent among students who have had psychiatric care (and now want to be psychiatrists, too) that I usually suspect any student who announces a desire to go into psychiatry of having had emotional problems.

Where Father is the hero, the fine line between outright parental influence and the effect of hero worship is hard to draw. Fathers are quick to point out that they bend over backward not to influence their sons, but influence is probably impossible to avoid; if the father is clearly and genuinely involved in his work, that is persuasion enough. (Occasionally, however, real enthusiasm for the work produces an opposite effect. Numerous boys have told me during college interviews that they did not want to be doctors, lawyers, or sales representatives, despite Dad's success in the field, because they had seen what it did to him.) Nevertheless, emulation has always been the sincerest and easiest form of flattery, and Father is a usual subject for emulation, regardless of how vehemently he may deny it, or how otherwise restive this son may be concerning parental influence and control.

Just as indirect parental influence can be a powerful force, so obviously can direct influence. The impact of what parents want, or feel is right for their children, can be seen in career plans and college choices, and in the attitudes of the student himself. Thus a parent will produce pressure in various ways, subtle or otherwise, to get his children to perform the chores that will make the parent a vicarious success. The child's concept of vocationalism is most likely to be inspired by parental concern over making enough money to live comfortably. Thus some of the lack of success in school and after may well come from the fact that the person's attitudes, parents, upbringing—in short, his environment—pushed him into courses of study or a career in which he had little real interest, but which seemed expedient at the time.

The prime urgency of expediency pushes both students and parents into situations which are not tenable. I have known too many parents (and students who want to do the right thing) who have pressed for one of the service academies, on the specious ground that it is both a first-class education and free. It is not free, and any young man involved in the rigors of plebe summer at West Point, for example, quickly realizes at what cost he is getting his education; and if he is temperamentally unsuited for military education, the cost can be enormous. In the same way, many others have been unhappy in business and engineering schools, secretarial schools, and the like, to which they have gone because this seemed to be a more practical and sensible course to take. Even the concept of college is one which has been forced by the pressures of public opinion and fashion on too many students and parents who dimly understand that it is necessary and therefore should be done, but who really understand college not at all and enjoy it even less.

Success or lack of it in college is usually attributed to maturity, which in this context may well mean being old enough to know you have to do some things you do not want to do. It is sometimes surprising to me to see a sudden flash of true feeling in a successful student which reveals him as someone who would probably have never gone to college if his deepest personal inclinations had been followed. For example, I was recently talking with an excellent engineering student who had visited Williamsburg and was profoundly impressed by the historical recreation of previous time. "You get a sense," he said, "of what a great thing it would be to be a really good silversmith in a time like that." This is certainly not the reaction of an inherent intellectual, and it immediately set me to wondering what that undergraduate might have done without the pressures of suburban parents and schools and the other external forces which had put him into college and into a career for which he was well trained but ill suited.

Not only do the external forces of society shape whether a young man or woman goes to college, but the fashion of the moment often has great power also to determine what will be studied and what the goal of the moment is. For example, at the present time, science, particularly physical science, is in disrepute with much of the student generation. Whether this feeling has been generated by antiwar feelings and concern about the science that could produce nuclear weapons and napalm, and which flourishes on many campuses because of government support, I cannot say. Nevertheless, it is true that engineering enrollments are shrinking despite strenuous efforts on the part of institutions to have enough students to maintain large investments in faculty, equipment, and buildings.

Yet curiously, as fashions in education veer toward the new frontiers, some of the by-passed favorites enjoy a peripheral revival. Physics was a new frontier ten years ago and attracted both the brightest and most imaginative students. Now biology is seen again as the most interesting frontier in science and, because of the most recent developments, bio-engineering and biophysics have become important.

But all the science enrollments are dropping, probably for two reasons. The first is that science is out of style for the moment, and the second is probably that science courses in high school are considered too hard and should be avoided lest they pull down the overall average and make college admission that much more complicated. With high school physics enrollments down, it is not surprising that subsequently college enrollments in the "hard" sciences are dwindling.

Fashion, however, is currently dictating a rage for the "soft" sciences—political science, sociology, and psychology. Enrollment in these courses has soared in response to the student's "discovery" of the social problems of this country.

In the same way, the career plans of the recent college graduates are apt to be strongly influenced by the current response to fashionable trends. One of the strongest of these is antibusiness, and one of the most remarkable countertrends is teaching. This does not mean that no one goes into business after graduation from college, but it does mean that the numbers interested have been dwindling and that, from certain colleges to which business has traditionally gone to recruit its raw material for executive training courses, the take is virtually nil, a trend which understandably concerns big corporations and which they are trying to counteract in various ways—without notable success at the moment.

One of the most interesting and imaginative campaigns has been carried on by the Harvard School of Business Administration together with about twenty-five major corporations. A number of colleges are given the option to nominate two students from the top quarter of the junior class to attend a program during the summer. The students first attend a short orientation program at Harvard, then work for the company for the major part of the summer, during which time they have a chance to see all of the operations of the company, meet with officers, directors, and the president, and then return to Harvard for a recapitulation. In addition to the inside view, the selected students are well paid, the business has had its crack at the brightest people in the colleges who otherwise would probably go to graduate school without considering business. Although my impression is that the program has not been a great success, it is certainly the proper approach.

While one of the antibusiness factors that affects student choices is an antipathy to restrictions ("I don't want to work anyplace where I'll be tied to a desk all day"), it is certainly not pure altruism which is pushing young graduates into teaching. It is the draft and the war lurking behind the draft. This curious, much-talked-about war may have greater long-term influence on the life and social patterns of this country than any other conflict the United States has gotten itself into. By bottling students into pressure situations in colleges and threatening them with the draft if they leave, the student's frustrated, immature, explosive, and blindly retaliatory response will undoubtedly change education in a variety of ways, and quite possibly a good chunk of the rest of society as well, before the pendulum swings back and/or the war is brought to an end.

That the pendulum will swing seems inevitable to anyone who has watched student fads go from one extreme to another. Possibly an extensive number of programs like the one that business and the Harvard School of Business Administration undertook jointly will start the trend, or it will be started by the intensive advertising campaigns that a number of large corporations are beginning to launch to attract good students from those universities that used to be a major source of supply for executive trainees. Such a change has been predicted privately by an administrative officer at Harvard, whose skills in classifying personality types, and predicting academic success in college on this basis, make him particularly worth listening to: "Some day, one of the more imaginative bright guys will see the challenge of business—and they'll all be running in a new direction." While it has not yet happened, it probably will.

The period from fifteen to twenty-five is one of great change, when responses to external stimuli are probably at their greatest, when internal reactions are settling into a pattern which will finally establish the tastes, direction, character, and career of the person involved. Traditionally an age of upheaval and uncertainty, this is generally not a euphoric period to live through, either for the adolescent or his parents, who continue to watch him anxiously even as he moves toward his middle twenties.

In the struggle to find "self," there will unquestionably be a number of false starts, new beginnings, crushed hopes, and, inevitably, bitterly disappointed parents. The last is probably the inescapable result, because parents, whatever their wisdom, do make plans and live vicariously through their children. The children in turn respond to their parents' concerns about the future by announcing goals—"I'm going to be a lawyer"—and these predictions, which often have no basis in fact, are too often accepted by parents as established fact.

As I have tried to say over and over, the college experience particularly is a time of change and response to new ideas and new situations. The young man or woman of college age, but not in college, is probably also susceptible to change, but only in college will the young adults be systematically bombarded with ideas, attitudes, and possibilities for the future that they have never had before.

The shock both to parents and students is greater, I think, when the parents are themselves not college graduates and less inclined, therefore, to understand what kinds of changes and temptations are likely to take place. So the son of a bricklayer who goes off to college to be an engineer, but discovers art and art history, will have a difficult time at home explaining a change that he understands only dimly himself.

Although the best possible advice is to let the student decide for himself what he should study and what he will eventually become, it is considerably more difficult to follow this advice than to give it. More often than not, the student will be asked questions which deepen both his own discomfort and the gulf between him and his parents. Questions like: "What are you going to do if you study art—be an artist? Starve to death?" "What's wrong with engineering, law school, going into business, with me?" "How can you study something so impractical after all the sacrifices your father and I have made?"

A major failing of most parents is that they never change their perspective on their own children; they see them as the irresponsible children they once were even after the children have long since reached the age of discretion. Moreover, as Archibald MacLeish has said, youth is a time of "generous and impatient" idealism, while parents have come to grips too often with practical reality. Having therefore settled their children in some practical and sensible educational rut which will produce sensible results with no worries and no chances involved, they are always annoyed, and even frightened a little, by the implied threat of sudden change. Accordingly, when Tom or Mary announces an academic change which seems to be a major reversal of direction, parents get nervous and quite often tend to throw their weight around.

The amount of pressure, emotional and financial, which parents can put on their children is enormous and, in turn, frightening in its own right. Carried to extremes, I have seen it produce suicide in a student who was unable to justify his desire to leave a "practical" premed program to his mother, a nurse who was slaving to support her son and an invalid husband. That her son was willing to abandon a sensible income-producing profession to take up the study of English and possibly become a teacher seemed to her a mockery of the considerable sacrifice she had made, and she said so. Her son, an intelligent and sensitive boy, finally resolved the two opposing views in the only way he could think of—but only after considerable agony, depression, and soul-searching on his part.

Few family differences reach such an awful climax, but the consequences can still be uncomfortable for both parties. If the prime rule for parents in this situation is "Don't you be mad at him," the corollary is equally clear: "Don't let him be mad at himself."

Self-confidence and self-esteem go hand in hand, and of all the ingredients necessary for academic success, self-confidence is one of the most important. While not more important than motivation, the willingness to work, it is certainly more important than raw ability, the potentiality, the promise of what could be possible under ideal conditions. The student who is made to feel guilty, or whose self-confidence has been blasted by parental disapproval of what they maintain is a patently bad decision, is much less likely to have a successful college experience than the equally capable student who is allowed to go about his business with a clear conscience. The other alternative, from my observation of students over the years, is the alienation of the student from his parents. While independence and separation of parents and children is normal and healthy, it is possible to accomplish this in a way which leaves both sides of the separation with love and respect intact. Put another way, parents must and should give their children credit for having the necessary experience or wisdom to make major changes in direction, however mysterious and inexplicable such a change may seem at the time. Change is the best indication of growth parents have, and as such, should be welcome.

Although college is the expected time for change, not all

the developments in a lifetime will necessarily occur so neatly on schedule. College is the time for intellectual experimentation which can have an important bearing on what the student eventually decides to do, but it does not necessarily produce the hoped-for results in the long run. For this and a number of other reasons the immediate post-college years are still times of change, and sometimes the change seems to negate an enormous investment in training and effort. For example, the dean of admission of a distinguished university completed his medical training and was practising for a number of years when his interest in alumni work for his college led him to accept the job of heading the admission activities. A similar case is the recently retired headmaster of a famous independent school whose original training had been as a psychiatrist until he became involved in academic administration. Changes of this sort are the decision of men who are clearly courageous enough and flexible enough to realize that the investment of time and effort means little if it does not bring the personal satisfaction that was hoped for.

In interviewing students for admission to college, I find that the great majority of high school students think about a career in service—working with people and for people. In recent years this point of view has grown enormously (with the concomitant drop in interest toward business), with teaching, government service, and social work becoming the favored choices, or at least the choices favored up to the time it becomes necessary to live with the choice.

Recently a young graduate of Brown who had majored in English and who had looked forward to teaching came in to say that, after a year of teaching, he was completely disenchanted with it. "I have to admire the people who really get wrapped up in their students, who want to listen to their problems and want to help them," he said. "It must be a great gift, but I don't have it."

This statement came from a veteran of one of the services

who went into teaching because he thought it was right, not because he was forced into thinking it was a good thing by the draft laws. The drive to service that the draft has generated is quite spurious in many cases and has produced its own share of quiet desperation, even while sending many young men into teaching who would otherwise not have been deferred.

The reverse, of course, is true. A number of recent graduates I have known have gone into business on leaving college and, finding no personal satisfaction in their jobs, have decided to try other fields. Thus an office manager in her mid fifties (scarcely a recent graduate) who had taken only commercial courses in high school elects to go to college so that she can teach, and, thanks to the flexibility of the junior college concept, she can. A young business school graduate with a wife and two children decides that law is more interesting than accounting and accordingly takes the requisite test, makes the necessary applications, and goes off to law school. The ultimate in courage of this sort was a graduate of Brown, a married man, a father, and a homeowner, who had been in business for several years. He decided that medicine was his life work and thereupon sold his house and returned to college to get the necessary preparation to enter medical school.

The frequency and ease with which this is done suggests that the age of quiet desperation is over, that now, with enough experience, self-knowledge, and willingness to be unsettled, the ideal vocation is possible for everyone.

The truth, of course, is that this is simply not so—that a degree of desperation will always be a standard fixture of human misery for some of the best reasons in the world: not everyone wants to work; not everyone really knows what he wants to do and apparently cannot always find out; and finally, the usual number of young men or women plunge into matrimony, encumber themselves with houses and babies, and then discover, when they are thoroughly enmeshed, that they have gotten themselves into careers which bring no satisfaction.

While not a great deal can be done to combat laziness or impetuosity, the question of what any one man should want to do with his life has been the subject of considerable research. Nevertheless, psychological testing is not perfect as a measurement or a source of absolute truth. It is, however, a useful tool, and its usefulness has been discussed in another part of this book.

In a sense, a change in direction during or after college represents the development of new resources and abilities, and as such comes under the heading of that most exciting educational phenomenon—the late bloomer. No single aspect of the educational process (or the life process) causes more speculation, argument, hope, and disappointment than the concept of the late bloomer. Every parent whose child is less than a good student hopes that he has a late bloomer—a student who will suddenly emerge from his cocoon alert and interested and, above all, capable.

A good deal of argument in educational circles centers about whether the late bloomer ever really blooms or not. Teachers are inclined to think so—but of course they are professional optimists or they would not be teachers. Headmasters of schools are in the same optimistic category; all have their favorite stories about a student who suddenly decided that productivity was good and that failing grades were bad. In the best cases the force for good is internal, but quite often it is external, as described in the following recommendation, written by one of America's most articulate headmasters, Frank Ashburn of the Brooks School:

> For a considerable time, print in any form affected Tom adversely; the dance roused all his energies to extraordinary results. A year ago his college chances looked about as bad as possible. Since then he has met Louise, who gets all A's at Wellesley and takes a dim view of uneducated men. He has to send her regular reports of progress. He

now writes, enjoys reading, is eager to get to college,
voluntarily attended summer school, and is not the man
he was. He has always been unusually generous, tolerant,
and friendly. If Louise survives I can see no limit to
possibilities. I recommend him, with the qualification
that even now Tom is not the intellectual type.

Admission officers, on the other hand, tend to look at the
late bloomer with cold suspicion, wondering if the external
force which is goading students to improve grades is the
need to get into college rather than any remarkable reversal
of character. "The late bloomer is the no bloomer," comments one veteran admission director noted for his acerbic
outlook. Similarly a psychologist noted for his work in
establishing motivational profiles felt that the late bloomer
did not exist; by the time a student has gotten to college, the
determining aspects of his personality had hardened beyond all possibility of real change.

Despite the determined professional cynicism shown by
so many of my admission colleagues, my experience says
that late bloomers do exist, that their appearance is unpredictable, and that the cause of their cure, if it can be
called that, is as difficult to judge as any part of the disease.

The most fascinating and baffling are those who "cure"
themselves. Claude Allen, headmaster of Hebron Academy,
describes it this way: "One morning a boy gets up and
decides it will be different from now on. He's turned a
corner. And it is different from that time."

One of the most remarkably versatile students I ever
knew explained his drive in much the same way. "In the
seventh grade I was a fat little slob, so I decided to do
something about it." He made himself into a competent
athlete and a highly competent student with an inner drive
and determination that made him a leader in his class at
Brown, a highly successful graduate student, and currently
a college instructor in his field. Not all students arrive at a

change of heart so suddenly. As a matter of observation, I would say that most of the very good students whose college applications I have read have always been good students, even in primary school, and in many cases have always been considered unusually bright. Thus the doctrine that "good students are made, not developed" has supported the belief that the late bloomer is the never bloomer.

Yet there are enough exceptions to make any parent take constant heart and to make any broad generalizations about late bloomers unwise.

One possible reason for underachieving, the disparity between academic ability and performance, is perhaps so simple that it is seldom thought about and it shows up occasionally in the successful late bloomer. What is involved is a fallacy concerning the student's awareness of the need for education. All parents understand that education is absolutely necessary for success, advancement, self-development, and a variety of other virtues. Since students are a part of the system, the general assumption of parents and teachers is that they, too, understand and appreciate the need for education when, in reality, they do not. The fact that education is so much talked about and that students are figuratively breaking down the doors to get into college supports the myth, and teachers have perhaps relaxed and come to see themselves less as generators of intellectual excitement among their pupils than simply as purveyors of information who lay it out for view and assume it will be snapped up.

For the action-minded boy or the pragmatic girl, there is often an enormous gap between life as they see it and the education that is presented. Spoken of in terms of "relevance," this gap has become the rallying point for much student protest about curriculum. While changes in the curricular pattern to bring it up to date have been going on in universities (with appropriate academic reluctance, of course) since the thirteenth century, such change will not solve the problem of the late bloomer because his problem is one of *individual* relevance. Thus I have known a restless contemporary who drifted through four or five different secondary schools, served in the Marines, and subsequently took a bachelor's degree without any distinction whatsoever, who has become a leader in a field where intellect and articulateness are of paramount importance because the solution of the problems involved were relevant to him.

For the practical-minded male student, the theorizing about abstracts which so characterize the liberal arts curriculum is occasionally bewildering but more often dull, and it is not surprising that many run-of-the-mill students in college really blossom either in graduate schools of business or in business itself. I have written the phrase "when faced with the requirements of a more practical curriculum, Jim will undoubtedly prove to be a better student" so often that it has become a personal cliché, yet I have so often seen mediocre liberal arts students become such good students in business schools that there is little doubt in my mind that personal relevance again is the determining factor.

What also appears to be late blooming—or more properly—what a colleague called the "reluctant burgeon"—is often instead a quiet but stubborn form of rebelliousness. In its simplest form, underachieving is a revenge, a fighting back. A pleasant and nostalgic form of this phenomenon was recalled by an old friend, recently retired as a professor of English. He recalled a student of his, obviously bright, who never got to class on time, never got his papers in when they should have been in, was a good-hearted, unmalicious clown in class who simply refused to take education seriously. The explanation offered was: "My father expects me to take over his drug business and I don't see much of a future beyond that. I don't need college to assure my future, so I'm going to have fun now before I get caught up in the drug business."

More timely is the comment in the College Board Review

that higher education is so necessary for economic survival (or exemption from the draft) that young men have no choices except college, whether they are inclined that way or not. It would be oversimplification to suggest that student activity against irrelevant curricula, the "system," the war, civil injustices, the profit motive, or the structure of society is entirely the result of being tied up in a no-escape situation which requires that they go to college (and at least be good enough students to stay in college), but it is reasonable to consider this as one of several causes.

This interesting reversal, in which the student adheres to one set of standards set up by his elders (being a good student) while trying desperately to avoid becoming entangled in all of the others is still too recent for there to be any solid information on what this form of rebellion will do to the shape and standards of our society. It is possible that when the student realizes that society will not succumb to his idealistic assaults on it, he will give up and become a "member of society," but as yet, we do not know. There is, however, a considerable probability that the exigencies of marriage and family will snap the resistors into line much faster than any strong-minded dean or parent. The radicals and pacifists of the 1930 generation of college students have disappeared so completely that the current group of undergraduates is reluctant to believe in their existence. In the same way, time will probably cure the greatest number of the late bloomers or underachievers, even though in a way which may not be to the entire satisfaction of the father whose son did not become a doctor, go to the "right" college, get into law school, or who simply has hair too long and a loudly expressed disrespect for the world as it is.

The unspoken complaint of the present college generation is that they are being pushed willy-nilly into college, and their loudly voiced complaint (one of many) is that what is offered at college is not "relevant." For me, one of the greatest difficulties in counseling college students in the liberal arts curriculum has been the attempt to point out that the relevancy of the liberal arts is for an entire existence, work and after work, a career and a subsequent lifetime of retirement. By the time a college student has finished four years of liberal arts, he probably has a better understanding of how all things he has learned fit together into an understandable, and hence, appreciable pattern. By the time a man has finished enough years at work to consider retirement, he probably has an even greater appreciation of the relevancy of the irrelevant arts curriculum, and as he moves into the uncertain vacuum of retirement, he will appreciate it even more.

The enormous threat of leisure—early retirement, longer weekends, and the shorter working day—hangs over this country and will grow steadily more menacing. Not only is life expectancy increasing measurably, but the age at which retirement is acceptable is diminishing as well. Even more immediate is the threat of automation and what it is doing to the work force and the workweek. Although paper shuffling executives and maintenance and construction workers of all sorts are affected only in a peripheral way, the production of most goods is increasingly controlled by automatic processes or governed by computers, or both. As the need for production workers diminishes, the workweek will be lightened, but at no loss of income, and this labor pattern will inevitably have an influence on the rest of the work force.

What happens when an able-bodied man has time on his hands? Apparently he finds another job; at least this is the pattern, not only in the United States, but in the countries of Europe that face the same problems we do. The reasons for it are at once self-evident and obscure. The extra job obviously brings in more money, which is always welcome, but another point is that the laborer who takes a second job does so because he has never learned what else to do. As William Faulkner observed, the only thing that man can do eight hours a day, day after day, is work:

You can't eat eight hours a day nor drink eight hours a

day nor make love for eight hours—all you can do for
eight hours is work. Which is the reason why man makes
himself and everybody else so miserable and unhappy.

It is doubtful that the urgency of informing high school
and college students about the threat of leisure can be
effectively communicated, since, until faced with it, it
seems a very pleasant dilemma. But for many purposeful
adults the sudden excess of leisure time is a genuine
burden.

"My father nearly went out of his mind for the first two
years of his retirement," a young college professor told me,
and this is not an atypical reaction. Although not scientifically documented, all of us have known recently retired
men who have died from no discernible cause, except what
might be called boredom. The problem of how to prevent
the agony of a sudden shift really separates into several
distinct areas: the proper preparation (education) of the
young to anticipate the problems of leisure; the appropriate
guidance of the recently retired or overly leisured on what
to do with their time; and finally the provision of the
necessary training to accomplish the new career.

The first is probably the most difficult to implement
because of the difficulty of impressing the young with the
practicality of preparing for leisure. Since it is a problem
they have not had to encounter (except on rainy days) it is
difficult for them to imagine. But chiefly it has not been
incorporated into the curriculum, just as a truly meaningful
view of race and social situations has not been realistically
handled. A major effort then should be made to adjust the
curriculum to meet the problems of society. There is an
immediate conflict here with the existing curriculum,
which is already bulging with too much for a student to
learn in too little time.

Perhaps the answer is in the division of the curriculum in
the same way life is divided—that is, into work and leisure.
For nine months of the year the school curriculum, whether

for college or vocational preparation, would be concerned with the practical subjects needed for survival or advancement. This part of the curriculum would include physics, machinery design, foreign languages, all dependent on the student's future plans; it would also include a core of special history, psychology, and economics courses for all students, to enable them to be knowledgeable and aware citizens, and a course in the mechanics of communication, reading and writing, equally essential to all.

In order to get all of these ingredients in, there would of necessity be a longer school year, and in the summer months the subject of leisure would be taught according to the tastes and inclinations of each student—individual sports, studio art, woodworking, music, art, philosophy, literature, with a central core of aesthetics and the philosophy of leisure for all. By devoting a substantial amount of time and energy at one time to "leisure" subjects, a distribution of instruction could be arranged according to individual interests, instead of the blanket approach to art and music which is now necessarily used in our high schools. And because the students would be studying chiefly those subjects which were of interest to them, this period of school could well be considered a form or organized leisure.

The problems inherent in such a system are obvious. First, one man's drudgery is another man's leisure. Second, and linked to the first, is a need to have the interests and abilities of every student carefully catalogued so that each vocational and leisure curriculum is as individually planned as possible. If it were to work, it would have to be flexible and responsive to changes in direction and interest as the child himself changes in the process of growing. The really important part of this curricular idea is not so much that it uses up the entire calendar year instead of three quarters, or that it divides subjects arbitrarily according to their putative subsequent use. Rather, its chief value is that it impresses on the student, by its placement in a formal course of studies, the need for him to learn how to spend his leisure time.

In taking leisure seriously, in organizing idleness, such a program may overcome the opprobrium which our society has always attached to "idleness." On the surface, organized idleness sounds reprehensible, but we have only to look into the near future to see that large chunks of idleness undigested by some form of organization would be far worse.

Changing the school curriculum so that students are steadily inculcated with a feeling of respect for leisure is only part of the solution, since the current adult population is faced with the problem increasingly, and without the benefit of any orientation. The closest approach to doing anything about the leisure crisis at present is the adult education program run by many communities as night courses in the high schools. These run the gamut of subjects from elementary reading and writing to arts and crafts. For many of the night school students, adult education provides them with training they have never had before, but for the most part depending on where the school is located, the adult education program is an auxiliary, an enriching course of study which might well come under the heading of the organization of leisure.

For the newly retired man or woman, there is a need for organization or stabilization in his life. After the initial thrill of "freedom," the destructive vacuum of having nothing to do and no goals in view wreaks its havoc. It is feasible, even necessary, to consider the possibilities of a second career or an extension of the first.

The group that handles this problem best, in my opinion, is the military. Twenty years of service entitle a man to retire with a reasonable pension in early middle age. With the pension as a sea anchor, the retired military man can branch out into a variety of areas, but a favorite, in my observation, has been teaching. The reasons are clear: for officers it is a continuation of what was essentially a

personnel job, with good vacations, rewarding psychological aspects, and a position of community respect. Having
operated in an atmosphere of controlled discipline, these
teachers are good disciplinarians, probably because there is
a certain air of authority which is infectious and which
both parties, students and teacher, understand almost intuitively. (I knew a retired admiral who was principal of a
high school in Virginia. He ran a taut ship!)

Teaching, of course, is not the answer for every newly
retired man or woman. I mention it only as a popular choice
among a group of men who are forced to retire earlier than
most and who perforce give the subject greater thought and
preparation.

The point is, if a second career is possible, and early
retirement makes such a supposition increasingly likely,
why not treat the second career in the same way as the
enterprising younger man who changed career choices in
midstream? In other words, if you have a second chance,
don't involve yourself in a second life of quiet desperation.
This is your chance to do what you want.

Again the dilemma arises, does everyone *know* what he
would like to do, given the opportunity, or is it best to be
shown? It seems to me that in a lifetime of business so
many idle thoughts and inclinations would be marshaled
off to one side and dismissed as not germane to business or
a career, that after a while they might be submerged or forgotten. Thus it seems sensible for the newly retired or about-
to-be-retired man to undergo a complete battery of interest
tests to reevaluate his talents and reestablish new goals.

The new goal, once established, can be prepared for in
many ways, but again the junior colleges, the most flexible
of our current academic institutions, probably offer the
widest choice of courses and the least demanding entrance
requirements. The question of whether additional training
is necessary—or of what to study if it is—is a guidance
problem which is not easily solved because it is outside the
usual purview of guidance counseling, which is more

usually thought of as guidance for the young. However, with the increase in the number of retired, communities are increasingly aware of the need for this kind of counseling as well. If it is not part of the services offered by the United Fund or another community agency, the testing service itself will offer some guidance as a part of its service, and unquestionably will be able to refer their clients to appropriate agencies. The psychological testing agencies themselves may be public or privately supported; they are often an arm of the state or municipal university. They can be found in the classified telephone directory under "Psychologists" or "Vocational and Educational Guidance."

Of course, actual employment in a formal second career is not essential, provided that the man just retired has a clear view of what he wants to do and the self-discipline to do it. It has been suggested that the disappearance of individual production, the rise of automated machinery, and the great increase in leisure, at the end of a week or a career, may engender the development of a new artisan class, devoted to the production of the intricate and beautiful handmade things that may otherwise disappear. An avocation, then, may be expanded into full-time occupation.

In the same way, reading or personal scholarship may become a full-time occupation. The important consideration is that the leisure be used to promote a sense of accomplishment and satisfaction. Ideally it should be a means of permitting people to change their vision of what they can and should do with their lives, and to attack the remainder with enthusiasm and pleasure.

Index

285